Emotionally Focused Couple Therapy

FOR

DUMMIES®

A Wiley Brand

Emotionally Focused Couple Therapy

FOR

DUMMIES

A Wiley Brand

by Brent Bradley, PhD,
and James Furrow, PhD

FOR

DUMMIES

A Wiley Brand

Emotionally Focused Couple Therapy For Dummies®
Published by:
John Wiley & Sons Canada, Ltd.,
6045 Freemont Blvd.,
Mississauga, ON L5R 4J3,
www.wiley.com

For general information on John Wiley & Sons Canada, Ltd., including all books published by John Wiley & Sons, Inc., please call our distribution center at 1-800-567-4797. For reseller information, including discounts and premium sales, please call our sales department at 416-646-7992. For press review copies, author interviews, or other publicity information, please contact our publicity department, Tel. 416-646-4582, Fax 416-236-4448. For technical support, please visit www.wiley.com/techsupport.

Wiley publishes in a variety of print and electronic formats and by print-on-demand. Some material included with standard print versions of this book may not be included in e-books or in print-on-demand. If this book refers to media such as a CD or DVD that is not included in the version you purchased, you may download this material at http://booksupport.wiley.com. For more information about Wiley products, visit www.wiley.com.

Library and Archives Canada Cataloguing in Publication

Bradley, Brent A., author
          Emotionally focused couple therapy for dummies / Brent Bradley, James Furrow.

(For dummies)
Includes index.
Issued in print and electronic formats.
ISBN 978-1-118-51231-9 (pbk.)–ISBN 978-1-118-51233-3 (pdf).–ISBN 978-1-118-51240-1 (epub)

          1. Couples therapy. 2. Emotion-focused therapy I. Furrow, James L., author II. Title. III. Series:
For dummies

RC 488.5.B73 2013   616.89'1562   CS2013-903235-5
                                                                CS2013-903236-3

ISBN 978-1-118-51231-9 (pbk); ISBN 978-1-118-51239-5 (ebk); ISBN 978-1-118-51233-3 (ebk);
ISBN 978-1-118-51240-1 (ebk)

Printed in the United States of America

10 9 8 7 6 5 4 3 2 1

Contents at a Glance

Table of Contents

Introduction

• •

*E*very day, we talk to couples who want something more from their relationships. Some are struggling to renew a passion they once had. Others are fighting to survive as a couple. The turning point for most couples is not resolving a particular disagreement or making a new decision but finding new ways to face each other through these challenges. For some, this change is about regaining the love they once had, and for others it's about finding love for the first time. The key to transforming a relationship begins with an emotional connection.

Over time couples learn to get along, make adjustments, and sometimes settle into predictable patterns. If you and your partner are one of these couples, taking a hard look at how you get along and what you do to keep the peace will open new doors for growth. Resilience in a relationship begins with making positive emotional connections and new investments in the love you share.

Emotionally focused therapy (EFT) was developed by psychologists Susan Johnson and Leslie Greenberg at the University of British Columbia at a time when therapists and researchers were focused on changing *behaviors* to improve a couple's relationship. Behavior change helped partners make significant improvements in treatment, but for many couples these gains didn't last. EFT pioneered a new approach to improving relationships through emotion-based change.

Research studies have found that EFT is an effective treatment for distressed couples. More than 70 percent of couples receiving EFT recover from symptoms of relationship distress; up to 90 percent report seeing improvements in their relationship. Over 25 years of research has documented EFT's benefits to couples who are also facing other challenges, including depression, sexual disorders, traumatic exposure, depression, breast cancer, and childhood illness.

EFT is more than a clinically proven approach. It offers couples a new experience of their relationship, one that provides renewed trust and a deeper level of intimacy. EFT principles and practices enable couples to identify common patterns that define their conflicts and enable partners to shift out of positions that often keep them stuck. Partners are able to face their challenges together and find safety and a deep sense of well-being in the love they share.

About This Book

The purpose of this book is to provide you with an experience of EFT. We take you inside the EFT process and offer insights and activities that will strengthen your relationship. Our goal is to invite you to better understand your own emotions and share those emotions with your partner. We hope your partner will join you on this journey and that, together, you will take new steps to deepen your commitment to a relationship you can count on in the years to come.

In this book, you find

- The power of emotions to organize you and your relationship
- Key differences between types of emotion
- Ways to identify your conflict style and the role you play
- Predictable strategies couples use to manage difficult emotions
- Ways to overcome fears and resolve unspoken needs
- Steps for facing obstacles to a more caring and intimate relationship
- Rituals that will strengthen the emotional connection you and your partner share

EFT works with experience, and we've written this book with that in mind. Each chapter includes examples of couples working through various challenges. These stories take you inside the experience of couples in the process of EFT. We hope that these examples speak to some of the issues you and your partner are facing as well. You also find activities that invite you into an EFT experience. You'll get the most from this book when you follow these examples and practice these exercises with your partner.

This book is a reference, which means you don't have to read it straight through from beginning to end. Instead, you can dip into the chapters that you and your partner need most today. You don't need to have read the chapters that come before — you can dive right into the middle of the book and find what you need.

You can skip two types of text without missing crucial information:

- **Sidebars:** These shaded gray boxes include information that may interest you but isn't critical to your understanding of the subject at hand.
- **Anything marked by the Technical Stuff icon:** For more information on the Technical Stuff icon, see "Icons Used in This Book," later in this Introduction.

Finally, within this book, you may note that some web addresses break across two lines of text. If you're reading this book in print and want to visit one of these web pages, simply key in the web address exactly as it's noted in the text, pretending as though the line break doesn't exist. If you're reading this as an e-book, you've got it easy — just click the web address to be taken directly to the web page.

Foolish Assumptions

We're going to take a wild guess that you're reading this book because your relationship is important to you. Reading this book could have been your idea or your partner's idea, but either way you're looking for clear ideas on how working with emotions can give you a stronger and more vital relationship.

You may be reading this book because your therapist recommended it — but you don't have to be in therapy to benefit from *Emotionally Focused Couple Therapy For Dummies*.

Finally, you may be a therapist yourself. If so, we hope you find this no-nonsense approach to EFT a practical resource for supporting your work.

Icons Used in This Book

Icons are a handy way to catch your attention as you read. They can help you pick out key concepts throughout the book. The icons come in several varieties, each with its own special meaning:

The Activity icon indicates an exercise that you may want to do with your partner. Make sure you have a notebook to record your answers and responses to these exercises.

The Real-World Example icon marks stories of couples we've worked with in therapy. None of these stories is based on an actual couple. Any resemblance to a specific person, either living or dead, is purely coincidence. The stories themselves are based on composites of couples we've worked with and provide an accurate representation of the process of EFT.

The Remember icon highlights information that you'll want to remember after you've set down this book.

When we get into some details that only a therapist might find fascinating, we mark it with a Technical Stuff icon. If you're not a therapist, you may still find this material interesting, but it isn't essential to your understanding of the subject.

The Tip icon points out practical information that is likely to help your relationship.

The Warning icon draws your attention to things you want to avoid because they can cause you or your relationship pain or harm or just slow your progress.

Beyond the Book

In addition to the material in the print or e-book you're reading right now, this product also comes with some access-anywhere goodies on the web. Check out the free Cheat Sheet at www.dummies.com/cheatsheet/emotionallyfocusedcoupletherapy for warning signs of a struggling relationship, six keys to a resilient relationship, tips on reigniting the passion in your sex life, and advice on how to rebuild after an affair.

Where to Go from Here

You can read this book however you like, using the Table of Contents and Index to locate the information you need. If you're not sure where to begin, we suggest that you start by reading Part I, to get an overview of EFT.

Wherever you begin, remember that emotional safety is key. If you're walking the tight wire of your relationship in doing one of these exercises, your insecurity will undermine your ability to take new steps as a couple. Work up to some of the later exercises in the book as a couple. When needed, seek the help of a competent couple therapist.

The steps you and your partner take together to invest in greater security and a deeper commitment of love will bring growth and well-being for you and those you love.

Part I
Essentials of Emotionally Focused Therapy

The 5th Wave   By Rich Tennant

"In this session, Barbara, I'm going to ask you to put down your emotional guard, and Ted, I'm going to ask you to put down your banana cream pie."

In this part . . .

Emotion plays a powerful role in relationships. In this part, we spotlight emotions and the influence they have in shaping how couples get along. Here, you find an overview of emotionally focused therapy and its innovative approach to strengthening intimacy and love. We describe recent developments in neuroscience and why emotion is now understood as a major player in how people respond and react in their most intimate relationships. We also show you different levels of emotions and how you can recognize their influence in your relationship. The exercises in this part will help you gain a better handle on your emotions and how they can bring you and your partner closer to one another.

Chapter 1

The Basics of Emotionally Focused Therapy

Many men's stomachs instantly churn when they hear the words *couple therapy*. They often believe that if they go to therapy, they'll be blamed for everything that's wrong in the relationship.

"I'm not going to couple therapy," Mike told Angelina. "No way. I'll get in there, and you guys will eat me up."

The fear is that two women — the wife and the therapist — will team up against him, like a tag-team wrestling match, except this will be real. More like a tag-team UFC match. And when that cage door is shut, there's no turning back!

Many men see couple therapy as a lamb being led to the slaughter — and they're the lambs!

Men do have cause for concern. We've both seen men being unduly blamed. But we've also seen this done to women. The family therapy field is littered with old textbooks from the '70s and '80s, pinpointing women as the villains.

Emotionally focused therapy (EFT) is different. In this approach, the relationship itself is the client. The emotionally focused therapist believes that partners have a good reason for their behavior, even if it often isn't the best course of action for sustaining a loving relationship. There are reasons for your behavior and your partner's behavior that make sense, and it's up to the therapist to help you and your partner uncover these reasons.

A funny thing happens on this journey: As you begin uncovering the reasons behind your destructive behaviors, these pesky things called *emotions* emerge. We're not talking about just anger, frustration, and jealousy. We're talking about hurt, sadness, and fear. Vulnerable emotions. Emotions that couples rarely, if ever, show to each other.

Understanding the Emotionally Focused Therapy Approach

Change happens in EFT by heeding your gut-level, core emotion in response to your partner in key relationship situations. These core emotions too often occur outside your daily awareness. Your hurt, for example, immediately occurs when your partner forgets something important to you, yet again. This hurt is powerful, and you feel it in your body. But the core hurt is quickly replaced with an emerging anger that begins coursing through your veins.

"I can't believe you forgot again!" Mary shouts at Mason. Right then and there, she mobilizes around her anger. She inadvertently pushes her hurt as far away as her anger will take it. "How many times do I have to tell you that this is important to me?!"

Mason is confronted with what he sees as the following viable options:

- **Admit his mistake and apologize.** This option sounds good, but Mason knows that he has gone this route many times before, and although it used to be helpful, it doesn't turn out well anymore. Mary only gets more upset with him. She isn't ready to hear his apologies.

- **Downplay the importance.** Mason has been really busy at work — and he's working for the *family!* He could stress this, and say that it's impossible to remember everything. "C'mon, gimme a break. Is it that big of a deal?" Mason knows that this approach usually makes Mary angrier.

- **Attack back.** Hey, he's only human! Mary forgets things, too. In fact, last month, she forgot to pick up that thing at the store that he asked her to pick up. That was important to him. Maybe she needs to back off a little and stop nagging him about everything. This option throws Mary off track, and lessens the direct heat on Mason. But it also creates a wider divide between them than the preceding two options. If Mason goes with this option, he's looking at a day or two of extreme awkwardness and even silence in the home. That gets exhausting.

- **Take it mostly in silence.** In his mind, Mason has been nailed. He messed up again, and he knows it. What's he supposed to do now?

Mason doesn't have a clue. To him, all roads lead to Mary being more disappointed in him. So, although he feels terrible inside, he goes quiet in the hopes that it'll all blow over as soon as possible. The problem is, this signals to Mary that Mason doesn't care.

As you can see, none of these options is working for Mary and Mason. In effect, neither partner knows how to get out of these situations without damaging the other person and the relationship.

"We get caught in these types of situations all the time," Mason says.

"It's terrible," Mary adds. "It just keeps happening more and more between us."

Mason and Mary are caught in a seemingly never-ending trap of blame, disappointment, and hurt. Each person plays a role, but they can't seem to change the script. As the fighting and emotional disconnection mounts, more damage is done to the relationship. "We're growing apart," Mary says. "With every fight, we're growing apart."

EFT is designed to target these negative cycles that result in couples too often upset, arguing, and walling off from each other. Most couples argue, but when you step into repeating negative patterns that increase in intensity, you've stepped into the danger zone (see Chapter 5).

EFT targets the destructiveness of ongoing arguing cycles by helping partners go below the surface anger and frustration and into the more vulnerable emotions of hurt and fear. These emotions stand in stark contrast to the reactive emotions driving arguments. They're also more powerful.

Considering Your Own Arguing Cycle

Can you find yourselves within the example of Mason and Mary (see the preceding section)? Do you fall into similar patterns of arguing? Almost all couples do. The ones that remain emotionally connected while working through conflict are the ones that most often make it in the long run. Remaining emotionally connected doesn't mean that you aren't upset with each other. It means that, although you *are* upset, you aren't putting the relationship on the line. Neither of you sees the argument as *that* serious.

Compare your own arguing style with that of Mason and Mary. When you get angry at your partner, do you act similarly to Mary? If you find yourself in the shoes of Mason more often, is his experience similar to yours? Think about it separately first, and write down your responses:

I find myself relating to Mason in the following ways (for example, "I attack back when I hear my partner's anger . . ."):

_____

_____

_____

_____

_____

I find myself relating to Mary in the following ways (for example, "I seem to get angry with my partner, and I . . ."):

_____

_____

_____

_____

_____

When you're both finished, share and discuss your responses with each other.

During typical arguments, neither Mason nor Mary has much of a clue as to what the other is really feeling deep inside. Plus, awareness of their own deep emotions during such exchanges remains vague. One thing that *is* clear to each of them is the anger and frustration they feel toward each other.

After they argue, Mason typically goes into another part of the house, outside, or for a drive. Over time, Mary has grown to understand her own deep emotion more and has gotten in touch with a real sense of loneliness after she and Mason argue and emotionally disconnect. "After we argue and he goes off," she says, "I'm initially angry, but on another level, I'm really lonely."

Of course, Mason doesn't see or know any of this. All he sees is an upset Mary who is once again disappointed in him. "I've messed up again," Mason says. "I failed her once more."

In turn, Mary has no idea what Mason goes through after he withdraws from the arguing. "It's awful," he says. "The fact that I'm disappointing her plays over and over in my head."

In time, Mason was able to recognize and experience a deep sense of failing Mary. He was afraid that she might get fed up with him at some point.

On their own, Mason and Mary couldn't stop the momentum of their relationship strain. No amount of communication techniques (for example, "I statements," speaking one at a time, replaying back to each other what the other said, date nights) worked. It certainly wasn't for a lack of effort on their part. You and your partner may find yourselves in a similar situation.

De-escalating Your Conflict Cycle

As couples begin to recognize and reveal each other's authentic core emotions lying beneath the surface of habitual anger and other more-reactive emotions, they begin to see each other's responses differently.

"Learning that she gets louder when she really needs me or feels like I'm not there for her makes a big difference," Mason said. "That has really helped me. I'm beginning to see through her anger, realizing that behind it is a more legitimate emotion like fear or sadness. She needs to know that I'll be there for her. I mean, anger is legit, too, but what she really needs is happening behind her anger."

That's huge progress for Mason.

When partners start talking like Mason does here, they enter into what is referred to in EFT as the *cycle de-escalation* phase of treatment. This basically means that couples still argue and fight, but not nearly as often and not nearly as intensely. Mason, for example, is able to withstand Mary's anger without withdrawing — in part, because her anger isn't as intense as it was before. He's also aided in realizing what's going on for her behind her anger.

Similarly, Mary is able to "de-escalate" her anger, in part because she no longer views Mason as not caring when they get into an argument. "I've seen what's going on inside of him when we argue," Mary said. "He gets overwhelmed. He cares. It's just that he sometimes doesn't know how to respond or what to do. It's the opposite of what I thought before."

Mary used to think that when they argued, Mason just didn't care as much as she did. And for good reason — what she mostly saw was a man who argued with her, made excuses, said a few things or nothing at all, and then withdrew.

"When I saw how genuinely worried, even afraid, he gets after we argue, that changed me," she said. "No one that doesn't care feels that kind of pain," Mary said. "He gets stuck when I show too much anger. On some level, he actually fears what may come next — his having to withdraw and face a kind of misery alone. I had *no clue* that was going on for him. No clue."

As partners experience each other's vulnerable emotions and begin describing and sharing them with each other, cycle de-escalation is ushered in. They don't fight as often. Things between them really begin to change. This phase is a normal part of the unfolding process of EFT.

"I'm learning that Mason really isn't the enemy here," Mary said so well. "The enemy is our hiding behind our anger and frustration instead of slowing down and dealing with the real emotions behind these. The fear, the loneliness, the sadness — that's what gets triggered. That's what must be handled with care, together."

Relationship closeness in EFT is built as each partner *authentically experiences* the vulnerable emotions of the other person — up close and personal. When you actually walk in your partner's underlying emotional shoes, so to speak, you "get it." This makes EFT different from other approaches to couple therapy.

Finding Each Other in New Ways

As couples' arguing cycles decrease and calm down, partners often start growing closer to each other. They no longer see the other person as the enemy so much. The enemy is the destructive anger, frustration, jealousy, and other reactive emotions that fuel the arguing in the first place. The enemy is in hiding the vulnerable emotions beneath the reactive anger and frustration.

As couples begin feeling closer, the door leading to increased intimacy opens up. Partners can begin sharing their relationship needs with each other more freely. Whereas before maybe they could talk about needs, the environment between them was often tense, and the talk of "needs" was often met with resistance.

Caring About Each Other's Needs

Distressed couples tend to use "needs" in ways that blame each other. "We used to love throwing our needs at each other," Mason said. "You know, like, 'I need someone who cares about me!' or 'I need you to do this!' It was just another way to try to make the other person feel bad."

Couples have to be active and work at it to increase the intimacy between them at this point, however. Decreased arguing doesn't simply correlate to a closer relationship. But it is instrumental in making a closer relationship a possibility.

"As we learned to argue less, and understand our more-vulnerable sides," Mary said, "we began to feel closer to each other. The tension between us faded drastically."

With the fear of arguing and isolation greatly lessened, couples have the opportunity to significantly increase the intimacy between them. With Mason, this meant he didn't feel the need to withdraw or hide nearly as much. Mary wasn't a "threat" to point out his deficiencies so poignantly anymore. This allowed him to feel safer around her, to feel like he could show himself more, and speak up more.

"I went from walking on eggshells to walking on the beach with my wife!" Mason said. "Really. It sounds crazy, but that's how I see it." Whereas before he would hide his vulnerability and relationship needs from Mary, he now felt like he could open up to her more. This allowed him to share more of himself with her. And the more he did this without somehow starting an argument, the easier it became for him to risk opening up to Mary more.

From Mary's viewpoint, this was exactly what she had wanted for some time. "The thing that drove me the most crazy was his refusing to open up to me. I never knew what he was feeling," she said. "Now I know how he feels. And if I'm wondering, I know how to ask him and listen in a way that makes it easier for him to risk sharing deeper emotions with me."

Opening Up to Each Other

Mary opened up to Mason more as well. She shared with him when she started feeling isolated or alone, for example, instead of criticizing him out of a place of anger. Mary's anger pushed Mason away. When she confided in him that she was missing him or feeling alone, it made him want to comfort and reassure her.

"When she opens up to me," Mason explained, "and lets me know when she's starting to feel a tinge of loneliness, or a small fear that I'm not hearing her concerns — when she does this now, it's not from anger. It's from a place of . . . kind of fear. It's like she needs me. It feels good to be needed."

Mason is describing how they're using their primary or attachment-related emotion (see Chapter 2) to learn what each of them needs from the other. These needs are healthy, and they appeal to the other person. Mason likes that Mary needs him. And Mary likes that Mason opens up to her, and that she more clearly knows where she resides in his heart.

Couples that find new ways of relating and increase intimacy between them find that they

- Argue and fight less
- Argue with less intensity
- Are much closer emotionally
- Feel safer to open up with each other
- Become closer friends
- Have sex more often
- Have a better sex life
- Handle life as a united team
- Are more loving parents
- Are more effective parents
- Rely on each other to parent together as a team
- Can count on each other in times of distress

The end goal of EFT is the creation of a sustaining emotional bond between you that can withstand the tremors of life. In real life, this emotional bond is referred to as *love*. EFT is about creating a lasting love between you — a love you'll have to work at to sustain, and yet from which you'll draw a large part of your very sustenance.

"We can talk about anything now," Mason says. "My friends can't believe the things we talk about. But that's who we are now."

Facing the Future Together

The final phase of EFT concerns a future best served by the two of you supporting each other and together making decisions. EFT is a powerful vehicle that, when utilized properly and carefully, can greatly help strengthen emotional bonds.

Some psychological theorists take themselves and their approaches far too seriously. We want to present EFT in its proper context. EFT does not critique culture or lay down a blueprint for a better society. It does not promise to cure personality disorders, anxiety disorders, addictions, and such. It isn't a substitute for religion, spirituality, or anything remotely close to that. It's simply a theory and ensuing plan for bringing people together emotionally.

What EFT can do — and solid clinical research documents this — is help couples reorganize their relationship toward a greater level of intimacy, closeness, and friendship than often previously imagined.

When couples move into the third phase of EFT — facing their future together — they're often closer to each other than ever before. Some couples report feeling close when they were dating, but not to the mature level that they do after going through EFT.

"When we were first dating, everything was new and exciting," Mary said. "But the kind of excitement we have now is better. It's excitement rooted more deeply in real love than before. And while we had sexual passion then, the passion we have now tops it. Not always, mind you," she says, laughing. Mason fakes a shameful look down. "But we're so much more comfortable with each other now."

Tackling Problematic Issues Together

When couples are at ease with each other, as opposed to being at odds, previous problem areas aren't as difficult to navigate. That's because partners are working together, rather than against each other.

Couples often argue about their relationship through issues that have nothing to do with their relationship. Take going to the grocery store, for example. When Mary and Mason were in the middle of an argument, Mason would intentionally pick up something from the store or fast-food restaurant for himself to eat, and not get anything for Mary. He knew that this would upset Mary. A part of him cared, but another part of him wanted to take a shot back at her.

When couples see their relationship as a resource for security and support, things that used to come between them are often seen as opportunities to show the other person that you care.

"Many times now," Mason says, "I'll stop to get myself a drink or a snack, and I'll make sure to pick up something for her, too. A pack of gum, a bag of chips I know she loves but rarely buys for herself. Now I want to do things like this."

In EFT, it's not ideas to solve problems that are of central importance. It's getting the two of you together and on the same page at a deeper emotional level, which then allows you to solve old problems as an intimate team.

Chapter 2

Understanding the Power of Emotion in Relationships

*E*motion is the glue in romantic relationships. Couples stick together because of the attachments they make to each other. Over time, couples form emotional bonds that organize and prioritize their lives. They can see this clearly when they're "falling in love," because they're focused on being romantic. But over time, the influence of emotion can be taken for granted unless a couple falls into problems and chronic arguments begin to take over the relationship. Emotions can pull couples together, but they can also push couples apart.

Getting a clear grasp on emotions and their role in your relationship opens new ways to engage your partner and understand yourself. Key insights from the field of neuroscience highlight the influential role of emotion in the thoughts, values, and decisions that couples make. Research advances have shed light on new ways in which couples can more clearly see their emotional reactions and the resources they need.

Trusting Emotion

Couples have to make decisions all the time. Some partners trust their "gut instinct," while others prefer "just the facts." These are just preferences — no one lives by pure reason or pure emotion. You use both in making judgments and decisions, but you put your trust in one more than the other.

Emotionally focused therapy (EFT) doesn't make you more emotional. EFT enables you to be more effective with your emotions and your relationship. This requires trusting that emotions are helpful and necessary. We aren't talking about blindly trusting any emotion you have. By asking you to trust your emotions, we mean for you to tune into your emotional experience — and use that emotional experience as a source of information and a way of paying attention to the reactions you have in the moment.

Emotion is not the opposite of reason. Instead, emotion provides information that reason can use. You make better decisions when you're able to work with your emotional experience and use it in your responses and decisions as a couple. Emotion and reason work hand in hand.

Increasing your trust in emotion requires becoming more self-aware at an emotional level. The more you trust your emotion, the more effective you'll be in understanding yourself and others.

When you trust your emotions, you're better able to

- ✔ Notice an emotion when it shows up.
- ✔ Manage an emotional response for a reason.
- ✔ Use these responses to motivate action.
- ✔ See your impact on others.
- ✔ Manage your responses to others and their reactions.
- ✔ Choose actions with greater awareness of your relationship.

Consider the example of Robert and Candice. Robert has little use for his emotions. In his mind, emotions are a nuisance, especially at work. He tires of the seemingly endless conversations focused on this "issue" or that "issue" and how his colleagues need to be more understanding. He doesn't see himself as cold or uncaring — just practical and pragmatic. At home, Candice tells a different story: "He's out of touch. I could have had the worst day of my life, and Rob's response is 'Oh, sorry to hear that.'" Candice mocks Robert's half-hearted response. "You know, if he really cared, he would show it. But he doesn't. He just moves on," she says with disgust. "Rob's just too busy, his work is too important to be bothered with my day, my feelings, or whatever. . . ." Candice throws up her hands and slumps into her chair. "It doesn't matter what I say — he never listens." Robert sits silently, looking at the floor, seemingly bewildered. Candice winces, "It's like being married to a robot."

In moments like these, Robert freezes up. He describes being flooded with Candice's intensity and anger. All he remembers in the moment is the angry look on her face, and then he shuts down. His experience tells him that it's best to ride out the storm. Stay quiet and say little. "This storm will pass," he says to himself. Inside, Robert has little sense for what he's feeling other than admitting that these kinds of situations make him feel bad about himself and his marriage.

This has become a typical fight for Robert and Candice. Neither strategy is working for them. Candice angrily demands a response. Robert withholds in return. This goes on until one partner gives up. After giving up on so many fights, some couples move on to giving up on the relationship. Both Robert and Candice lack awareness of their own experiences and their impact on each other.

Too little or too much emotion *both* can result from not enough emotional self-awareness.

Here are some signs that emotional awareness may be lacking:

✔ Your partner understands your emotions better than you do.

✔ Your emotions often get the better of you in arguments.

✔ Your emotions are so strong that they're overwhelming.

✔ You often react rather than respond to your partner.

✔ You don't have a clue why your partner reacts so strongly to what you say or do.

✔ You don't know what you feel.

✔ You don't know why your arguments end in a worse place than where they started.

Think of a recent time when you were blindsided by an emotion. Maybe it was your own. Maybe it was your partner's emotion. Then follow these steps:

1. **Think about what happened, and ask yourself the following questions:**

   • How did the argument start?

   • What was the first sign that told you things weren't going well?

   • What were you feeling in that moment?

2. **Once you can name that feeling, ask yourself the following questions:**

   • Did you trust that feeling? Why or why not?

   • Did you listen to it? What was the meaning behind it?

- Did you act on it? What did you do with this feeling?
- How did your partner respond to this feeling?
- How might being more aware of this feeling help you in the future?

3. Discuss the questions in Step 2 with your partner.

Don't focus on the fight — instead, focus on the feelings behind the fight. Focus on your emotional responses and what you did with it. Then talk about how being more aware of this feeling may help in the future.

Increasing your emotional awareness increases your ability to understand your relationship and your partner. You're better able to anticipate and respond to the emotional signals in the moment when you're more aware of your own.

Many couples see their emotions more clearly after a fight rather than in the middle of it. This makes sense because partners are picking up the emotional pieces and can better see what was going on after the heat of the conflict.

Trusting emotion gives you an advantage in those moments by making you more aware of yourself and your partner. Emotion gives you information you need about yourself and your partner, especially when the stakes are high and the topic is a challenge. The key is having access to this information when you most need it — and that's in the moment!

Defining the Role of Emotion in Relationships

Emotions play a critical role in your life together as a couple. Couples rely on emotion to communicate their values, priorities and love. From the simple joy of an ordinary moment to imminent needs in a time of despair, emotions connect couples to the experiences they share. Here are some ways in which emotion makes a difference in your relationship:

✔ **Focusing attention:** Emotions highlight what's important. Your emotional responses draw your attention to what matters in the moment. If you're feeling alone and your partner ignores your sad expression, you may feel angry at your partner. In that moment, the feeling you have is emotion getting your attention.

Juan said, "I felt my anger flare. Rosa gave me one of those looks, and I knew in that moment that we were headed for a fight." Later, Juan explained, "When she started to cry, I dropped my anger and took her hand. It wasn't worth it." In both of these instances, Juan gave his attention to the emotional experience. Whether anger or compassion, his emotions spotlight what's important.

✔ **Setting priorities:** Emotions point to what you need. Emotions are part of our motivational system. When you're dealing with something important, you feel strongly about it. You make it a priority. This is true in relationships. Couples often argue about the issues they have strong feelings about.

Holiday events trigger an ongoing conflict for Carrie and Lee. Lee is from a close family that puts a high price on loyalty and attending family events. Carrie feels excluded and feels that Lee minimizes her needs for more couple time. Lee feels forced into an uncompromising position with his family. Both Lee and Carrie feel passionate about their needs, and this shows up in their arguments.

✔ **Providing meaning:** Emotions color our memories and experiences. If you've had a bad experience in the past, this experience may influence how you anticipate the future. The same can be said of the positive experiences and memories you share. The way you understand what's happening in the moment or has happened in the past is remembered at an emotional level.

Larry and Tamara make special plans to get away for a weekend several times a year. These getaways make them feel close as a couple. The positive experiences they've shared remind them of the importance of their relationship and what they mean to each other.

✔ **Priming action:** Your emotions put you into motion. If you're afraid, you may keep your distance. If you're angry, you may demand to be heard. Either way, your emotions are pushing you to respond to a situation in a particular way. The same can be said for tender moments in a relationship. Hugs, kisses, or caresses all can be responses to feelings we have of love or concern.

Terrance knows himself well. When he's stressed, he prefers to be alone. Sharon is more prone to talk and seek his reassurance when she's worried. Each action makes sense to the person doing it, because seeking or withdrawing is an emotional response. You can see how these differences could be difficult if both partners are facing a difficult situation as a couple.

✔ **Triggering core beliefs:** Emotions shape how you understand yourself and your relationship. The warmth and good feeling you have in your partner's arms tell you that you're loved, you're important, and you matter. Similarly, your partner's harsh words and stinging anger can call all these previous beliefs into question. Couples are always making sense of what they experience together. Your emotions color your memories and how you make sense of your relationship.

Emotional growth for both of you

EFT works at an emotional level to transform couples' relationships. The focus of much of the therapy is on what happens between the two partners as they work out difficulties in their relationship. At the same time, the EFT process helps each partner develop greater awareness and capacity for working with his or her own emotions.

Here are four areas where you may grow in your own ability to work with emotion through EFT:

✔ **Self-awareness:** Emotionally focused therapists help each partner become more aware of his or her emotional experience. This involves being able to label your emotions and develop a language for your experience. In EFT, we're less concerned that you come up with a specific feeling word and more concerned that you can put some meaning to what's happening in the moment. This includes being able to name what you feel in the moment — it's the emotional meaning that's key. Self-awareness begins with being able to simply accept what you're experiencing. Allow for it to happen, and then get to know it. Sometimes an emotionally focused therapist will figuratively ask you to "walk around" in your experience. Just as you might take a stroll through a new neighborhood, you need to get to know your emotional world, so when those feelings show up, you know where you are.

✔ **Self-expression:** In EFT, therapists invite partners to experience and understand their emotions. Research has shown that just expressing emotion isn't enough. You have to unpack these experiences and be able to make sense of them. Some people would be happy to discuss their emotions at a distance instead of experiencing them firsthand. They've been told directly or learned from experience that emotions are not to be trusted — so it's safe to analyze emotions and describe emotions, but it's not safe to feel them. The emotionally focused therapist works with emotion to help partners express their emotions directly with new understanding and greater confidence.

✔ **Regulating emotion:** An emotion must be regulated to be of use. Emotionally focused therapists provide people with a therapeutic relationship where emotions are understood and supported. In a relationship, partners' reactions can be misunderstood and sometimes rejected. Often, when you have a mix of emotion or a strong emotion, it's difficult to make sense of the feeling, much less explain it to your partner. In these situations, a therapist's validation and empathy can open new levels of understanding and clarity in making sense of intense emotional experience. Being able to be seen and heard in this way provides an important soothing and calming effect. Emotionally focused therapists engage these experiences to work through these emotions as a team.

The same is true for partners who tend to stay away from their emotions and lack the necessary awareness to engage an emotional experience. The EFT process enables partners to gain a greater ability to engage, accept, understand, and expand their emotional experience. As partners do this together, they're better able to work alongside their emotional experience rather than against it.

✔ **Emotional reflection:** The successful experience and use of emotion brings new levels of self-understanding. The stories you tell about yourself are a way of expressing who you are. These stories of triumphs and tragedies carry with them emotional experiences that shape what you know and have come to expect of yourself and others. In EFT, we open up new opportunities for partners to experience themselves and each other in ways that expand how they see themselves. They experience new levels of confidence and competence that provide a new basis for seeing themselves and their partners.

Dave felt alone and often neglected. He shared these concerns with Cheryl. She challenged him to find more "guy friends" and to "not feel sorry for himself." Dave felt his stomach drop as fear raced through his body. Old thoughts from his childhood raced through his mind: "You're not important, you don't matter, and you're all alone." These feelings left him doubting whether he could ever be loved as he had hoped.

✔ **Communicating by showing emotion:** A subtle smile or an angry look at your partner will trigger a response. Communicating care, attention, and love involve displays of emotion that signal approach. Similarly, emotions like anger, disgust, and contempt signal messages of distance and rejection. Even the absence of showing emotion can communicate that something is wrong.

Joanne knew that Thomas's day must have been bad. He looked upset, and he dismissed several efforts she made to check on him. She kept her distance, hoping for an opportunity to talk about what happened. Thomas would prefer to keep the matter to himself, but his emotion was communicating that something was wrong.

Couples rely on emotion to share their values and priorities. Keeping your verbal and nonverbal messages clear and in agreement makes a difference. If your face is saying one thing and your words are saying another, your partner won't trust what you're saying. Your feelings can show up in subtle ways that your partner may notice even if you don't. Matching your words and feeling requires emotional self-awareness. Couples are always communicating at an emotional level, and what they're communicating can bring them closer together or drive them farther apart.

Identifying the Differences between Positive and Negative Emotions

The process of change in EFT is guided by changing emotional experiences. EFT pioneer Leslie Greenberg makes clear that transformative change occurs when one emotion is replaced by another emotion. When you experience a more adaptive emotion like joy or surprise, it will push away more problematic emotions like distress or anxiety.

Lawrence waits pensively for Shannon to return from work. He's grown accustomed to Shannon's frustration about his unemployment. Typically, Lawrence feels anxious when she returns home, but to his surprise, Shannon greets him with a kiss and shares her appreciation for his support and commitment during this difficult time. Lawrence settles into the moment, feeling more at peace and actively engaging Shannon in a conversation about her day.

The experience of more adaptive (or positive) emotions tends to push out more problematic (or negative) emotions because the two experiences won't work together. You can't frown and smile at the same time — they're incompatible. In EFT, emotion is a key ingredient and agent of change.

Recent studies suggest that positive emotions can undo the effects of negative emotion. Often the role of negative emotion is focused on survival. When threatened, you may defend with an angry attack or retreat in fear. Either response is a powerful negative emotion that focuses and concentrates your attention on a specific threat. Positive emotions expand and broaden your focus and emphasize growth. These emotions help you move toward exploring new views of yourself, your partner, and your relationship.

Here's a list of some positive emotions:

- ✔ Amusement
- ✔ Awe
- ✔ Compassion
- ✔ Contentment
- ✔ Gratitude
- ✔ Hope
- ✔ Interest
- ✔ Joy
- ✔ Love
- ✔ Pride
- ✔ Sexual desire

And here are some negative emotions:

- ✔ Anger
- ✔ Contempt
- ✔ Disgust
- ✔ Embarrassment
- ✔ Fear
- ✔ Guilt
- ✔ Sadness
- ✔ Shame

Positive emotions can provide antidotes to negative emotions. Of course, it isn't as simple as wishing away sadness or grief or forcing yourself to think positive in the midst of a bad day. If you acknowledge your frustration and disappointment, and get to know it a bit, you may find some sadness there as well. Here's the key: Slowing down to experience this sadness gives you more to work with, such as greater awareness of yourself and others. Facing your sadness opens up new possibilities for self-understanding and seeking support. You'll feel more effective and have greater vitality in working through these emotions and greater clarity about yourself. Your sadness transforms your irritability, and the actions you take in response can promote a new feeling of confidence and well-being. Transformational emotional experiences result from working through emotion rather than getting away from them or being overwhelmed by them.

Often we see couples make strides in their relationship as the negative emotions that drive a partner's painful past are replaced by new experiences of success and growth. Think of these emotions as steps of growth. As you and your partner make a new step together, you make reaching the next step even more possible. Growth promotes growth, and positive emotions promote positive emotions — enabling you to be more resilient in facing the everyday challenges of life.

Broaden and build: Positive emotions are key to resilient relationships

Research by psychologist Barbara Fredrickson highlights the specific ways positive emotions make a difference in our everyday lives. Fredrickson's theory suggests that negative emotions are particularly important for our survival. Responses to fight or flight in a situation narrow your attention and keep your focus on some potential threat. This works well when facing a dangerous threat or harm because you're focused and ready to respond.

Positive emotions work in the opposite direction: They broaden and expand your attention and increase your flexibility and range of responses to a given situation. Positive emotions help you be more adaptive and responsive to your circumstances. You're more likely to engage others and explore new opportunities and possibilities. As you explore with greater curiosity and openness, your positive emotions enable you to learn and possibly correct false assumptions about yourself or your world. Over time, these broader experiences make you more resilient and responsive to your

relationships and surroundings. Positive emotions enable you to build more psychological resources over time. These benefits accumulate, enabling you to live more effectively and to have a greater sense of well-being.

Fredrickson's theory helps explain why couples who've gone through EFT often describe a greater confidence in their ability to face adversity together. They become more resilient. This makes sense when you understand how the ongoing conflict in a couple's relationship can lock partners into a survival mode. Their arguments follow rigid patterns of negative emotion that restrict their emotional and cognitive resources. An emotionally focused therapist works with these negative emotions to transform partners' awareness and engage new opportunities for addressing a couple's underlying concerns. As this process unfolds, partners move toward engaging their emotions differently, broadening the understanding and building new resources in the relationship they share.

Seeing What Science Has to Say about Emotion

Decades of research on emotion, neurophysiology, and clinical and social psychology have opened new ways of understanding what happens when a distressed couple has an argument and what steps a therapist may take to effectively intervene. Research continues to demonstrate the developing role of the brain and its role in emotional functioning.

In this section, we review several findings that highlight the relationship of your brain, your emotions, and your relationships.

Recent brain research

For decades, neuroscientists assumed that the adult brain was essentially fixed in form and function, but not anymore. Today we know that the picture of a static, unchanging brain is incorrect.

The brain has a property called *neuroplasticity,* the ability to change its structure and function in significant ways. You probably know that your brain was like this when you were a child, but you may be surprised to learn that your brain maintains this flexibility throughout your life. You can affect the very structure of your brain through new experiences and changing your thinking.

The way you internally process and respond to emotion for yourself and with others is partially the result of brain circuitry imprinted in your early years by the genes you inherited from your parents. But it's also based on your current, ongoing experiences.

Early brain circuitry is *not* forever fixed. Your emotional style (the way you process and respond to emotion) is quite stable over time. But this is for your own good. Just imagine for a minute if you forgot how to respond to the cashier at the grocery story every time he offered a "Thank you" and a warm smile for shopping there. Talk about living the movie *Groundhog Day!* We need to habitually respond in typical ways for our own good. We come to count on these responses without thinking about them.

But when your typical response is to avoid emotion, get overly anxious, or hastily react to your emotions, this usually pushes others away. Your emotional style *can* be altered by new experiences and by conscious, intentional effort — at any stage of your life.

The brain's way of keeping us connected

In his book *Social Intelligence: The New Science of Human Relationships* (Bantam), Daniel Goleman vividly explains how a class of brain cells called *mirror neurons* sense — in real-time — what another person is feeling and is about to do. Now think about this for a minute:

- ✔ Your brain is built to sense what another person is feeling and what action she'll likely take — all instantaneously.

- ✔ Your brain is able to do the action of your partner in your mind, and anticipate the next action she may take, enabling you to share experience.

- ✔ Mirror neurons allow you to feel with that person. Not feel your own feelings, but feel the other person's feelings with her.

Whenever you make contact with another person — be it through talking, looking each other in the eyes, touching, making love — your social brains interlock. This obviously has enormous ramifications for your relationship. Together you can reshape the circuitry of your brains toward a more positive connection and intimacy in your relationship. You can "reboot" your brain, so to speak.

Consider the following exchange between Brian and Jackie in light of how our social brain's mirror neurons set us up to *feel with* the other person: Jackie had a decent day at work. She was looking forward to coming home and spending time with Brian and the family. Yes, it gets hectic at home, but it's "their hectic," not the world's.

Brian sees Jackie walk in and says loudly, "About time you got here. Ashley has already torn up three rooms! There are toys all over the floor, dishes everywhere, just a big mess. I can't keep up with her!" Brian has just dumped a load of his emotional reactions.

In rapid response to this, Jackie's brain is activating circuits of those very same distressing emotions. She's being *pulled* to respond from her own secondary emotion because her mirror neurons are taking on the experience of Brian's secondary emotional state. Her body is tensing. Her pulse is beginning to race. She's feeling hotter. Just like Brian. And all this happened in a matter of a few seconds, while she was shutting the front door, putting down her briefcase, and taking off her shoes.

Read Jackie and Brian's story with your partner, and talk briefly with your partner about the following:

> ✔ How do you imagine Jackie responded to Brian?
>
> ✔ How do you think Brian felt?
>
> ✔ Can you guess what's going on inside Brian? If you could get to his truest feelings, what would they be?

Take a step back for this situation. Can you begin to see this two-person interlocking brain feedback cycle happening almost automatically? The odds are stacked in favor of Jackie responding in either a defensive or critical manner. She doesn't have to respond in those ways, mind you. Throughout this book, we guide you to more helpful ways to respond when you're faced with similar situations.

Let's take a look at the same scenario, but this time with Brian doing a better job of trying to relate to Jackie from his truer and softer emotions: Jackie had a decent day at work. She was looking forward to coming home and spending time with Brian and the family. Yes, it gets hectic at home, but it's "their hectic," not the world's.

Brian sees Jackie walk in and says wearily, "It sure is good to see you. I know it's not what you want to hear right now, but Ashley has torn up three rooms, there are toys all over the floor, dishes everywhere, just a big mess. I'm feeling *really* overwhelmed."

Can you *feel* the difference?

With your partner, each of you briefly put yourselves in the shoes of Brian and Jackie in the following ways:

> ✔ Take a minute to share with each other how you *sensed* the second scenario differently from the first.
>
> ✔ If you were Brian in the second scenario, how would you have felt when saying what he said?
>
> ✔ In turn, how would you have felt being Jackie in the second scenario? (Psst! You're trying on those mirror neurons!)

As Goleman says, emotions are contagious. If you've ever caught a ball thrown hard your way, you can remember that inevitable sting in the palm of your hand. It's the same with emotion. When someone throws strong emotion your way, you'll feel it in your body. It may sting or it may light you with warmth, but you'll feel it — and fast.

Two brains are better than one

Two brains may be better than one, particularly when the bodies that belong to those brains are holding hands. Researcher James Coan found that his research participants who experienced a threat of pain experienced less stress while holding the hands of their partners. The stress in this case was measured using a brain fMRI that showed how much of the brain was active during a threat of pain.

The effect of hand holding was most clearly seen among couples who were very satisfied with their relationships. This research provides an important example of the ways in which your relationship with your partner can better enable you to face and manage the stresses that are part of life as a couple.

How fear works in the brain

Your brain has a number of emotional systems that enable you to actively respond in different ways. Your fear system acts as a guardian that alerts your body to various threats and dangers. This system may trigger a range of responses from fight to flight (see Chapter 3) when you're faced with either physical or psychological threats. This system functions at a basic level and may not discriminate well between the various types of danger you encounter. Fear can also run in the background, affecting your response to other people, so you may show anger in response to a harsh criticism, but what's running alongside that anger is fear.

Pam and Dave are a good example of fear at work. After a 12-hour shift, Pam returns home to find Dave half-asleep on the couch, dishes in the sink, and his work clothes strewn throughout the apartment. Pam gets Dave's attention: "Can't you try to be more considerate?" Hiding little of her disdain, Pam continues, "It's not fair that I have to come home to this."

Dave responds defensively and mocks Pam's concerns by exaggerating his efforts to clean up his dishes and clothes.

"Fine," Pam says. "At least I know where I stand with you. Jerk!" Pam slams the door and waits another two days before trying the conversation again. Meanwhile, Dave withdraws in silence, avoiding Pam's attempts to smooth over her angry and hurtful attack.

Dave's avoidance and Pam's anger are defensive fear responses. These interactions push them into a panic state where efforts to repair after a fight get blocked by the fear of being vulnerable. In these moments, you may be like

Dave and withdraw in self-protection or you may be like Pam and react with attacking comments to draw attention to your pain. Over time, this fear may organize your relationship, as you and your partner both begin to take fewer and fewer steps toward the vulnerability you used to share.

Understanding Attachment Theory and the Emotional World of Relationships

You can think about emotions as the signals that communicate with your mind, body, and social world. These signals carry important information about everything from love to survival. To understand emotion's role in romantic relationships, EFT follows John Bowlby's attachment theory, which provides a map for understanding the ways in which emotions guide relationships and relationships shape emotional experience.

Bowlby proposed a number of important ideas that highlight the importance of relationships from infancy to adulthood. Attachment relationships are those you turn to for security and significance. Your relationships may change over time, but the importance of your attachment relationships is a constant through your life.

Romantic relationships in adulthood may take up to two years to develop a level of significance. These bonds provide a source of emotional stability and support, promoting each partner's resilience and growth. The strength of an attachment bond is determined by a couple's ability to remain emotionally engaged, especially in times of trouble or uncertainty.

Couples are likely to experience a number of benefits associated with a more secure relationship, including the following:

- **Better management of emotion:** Couples are less reactive and more likely to seek support when needed.

- **Better processing of information:** Couples have greater openness and flexibility in problem solving and are better able to handle uncertainty.

- **Better communication:** Couples use more empathy and share more openly about their own needs and experiences.

- **Better self-understanding:** Partners are more clear and coherent about their own identities.

The foundation of felt security

Here are three characteristics of a secure attachment:

- **Someone you can count on:** Being human means you depend on others. Your survival depends on this. There is no escaping a basic human drive to seek and maintain relationships with others who are important to you. For couples, the key is not if or when, but *how* you rely on your partner.

  You stand strong as an individual when you have a clear sense of where you stand with those who matter to you. A secure relationship provides you with a clearer view of yourself. This happens in the light of a relationship with someone who cares about you.

- **Someone I can turn to in times of trouble:** Knowing that you can turn to your partner for comfort and care is essential to attachment security. Bowlby described this aspect of attachment as creating a "safe haven." Attachment security promises a relationship that offers protection and safety amidst the storms and stresses of life.

- **Someone who gives me confidence:** Having a secure attachment means having a relationship that encourages growth and self-exploration. Bowlby called this quality a "secure base." A secure attachment provides a foundation that partners can build upon so that they can take personal risks and explore life together.

The keys to strengthening an attachment bond are being accessible and responsive to your partner. An attachment bond provides a "felt sense of security." It's something you know in your bones. You must be able to experience a confidence that your partner will be there if you're in need and know that he or she will respond specifically to you.

If you boil attachment security down to one question, the bottom line is: "Can I depend on you when I need you?" The answer isn't just about what your partner *intends* — it's about what your partner *delivers*. This requires accessibility and responsiveness. Sue Johnson, in her book *Hold Me Tight* (Little, Brown, and Co.), identified a number of ways partners demonstrate being accessible and responsive in intimate relationships.

According to Johnson, being accessible to your partner means you will

- Give attention to requests or concerns.
- Be available at an emotional level.

- ✔ Give your partner priority.
- ✔ Make your partner feel included.
- ✔ Listen to your partner's deepest concerns.

Being responsive to your partner means you will

- ✔ Be there in times of need.
- ✔ Respond to your partner's need for closeness.
- ✔ Provide support in times of uncertainty.
- ✔ Make efforts to reconnect after an argument.
- ✔ Affirm your partner's value and importance.

Take a moment and test your own level of accessibility and responsiveness. Look through each of the previous items and answer the following questions. Start first with accessibility and then ask these questions again about responsiveness.

1. **Look at the list, and choose one item that you see as one of your strengths — something you do often or that comes more easily.**

   Remember a time recently when this was true of you. What did you do in that moment? How did you show your partner you cared?

2. **Look again at the list, and choose one item that you see as an area of growth — something you don't do often or find a struggle.**

   Remember a time recently when you had an opportunity to be more responsive or accessible. What did you do instead? What was its impact? What was going through your mind at the time?

People often get stuck in these areas, and when they do, they typically have a good reason for holding back or being more cautious. Think about your area of growth and name the reason you may give for holding back.

The goal of this exercise is self-awareness. We're asking you to think about areas of success and growth. In EFT, we also focus on how your partner experiences you in these areas. What you both experience really matters, but for now we want you to focus on your own assessment.

If you choose to share your answers with your partner, keep the focus on your own experience and awareness. Avoid discussing whether your partner's views are right or wrong. You'll have other opportunities to discuss these issues together, but for now we're looking for you to focus on yourself.

Doing this exercise gives you a glimpse into what EFT is all about. A primary goal of EFT is to strengthen both partners' ability to work effectively with their emotions in vulnerable ways. This means being there for your partner when it matters most.

Staying in sync

When couples work together at an emotional level, they often find a deep and powerful way to be in tune with each other. This involves the two working as one. Partners are in touch with one another in physical ways (for example, by making eye contact or holding hands) and emotional ways (for example, by displaying empathy or offering support). Couples who share moments in which emotion connects them in profound ways are able to grow in their relationship and as individuals.

Toni sat silently, tears running down her face, her chest rising and falling with each wave of pain. Conner leaned toward her, allowing their shoulders to touch. In the silence, they breathed together. "I am so sorry," Connor said. "I wish I could've been there somehow. I guess I want you to know that I'm here right now." He reached for her hand.

She squeezed tight. "It just hurt so much. I was alone and afraid. I couldn't reach you and I needed you, Conner." Toni looked into his eyes.

"Yeah, I see that now," Conner said, choking back his own tears. "I didn't understand. I hurt you so much. I wish I had been there. I am *so* sorry."

Toni relaxed into his arms.

Conner missed Toni's doctor's appointment and the news of her miscarriage. Toni had counted on his being there, but he was delayed. In the past, he had tried to explain and help her see that he'd tried to be there, but in this moment, he joined her fear and pain, and owned the moment with her.

Connecting at this level requires you to take risks and walk through vulnerability to meet each other. Just like a hiker who's traversing a narrow canyon wall, couples need to be intentional in staying in contact as they navigate vulnerable emotions. When couples are able to walk through these risky, sometimes painful moments, they find new levels of peace.

Here are four keys to staying in sync with your partner:

- ✔ Maintaining eye contact
- ✔ Sitting so you can see each other face to face

  ✔ Touching or holding hands

  ✔ Slowing down and making space for emotion and reflection

Key moments of emotional connection enhance a couple's felt sense of security. These moments in EFT often put couples back on a path toward closeness and a more meaningful relationship. Research has shown that couples who maintain a more secure relationship are more likely to reach out to one another for support, more clearly communicate their needs, and have more trusting and satisfying relationships.

Understanding reactive strategies of insecurity

Attachment works like a warning system in a romantic relationship. In times of distress or threat, it triggers partners to seek care, contact, or comfort from each other. In relationships with attachment security, partners depend on each other in their times of need to help cope with the emotional distress. Bowlby believed this was a person who had attachment significance — someone you would look to first.

The attachment system is a powerful motivator. Bowlby believed that being isolated and alone was a traumatizing experience for anyone. Humans don't thrive in isolation. For couples, isolation and withdrawal can be common responses to conflict. In these moments, the attachment alarm system rings, but no one is home to answer.

Attachment insecurity can be triggered by silent withdrawal as easily as it can by angry attack. Insecurity results from a lack of safety, not simply a lack of engagement.

Attachment insecurity results when a primary caregiver or other attachment figure is unresponsive and unable to respond to a person's needs in a situation of distress. In a couple's relationship, this occurs in moments of distress where efforts to seek comfort or care from another person don't relieve the initial distress. What triggers distress may be related to a couple's relationship or other threats to well-being, including physical pain, threats of loss, work-related problems, and stress associated with new situations.

Attachment insecurity can have lasting negative effects on a couple's relationship and the well-being of each partner. Research has shown that insecure attachment has been linked to a number of negative emotions:

- Loneliness
- Anger
- Anxiety
- Depression
- Physical complaints
- Lower self-esteem and self-confidence

If you're feeling distress and your partner isn't available or won't respond, you'll likely have three responses:

- **You'll recognize that regular efforts to reach your partner won't succeed.** Because of this, you'll give up on direct efforts to get a response to your needs.

- **You'll experience some negative thought about your partner and possibly negative thoughts about yourself.** You may think, "All he cares about is himself. He's an insensitive jerk!" You may also think, "She doesn't really care about me. No one does really. I'm just not worth it."

- **You'll turn to a backup strategy for addressing the distress that you're experiencing.** This distress now includes your partner's failed response, so the intensity of your distress is at a higher level than it was initially.

The attachment system works to adapt and regulate emotion through a safe and trusting relationship. Over time, as the attachment system fails to provide a safe and secure response, attachment insecurity results. A couple begins to rely on secondary ways to cope with the unresolved distress in their relationship, which is already compounded by attachment insecurity itself.

Juanita always felt one down in Drew's family. Cultural differences played a big role in her conflicts with Drew. She often expressed a need for reassurance after visiting his family because she never felt accepted by his parents. After a recent fight, Drew expressed his frustration: "I can't help my family. They are the way they are. I don't like it, but there's little I can do. I don't know what you want from me." Drew stormed away in silence leaving Juanita in tears, alone, and afraid.

Usually, Juanita was able to find peace by talking through her fears with Drew. But his anger this time threw her. Some of his anger was directed not at his family but at her. Her anxiety grew as a result. She felt angry at Drew because he dismissed her concerns, even though he knew how hard she struggled to deal with her fear. Now she was also afraid that the rejection she felt from his family was showing up in their relationship. This feeling was compounded by the fact that Drew was gone and no longer available.

Couples in moments of insecurity turn to alternative strategies for managing their emotional distress. These common patterns of coping are reactive. They're based on insecurity and the failure of the relationship to provide a means for addressing the initial emotional distress.

There are three basic patterns of coping that include anxious, avoiding, or mixed responses to the attachment distress. Anxious responses work to turn up the volume of the attachment alarm system, pleading for a response. Avoidant responses tend to minimize or mute the signals of distress. Partners turn to these coping responses in hopes of managing the ongoing distress each person feels, often in an intense way. Mixed responses can be confusing because they combine both over- and under-responding to times of emotional distress. Partners with this coping response send "mixed" signals.

✔ **Anxious coping strategy:** The anxious coping strategy is based on anxious ways of relating. Partners seek reconnection and reassurance by seeking physical and emotional closeness. Often, this pattern is associated with someone who comes across as "needy" or "dependent," especially to the partner whose attention is being sought.

Partners using this strategy tend to have more negative views of themselves. If you're prone to rely on this strategy, you're more likely to fear rejection and seek reassurance as a result. You're also more likely to see your partner in a positive light, as someone whose opinion and care ultimately matters.

Here are some common worries found among partners who would tend to use an anxious strategy:

- My partner doesn't care about me as much as I care about him or her.

- My partner may fall out of love with me.

- My partner may not want to stay involved with me.

- My partner could easily be interested in someone else.

Juanita has many of these fears. Over time, her fears have gotten worse, particularly as she has felt Drew's impatience with her frequent need for reassurance. Although he understands the tension in his family, he often feels like his reassurance makes no difference. He doesn't mind the questions Juanita has, but her anxious tone drives him away. No matter what he says, the tone keeps coming back.

✔ **Avoiding coping strategy:** Partners who use the avoiding coping strategy tend to minimize attachment emotions. If the alarm is ringing, they want to put a pillow over it or find some way to turn it off. Some common tendencies include avoiding closeness and more intimate experiences, suppressing thoughts to manage emotion, and minimizing a need for others. If this is your coping strategy, you likely value self-reliance and independence and have a more negative view toward others.

Here are some common thoughts that fit with an avoiding coping style:

- I prefer to keep my concerns to myself.
- I rarely talk about my personal needs.
- Being close makes me uncomfortable.
- It's hard for me to depend on my partner.

Drew clearly identifies with being more independent. He often feels intimidated by his family, and he found his relationship with Juanita a welcome change from the pressure and expectations of his family. In recent months, he has turned more inward, finding it hard to meet Juanita at an emotional level. He prefers to avoid the family issues and focus on work and their shared sports activities. He seldom lets on about his frustration with Juanita's neediness, figuring it'll just get worse if she knows how he really feels.

✔ **Mixed coping strategy:** The mixed coping strategy involves a combination of avoiding and anxious responses. Partners who turn to this way of coping often have the fears common to the anxious strategy and yet also struggle to trust closeness and intimacy, which fits with the avoiding approach. If this is your coping style, you may fear what it would be like to be rejected and at the same time keep yourself from being in a situation where that could happen. Partners who use this approach often adopt a more passive approach to their relationship and often sacrifice their own needs instead of risking being rejected.

These insecure strategies are ways of coping, not indicators of a psychological problem. People turn to these strategies when what they need is not available. The challenge for couples is that insecure patterns of relating tend to reinforce themselves. This is what's happening for Juanita and Drew. The threat of Drew's family rejection spun Juanita into her fear, and when she sought comfort from Drew, he turned to his strategy of avoiding. Over time, these coping responses become predictable patterns that couples practice without intending. When these patterns become fixed and problems remain, a couple relationship becomes emotionally insecure.

Think about a time in your relationship when you reached out to your partner for contact but didn't get what you needed. Look over the three strategies — anxious, avoiding, and mixed — and answer the following questions.

✔ Which of these strategies best describes what you do in moments of insecurity?

✔ What are the messages you say about yourself in these moments? What are the messages you say about your partner in these moments?

✔ How does this strategy help you? How does this strategy keep you from what you need?

Understanding the role of attachment in your closest relationships points you toward new steps you can take as a couple. The patterns that define relationships make sense when you understand the goals and motivations for the behaviors that keep these patterns in place. Attachment theory provides both a map and guide for building a more resilient relationship.

Chapter 3

Organizing Your Emotional World

. . . .

In This Chapter

▶ Looking inside emotional experience

▶ Discovering the deeper experience of your emotions

▶ Seeing emotion as a process

. . . .

According to conventional wisdom, it's good to "talk about your feelings." But this assumes you know what your feelings are and that you value what they have to say. Often, people assume that talking about feelings helps you get your emotions out there (as opposed to holding them in). However, the purging of emotion by just "letting it all out" is an ineffective strategy for dealing with emotions. (See the nearby sidebar, "What happens when you vent," for an example of why venting isn't a good idea.)

In this chapter, we identify the critical role emotions play in close relationships and explore how feelings inform your thoughts and actions. We focus on ways you can increase your emotional awareness and practice sharing your experience with your partner. Emotion provides glue to hold your relationship together, and in this chapter we help you see how that works.

Unpacking Emotion, Up Close and Personal

Emotions are more than just feelings. They pull together what you feel in the moment with how that registers in your body, as well as what you do to make sense of it all. By paying attention to your emotions, you're better able to put words to experience and get support from those around you. Building a deeper understanding of emotion begins with the core building blocks of emotional experience: affect, feelings, and emotions.

What happens when you vent

Bob vents his frustrations regularly. He's proud that he never keeps things in. If he feels angry, he lets it out.

"Honey!" Bob says loudly. "My keys are gone again!"

"Sorry, dear," his wife answers. "I haven't seen them."

"You always say that!" Bob yells. "And yet every time I lose my keys, it's because you had them last!"

"I really haven't had them or seen them Bob," his wife answers.

"Here we go again. I'll find them if I trace through your steps, not mine!" Bob scowls.

Bob throws things around while looking for his keys. Then he spots them, right over by the microwave . . . where he left them last night.

Venting how you feel may make you look like a fool. And you may get in a cycle of pushing your loved ones away from you. No one wants to be around someone who bursts out with anger.

If you're quick to vent, you miss important information that your emotions have for you. You steamroll right into another gear. Instead, what you need to do is downshift and listen for the real meaning underneath the anger. You may have never heard of emotions as giving you key information. But they're there, trying to get your attention.

There are many strategies for coping with or managing your emotions. Your best efforts to deal with your emotional world may prove ineffective simply because you don't understand how emotions work. And you may not understand how powerfully they impact others. You aren't alone.

Bob's anger gets the best of him and drives his wife away. Momentary frustration flares to anger, leaving a path of destruction in his marriage. If Bob listened to his frustration and tuned into his underlying experience, he would find the support of his wife. And probably his keys.

Now take a look at how Bob gathers himself and does this scene differently. Let yourself try to feel how Bob and his wife feel this time, as opposed to before.

"Honey!" Bob says with loud frustration. "My keys are gone again!"

"Sorry, dear," his wife answers. "I haven't seen them."

Noticing the intensity of his voice, Bob catches himself, slows down, and lowers it. "I can't find them, and I'm running late. I have to get to work right away. I can't be late again. I'm really stressing over it."

Bob owns his urgency and names his frustration. Can you imagine how this feels differently to Bob and his wife?

"Can I help you look?" his wife responds. "Last I remember, you had them in the kitchen."

"Found them!" Bob says with relief. He then pauses and offers an explanation for his emotion. "Sorry I was a little tense, but I can't be late for today's meeting. It's really important."

"It's okay," she responds. "I'd probably feel stressed, too."

Experiencing affect

Affect is your immediate emotional response. These automatic responses happen without your thinking about them — you simply respond. Your affective responses are biologically based. They're there to help you in situations of immediate need. These responses happen instantaneously in times of danger. Sometimes a potential threat is physical, like swerving to avoid an automobile accident. Other times, the threat may be psychological, like being on the receiving end of a hostile verbal attack. Either way, your body responds in a similar way — you may protect yourself or flee — and your response is immediate and automatic. This is your affect at work.

Affect is also at work to promote care for others. A baby cries and a mother instantaneously responds, for example. The mother is immediately prepared to act. She may go and comfort the child right away, or she may wait to respond, depending on the situation. But her immediate alert response is the same.

Adults respond to similar cues in their relationships. Sara receives word that her aunt has passed away. Tears well in her eyes as she puts down the phone. Paul hears her soft cry and goes to her side.

"What is it?" Paul asks.

"Aunt Mae is gone," Sara says. She sinks into Paul's embrace.

In this moment, few words are spoken, but few are needed. Paul is responding at an affective level to Sarah's vulnerable emotional signals.

Similar automatic responses can be triggered by threats. The possibility of divorce, a job loss, or unexpected serious illness may prompt more defensive responses to the threat of loss. Partners may automatically move to defend themselves. Affect provides more action than it does meaning. Act now and ask questions later. You don't think about these responses. You simply do them.

Affect-level responses are immediate and physiologically based. They're typically adaptive and effective responses to immediate threats. Affect motivates you to respond in the moment without thinking. This is a very basic system that works well in securing our survival and caring for others.

Fight or flight

The fight-or-flight response is a good example of affect at work. Your brain responds to a perceived threat at a basic or primitive level of defense. Your *amygdala* (the memory structure in your brain that is principally involved in emotional processing) and *thalamus* (the central structure located at the center of your brain that relays sensory experience) work together to make sure your body has the physiological resources it needs to respond to danger. The system fires quickly with limited information and triggers the following sequence:

- ✔ **Freeze:** You become hyperaware of what's going on around you. This is an alert response — think of the clichéd deer in the headlights. You stop, look, and listen.

- ✔ **Flight:** You try to get away from the threat. This is an exit response. You move away, hide, or flee from the threat.

- ✔ **Fight:** You attack in response. This is a defend response. You move forward with anger, assertion, and an effort to subdue the threat.

- ✔ **Fright:** You play dead. You become immobile. This is the surrender response. You know you can't win the fight, so you give in, placate, play dead. This response can open the opportunity for an escape.

These responses show up in couple conflict all the time. When your relationship is threatened, you can easily find yourself in at least one of these responses.

Your brain has two pathways in response to fear: The low road leads to immediate response where specific brain systems activate physiological resources to deal with the threat. The fight-or-flight response is a good example of this more automatic triggering system at work. Responses here are immediate and fast acting. The longer pathway or high road engages more cognitive resources in your brain to assess the threat and possible response. This is the slower road where there is more often a delay in response to a triggering event. Emotionally focused therapy works to reduce the threats couples experience through providing a context of emotional safety and a process for regulating and working with the fears that trigger these reactive responses.

Recognizing feelings

Your body has feelings — sensations that you experience in your body. You feel pain, tension, comfort, and warmth. Different from affect (see the preceding section), feelings have more to do with information than moving you to take action.

We talk with people (mostly guys) who say that they don't have feelings. In therapy, a man's partner may complain about her frustration that he's unresponsive, uncaring, and selfish because she can never seem to get through to him. Gradually, things change. After five minutes of this conversation, this "non-feeling" guy is feeling mighty uncomfortable. He shifts and turns in his chair, looks out the window and then down at the floor. A frown on his face shows with a hint of disgust. Five minutes of feelings but no words. He's in pain, and his body knows it!

Some feelings are simple and specific. Michelle has a sick feeling in her stomach after she realizes she has failed Robert again. She sees the hurt look on his face and says, "I feel awful about what I've done." Her bodily feeling response gives her information about what is happening for her in the moment. She can use this information to respond to Robert.

Feeling can also be more complex: "I feel bad about myself" or "I feel ashamed and embarrassed." These feelings are more complex because the responses also connect with how you see yourself as a person. Michelle may not only feel awful that she disappointed Robert, but also feel that she's awful as a person. The feeling is not only a response to a situation but also a response about herself.

Accepting your feelings is an important step in working with emotion. If you accept what you're experiencing, often noticed first in your body (for example, a sinking feeling in your gut), you've taken the first step toward change. You have to start from where you are. You may not want to be angry, but that's where you are. In emotionally focused therapy (EFT), we don't judge an emotional experience — we learn from it. If you're angry, it's important to be able to recognize your feeling and accept this experience. The more you're able to recognize your feelings, the better able you'll be to explore your emotions and put them to work.

Your feelings may show up in your body in a number of the following ways:

- ✔ Sweaty palms
- ✔ Cold, clammy hands
- ✔ Muscle tension (shoulder, neck, jaw, fist)
- ✔ Posture (open, slumping, leaning forward)
- ✔ Fidgeting
- ✔ Shaking
- ✔ Pounding heart
- ✔ A warm feeling in the chest
- ✔ Sighing
- ✔ Breathing deeply
- ✔ Nausea

- ✔ Blushing
- ✔ Paleness
- ✔ Quivering lips
- ✔ Pursed lips
- ✔ Smiling
- ✔ Frowning
- ✔ Tears
- ✔ A downcast gaze
- ✔ Avoiding eye contact
- ✔ Vocal tone (soft, excited, subdued, high pitch, flat)

Your bodily responses provide you clues to exploring your emotional experience. Increasing your awareness of your partner's emotional experience, as well as your own, will enhance your ability to stay in tune with the emotions each of you has and will share.

Try the following exercise with your partner to practice getting in touch with your common feelings. This exercise will help you make connections between your emotions and where you feel them in your body.

1. **Think of a time when you were upset with another person. Go back to that moment in your mind.**

   What was the first sign that told you that you were getting upset? Close your eyes. Imagine that moment. What was happening inside your body? Look at the preceding list for clues to your bodily responses. When they come to you, write them down.

2. **Now, consider each of the following emotions:**

   - Anger
   - Fear
   - Joy
   - Love
   - Sadness
   - Surprise

   Where do you feel them in your body? Take each emotion and ask yourself where you feel it. Don't rush. Give yourself time to find these feelings in your body. For example, you might say, "When I feel love, it often shows up in my body as a warm feeling in my chest."

3. Share and discuss with your partner your answers to these questions.

This will help you start to notice your own emotions and those of your partner.

Focusing on your experience

Focusing is an exercise that can help you develop a deeper awareness of your felt experience. Eugene Gendlin developed this approach to help people put words and meaning to their bodily felt experiences. A key assumption in focusing is that there is always more to your experience than you put meaning or words to. So, focusing is a way to explore and gain a deeper awareness of this unspoken and unnamed experience.

Focusing involves six steps. Each step sets the stage for moving deeper into felt experience. Your therapist can lead you through this exercise, or you can walk through each of these steps on your own. Following these steps helps you gain a deeper understanding of a bodily felt experience of emotion:

1. **Clear a space.** Focusing begins with exercises that promote relaxation and awareness of physical sensations. This step helps to free you of distractions and to begin to concentrate on what's taking place in the moment. After taking a few deep breaths, your therapist may ask you to focus on internal experience: "What do you notice inside?"

2. **Focus on a bodily felt experience.** The focus shifts to paying attention to places in the body where you feel your feelings. Attention is given to major issues you're facing, and freedom is given to focus on one issue at a time. Physical sensations that you find "inside" become the focus of attention. The goal is to help you make contact with a "felt sense" of your experience. The felt sense is always more than what can be explained in words.

3. **Describe in words.** This part of the exercise explores the use of words and images to describe what you've experienced. Find a phrase or image that captures the essence of the felt experience. Remember you must start by working from the experience.

4. **Explore the experience.** When you can describe the experience in words, you can then explore the fit between your felt experience and the description you have given to this experience. This step tests the fit by shifting back and forth between the descriptive words or images and your felt experience.

5. **Elaborate and accept.** Moving forward in the process requires listening again to the felt experience. Your experience evolves and a new awareness of the felt experience begins to emerge.

6. **Close.** As the experience concludes, you focus on new insights that have emerged from exploring your felt experience and receiving any new understanding as a gift.

Focusing captures a key element that is common in the EFT approach. The emotionally focused therapist works with couples to access bodily felt experiences and use these experiences to create new levels of understanding. Through greater awareness, new experiences emerge. Processing and working with your experience at this level enables you to have greater access to your experience, more effective means for working with your experience, and new ways to see your relationship.

For more information on focusing, go to the website of The Focusing Institute (www. focusing.org).

A partner's first clue about her partner's feeling is often a facial response. A smirk shows contempt, while a wrinkled nose signals disgust. Surprise is seen in wide eyes, while an open mouth and a big smile with teeth showing signal delight.

Look at the faces in Figure 3-1. Identify a feeling word or phrase for the emotion you see in each of these faces. Notice how quickly you identify these feelings. Identifying feelings in the faces of others is a simple exercise that you do every day.

Here are the answers: (1) joy, (2) sadness, (3) fear, (4) anger, (5) surprise, (6) love. *Note:* You may not have used exactly these same words to label the facial expressions in Figure 3-1 (for example, you may have said "happiness" instead of "joy" or "shock" instead of "surprise"), but the key is seeing whether you were on the right track.

Now step back from this exercise and answer the following questions about the feelings you saw in these faces:

- Which feeling was easiest for you to identify? Is this an emotion you feel often?

- Which feeling was most difficult for you to identify? Is this an emotion you find difficult to express or experience?

- How well does your partner know your response to these emotions? Ask your partner what he or she notices about you when you feel one of these emotions.

Communicating emotion

Emotion organizes *affect* (immediate response) and *feelings* (bodily felt experiences) into a meaningful experience. Emotion requires the ability to reflect and bring meaning to your experience. It's the integration of immediate reactions, bodily responses, and the meaning and language used to share about these experiences with others.

Emotions provide essential information that you communicate about yourself and your relationships with others. Imagine telling your partner that you love him without emotion. The words might sound good, but are the words believable? We doubt it.

Romano was better with actions than words. He kept his feelings at bay and considered himself the strong and silent type. After months of waiting for some sign of commitment, Cecelia told Romano she was moving on. Nervous and robotic Romano mustered a response: "C., I love you. I want us to work. I always have. I just don't know how to show it. Trust me!"

1   2

3   4

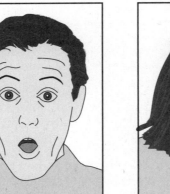

Figure 3-1:
Identify
the feeling
in each of
these faces.

5   6

After months of waiting, Cecilia didn't trust Romano's stilted response. "It's just too late," she said. "I hear what you're saying, but those are just words to me. Why do I only hear them now that I'm leaving?" She felt no passion, no heart — just excuses.

Focusing on your emotional experience provides insight and understanding into how you see yourself, how you see the world, and how you see the world looking back at you.

Emotions function like a GPS. You can think of this as your own built-in EPS — an *emotional* positioning system. Your emotions provide you with direction and motivation for taking action. Emotions help you navigate your social world. Emotions color your most important thoughts. These thoughts include your personal hopes, goals, and needs.

For couples, the experience of intimacy involves having shared goals and shared needs. Sharing at an emotional level helps couples clearly identify their needs and goals. Likewise, couples also struggle to connect around these hopes and needs, and this shows up in the conflicts they share. A couple's ability to communicate on an emotional level becomes essential in addressing differences in experience and expectations, particularly when these core needs are not getting met.

Lisa finds it hard to understand why Bill gets so upset with her for missing his social events at work. "Why do you still miss so many of my work parties?!" Bill says. "People are asking about you, and I'm tired of giving excuses."

In Lisa's mind, Bill's schedule often conflicts with her work-related travel. For Bill, the parties aren't his bottom line. The real issue is whether he can count on Lisa and whether he's a priority in her schedule, much less her life.

Bill continues, "If you cared about me — about us, for that matter — you would make more of an effort to show up like you promised!"

Lisa is silent. Then she explains, "I've missed three parties in two years. You know my job, schedule, and boss. It's not about us. It's not about you. It's the job."

"I find that hard to believe," Bill argues. "I need you, but I don't think you get that." Lisa responds, "I know that. That's what this is about. You don't believe me when I say that I really do care."

If you asked Bill and Lisa if they're committed to their relationship, they would both say, "Yes, definitely." The words sound right, but neither Lisa nor Bill believes the other *really* means it.

A change for Lisa and Bill requires a *new emotional experience*. An emotionally focused therapist works with emotions as the fastest and clearest route to lasting change. Each partner's experience is accepted as a first step to experiencing and expanding his or her experience. This focus on affect and feelings in session enables the therapist to work with the inside experience of each partner, in the context of the relationship.

One goal in EFT is accessing the emotions underlying the reactive emotional responses that lock couples in destructive patterns of conflict. An emotionally focused therapist seeks to make the implicit patterns and emotions more explicit. Through this, the therapist helps a couple to develop more effective ways to connect at an intimate emotional level.

Focusing on emotional experience provides a way into matters of greatest importance in a relationship. Often, the emotions experienced, especially in the heat of conflict, aren't the only emotions at work in those moments. Accessing and expanding the emotions that are working below the surface opens new doors for couples to begin to share what really matters in their relationship.

Discovering the Process of Emotion

Emotions involve your mind, your body, and what you do. When you're trying to break down a particular emotional experience, it's helpful to think about emotion as an unfolding process, like a series of steps, each building on the one before.

There are four parts to an emotional experience, and each has some important information to getting inside your emotional experience (see Figure 3-2).

- ✔ **Trigger:** What gets arguments started
- ✔ **Feeling:** Where you're impacted
- ✔ **Meaning:** Why things happen
- ✔ **Action:** How you respond

Think of a four-door car — any door will get you inside. The same is true for these four parts of emotional experience. Open any door, and it'll take you inside your emotional experience. (Hopefully, the doors aren't all locked. If that happens, turn to Chapter 11.)

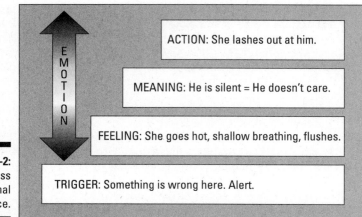

Figure 3-2:
The process
of emotional
experience.

Recognizing the trigger

Emotions respond like reflexes do. Your doctor taps your knee and you kick. No matter what, you can't keep your leg from kicking. Situations tap our lives, and we have an emotional response.

Consider the following negative situations, and imagine if this happened to you:

- A layoff notice at work
- A serious medical diagnosis
- Failing grades on your child's report card
- The unexpected death of a close friend
- Your partner talking about wanting a separation

Now consider the following positive situations, and think about how they would trigger an immediate emotional response:

- A long-awaited promotion
- The birth of your child
- Being reunited with an old friend
- An unexpected romantic gesture
- Making a hole-in-one on the golf course

Difficult situations such as disappointments or unmet expectations may cause you to withdraw and go quiet. Positive experiences may cause you to engage and express your emotions. These responses vary from person to person and from situation to situation, but they all begin with a trigger. The following examples point to some common triggers couples may encounter:

- ✔ Threats of divorce
- ✔ Harsh criticism and contempt
- ✔ Broken promises
- ✔ Defensiveness
- ✔ Withdrawal of affection
- ✔ Sorrow or sadness
- ✔ Genuine remorse
- ✔ Fear and uncertainty
- ✔ Expressions of deep vulnerability

Human beings are designed to sense danger. You respond to a dangerous situation before you're even aware of it. In fact, you may not know you were in danger until after you've already responded! That's how fast emotion works.

Helen knew something was wrong. She was alert, tense, eyes wide open. The house felt different. The minute she heard the rustling upstairs, her body went on high alert. As she was preparing to call 911, she caught sight of a cat scampering down the stairs.

You're hard-wired to respond to danger. Your biology is designed to respond automatically for survival. Whether a cat or a cat burglar, you're ready to respond. The sense of danger Helen felt was triggered by a sound she wasn't expecting.

Often, the triggers couples face are situations that are also a surprise. The husband who makes a special dinner and sets a romantic tone gets triggered when his wife is distracted by unfinished business from her day. A wife is triggered when her husband fails to follow through on his promise to do his part of the household chores. There may be logical reasons for these unexpected outcomes, but the trigger doesn't wait for logic — it fires in moments of the unexpected.

Triggers can be subtle. You can miss a trigger unless you're looking for one.

Look for the trigger in the following example: James was later than expected. He rushed in the door and saw an angry look on Katy's face. The look in her eyes said it all for him. "Just as I expected," she said. "You're late again. I can never trust you to be on time." Before she said a word, James knew the coming conversation. He sensed her scorn. His palms started to sweat. His face was stoic as he braced for her all-too-familiar tone. He was hoping this would blow over quickly. But he was also ready to escape from the room if it didn't. Fear was setting in. His trigger? The look on Katy's face.

Acknowledging the feeling

Emotions show up in your body as a feeling. You see something disgusting; it makes you feel sick. You feel the disgust in your gut. The emotion shows up in your body.

People experience their emotions differently. Everyone feels stress, but it may register differently in your body than it does in your partner's. For some people, it shows up in the neck and shoulders; for others, it shows up in the forehead. These physical sensations tell you something important about your experience.

These feelings carry important information. Tuning into these feelings really matters when

- ✔ You rarely think about what you feel.
- ✔ You seldom talk about your feelings.
- ✔ You struggle to come up with words to describe your experience with others.
- ✔ You have many feelings all at once and find it hard to determine what's happening inside of you.

Getting in touch with feelings often means slowing down and focusing on your bodily felt experience. Try getting in touch by doing the following:

1. **Take several deep breaths, breathing from your abdomen.**

2. **Close your eyes, and minimize distractions.**

3. **Focus on what's happening inside of you.**

   Tune into your physical sensations (for example, tightness in your shoulders, emptiness in your stomach, tension in your forehead). These are your feelings.

4. **Pay attention to the thoughts that come up along with your feelings.**

   What images come to mind as you pay attention to these feelings?

Being aware of your feelings begins with being aware in the moment. Bodily experiences often follow triggers. Something happens, and the body responds.

Think about how feelings make a difference in the example of James and Katy (see the preceding section). James often keeps his feelings to himself. He's a rational guy. But he can easily lose his composure when Katy is hurt. He hates himself for it, too. It makes him feel sick. When she's angry, he feels agitated inside. He feels, but he doesn't let on what's happening for him. Katy's anger is like fingers on a chalkboard. He can't get away from it fast enough. His feelings of dread and fear show up in sweaty palms, a sick feeling in his stomach, and tenseness in his chest. He's afraid, and his body shows it. These are James's feelings.

Naming the experience

Emotions carry vitally important information. When you experience emotion, it has a message for you. If your body feels pain when you touch a sharp object, the pain is communicating danger. Understanding emotions requires listening for the meaning in your feeling.

Roberta feels tension in her neck when Shawn starts talking about his frustrations at work. Her tension builds as his unhappiness spills out. Listening to the constricting feelings she feels in these conversations, Roberta puts words to her experience: "It's suffocating," she says. "His negativity has no end. There is no room in the conversation for me to say a word." Roberta's feelings help her better see what's happening with her and Shawn when he gets lost in his anger.

Read the case of Mark (see the nearby sidebar, "The weight of sadness"), and follow the therapist's questions. As you do so, imagine having a similar conversation about an emotion you find hard to get a handle on. Use the following steps to home in on your feeling and begin to make room for getting to know your feeling better. This activity will help you better understand your emotions, particularly when they're difficult to identify or at times overwhelming.

1. **Find your feeling.**

   Where do you feel this in your body? Describe it.

2. **Visualize your experience.**

   What does it feel like? Find a metaphor or word picture. Find words to describe this feeling. Check out various words and images until one best fits with your feeling.

3. **Put words to your experience.**

   Think of a story about this experience. Remember a time when you felt this particular feeling. How would you describe what this feeling meant in that moment?

4. **Share with your partner this story and what you see more clearly by paying attention to your emotional experience.**

This is the thinking part of feeling. Feelings aren't that helpful if you don't understand them, or if you can't heed their message. You might as well just turn them off if you can't use them. People have tried turning off feelings, but it doesn't work very well. Feelings are always there. They're part of life. They're part of you.

Consider how James hates disappointing Katy. He's often late. And even when he tries to leave work early, he often finds himself somehow late again. James tries to not think about the sting of her disappointment. And he hides how it impacts him. He doesn't want to make things worse. He skips over his feelings and promises to make things better in the future. Inside, he feels like he's a failure and he's afraid that he isn't living up to what she wants. He tries to push that feeling away because fear paralyzes him when he thinks she might give up on him. Fear is what he feels, and he would name this feeling the "fear of rejection."

You can't share an emotional experience you don't understand. Accessing feelings brings you a step closer to using emotions more effectively in your relationship. Putting words to your experience helps you better express not only the emotion but also the message that your emotion carries.

For couples, sharing at an emotional level is speaking from the heart. You make clear how you're impacted by your partner and what this means to you. You can't have one without the other — feelings and thoughts work together.

Moving to action

Emotions have links to action. They make you move. They can kick you in your pants.

Think about what you do

- ✔ **When you're angry:** How do you respond physically?
- ✔ **When you're sad:** How do you act?
- ✔ **When you're afraid:** How do you instinctively respond?

Emotions motivate us to act. This is important in understanding what happens when couples argue. Typically the actions you take with each other are tied directly to the emotions you feel in the moment. If you know the feeling, you can predict the action.

The weight of sadness

As therapists, we look for moments with couples where feelings are showing up and a partner isn't in touch with those feelings. Nonverbal behaviors are often the giveaway that more is going on in the room than what's being talked about.

Mark is one of those guys who have a tough time finding their emotions. In a therapy session, he was sharing about being a loner most of his childhood. As he shared various memories, he was talking about something sad and reporting it as if were the six o'clock news. His face seemed to drop at points, and his eyes softened with what appeared to be sadness. In these moments, one of your authors, Jim, invited Mark to explore his experience and try to put a name to his feelings.

"Help me out here, Mark," Jim said. "On the one hand, you're talking about all these lonely times like it's no big deal. But on the other hand, you look rather sad."

"Yeah, I guess I'm sad," Mark responded. "But I try not to dwell on that."

"Okay," Jim responded. "You try not to dwell on the sadness. You try to keep it at a distance, right?"

"Yes," Mark said.

"And I wonder, when you feel sadness, what's it like for you inside? Where do you feel it?"

Mark hesitated and seemed to look inside himself for the answer. "It's like a pit in my stomach," he said.

"Are you feeling it now?" Jim asked slowly. Mark slowly nodded yes, as his sadness started to slowly emerge into his focus more. "Can you describe to me what this sadness is like for you?"

"It's big like a rock," Mark said. "No, more like a boulder." Mark sank more into his chair and looked at the floor.

"The sadness you're feeling right now is like a boulder," Jim said. "And its weight is crushing. Is that close?" Jim asked Mark to begin to put words to his experience. This helped him move into it more — to more clearly experience it and understand what it was telling him.

"Exactly," Mark said, almost relieved that Jim understood him. "I can hardly breathe when I feel this!" Mark's voice was clear as he got a deeper sense of his sadness.

Mark was moving toward a deeper experience of his emotion. This is found in the feelings he experiences in his gut when this sadness shows up. He can talk about sadness, but it's all intellectual for him. By focusing on his internal sensations and asking him to explore them with images and words, Jim was able to help Mark come to a new understanding of what his sadness is about. He listened to his emotion and found relief as he was able to see and experience his sadness in a new way.

"So, if that boulder had a name," Jim asked Mark, "what would it be?"

"I'd name it Sadness and Hurt," Mark softly responded.

"And if that boulder had words, so that it could speak," Jim asked, "what would it say?" Jim was asking Mark to put more meaning to his experience.

"It would say, 'These memories are too big,'" Mark said. "'They can't be moved. They're stuck and just too big.' It's crushing me."

Jim helped Mark further understand what he was starting to experience about himself. "All this sadness has left you crushed," Jim said. "Like you can never get out from under your past. It keeps you stuck. Unmovable. Like this huge boulder."

Brandon seeks reassurance when he feels uncertain. He pursues LaToya for words of comfort. He feels anxious and responds by getting an answer for his uncertainty and getting it now. This also works the other way around: LaToya sees Brandon coming a mile away. She's seen this over and over, particularly after a fight. She knows Brandon won't stop with his questions when he feels insecure. She knows what's coming before the first word is out of his mouth.

Couples can predict the actions of their partners. But this can create problems, because these predictions aren't always right. It's more like forecasting the weather. There is a 70 percent chance of rain because the conditions are right, but those conditions can change. That's the way it is with couples. Partners can predict each other's behaviors most of the time — just not with 100 percent accuracy. Actions don't tell the full story of what's happening at an emotional level.

Putting it all together

Looking again at James and Katy, when James knows Katy is upset and unhappy with him, he moves cautiously. He's tentative — as if he's walking through a minefield. Any step could set off an argument that would end the evening. He appears awkward, clumsy even, as he asks Katie about her day. He tries to appear normal, but his actions betray him. His fear has him on guard and Katie knows it. See Table 3-1 for a summary of the four parts of James's emotional experience. Katy's responses are also included so you can see how each person's actions and responses play off one another.

Table 3-1	Inside James and Katy's Emotional Experience	
Emotional Experience	*For James*	*For Katie*
Trigger (what happened)	Katy's look of disappointment.	James's guarded response.
Feeling (what the person experienced)	Sweaty palms, sick feeling.	Tense shoulders, rigid posture.
Meaning (what the person was thinking)	"I'm a failure. She may reject me."	"I can count on him. I'm not important."
Action (what the person did in response)	Shuts down, becomes tentative.	Increases intensity, demands attention.

The key is recognizing that each person's emotional experience unfolds as a process and that this process happens both inside each partner and between the partners.

Review Table 3-1. Think of a recent argument you had with your partner. Put yourself back in the moment when the fight began. What were you doing? What was your partner doing? Close your eyes and see if you can picture yourself in that moment.

- What was the first sign that something was wrong? What did you notice?
- What was happening inside you as the conflict continued? What were you feeling?
- How did you make sense of what you were feeling in the moment?
- What did you do in response to the tension between you? What action did you take?

Using Table 3-1 as a model, identify your trigger, feelings, understanding, and action. What was your trigger and feeling? How did you try to make sense of what you were feeling and what action did you take?

You can also do this activity as a couple. First, decide on a recent conflict you had. Then walk through the steps individually. When you've completed your part of the table, invite your partner to review your trigger, feeling response, understanding, and action.

Notice how your actions may be your partner's trigger. These emotional patterns often play off each other in a relationship. Slowing down an argument and looking at what's happening for you and your partner opens up new understanding about yourself, your partner, and the relationship you share.

Chapter 4

Identifying the Three Levels of Emotional Experience

. . . .

In This Chapter

▶ Understanding the vital function of primary emotion

▶ Recognizing your own reactive secondary emotion

▶ Defining the role of instrumental emotions in your relationship

. . . .

*W*hen people talk about emotion, they usually oversimplify. They jam all emotion into one tight box and keep the lid on. It's common to hear, "Emotions get in the way of making rational decisions" or, "You're reacting too emotionally" or, even worse, "Take your emotions out of it!"

For many years, psychology has emphasized thinking over feeling. It's still largely the case today. But the field of affective neuroscience is pointing to a different reality, one in which emotional processing in your brain is central and rapid, and actually sets the stage for the slower process of thinking.

You actually feel *before* you think. Modern neuroscience has charted the brain's response to situations and found that emotions fire two and a half times more rapidly in the brain than thoughts do (see Chapter 2). We aren't saying that emotions are more important than thoughts. In fact, feeling and thinking should team up and work together to make you that much more aware and prepared to make the best decisions and to act in the most helpful of ways. But most people overthink and underfeel.

Emotions occur within three layers: primary, secondary, and instrumental. In this chapter, we help you begin to recognize these three layers of emotion as they occur within you. By becoming more aware and increasingly listening to your primary emotion, you'll be tapping in to a built-in source of information and guidance that you can count on. You'll begin to trust your own emotional experience, be clear in what you need, and be confident in what you say.

Discovering the Importance of Primary Emotion

Primary emotions are the initial, "gut-felt" emotional signals stemming from your immediate surroundings. You may feel primary emotion as a tingling or sinking experience in the pit of your stomach, a tightening of your shoulders, or a heaviness or constriction in your chest. Although you may not be aware of it, everyone feels primary emotion somewhere in the body (see Chapter 3).

Primary emotions are most often vulnerable or soft emotions. They reveal your underbelly, so to speak. Here's a list of common primary emotions:

- ✔ Sadness
- ✔ Fear
- ✔ Hurt
- ✔ Anger
- ✔ Shame
- ✔ Joy
- ✔ Excitement
- ✔ Surprise

As you can see, there are negative (painful) and positive (happy) primary emotions. Both are considered primary because they're the first emotions you feel in response to situations. Negative primary emotion tends to make you shrink down, such as when you're hurt or sad. Positive primary emotion usually leads you to expand outward, such as when you experience joy and surprise.

When a couple's relationship is in distress, the negative primary emotion is usually unspoken. It may even go largely unnoticed. It's important that you start to notice your primary emotion. For example, when you suddenly realize that you forgot to do something that's very important, you may get a kind of sick feeling in your stomach. This sick feeling is your body's experience of primary emotion.

Consider the following simple example demonstrating how primary emotion was at work in Brian and Stella's relationship one Saturday morning:

"Brian," Stella said, "where's the dog? I've looked all over for her."

"I haven't seen her," Brian responded, immersed in his laptop.

"Molly! Molly!" Stella called out, walking through the house.

And then it hit Brian like a ton of bricks: He had forgotten to let Molly inside before going to bed the night before. His stomach sank. He felt his heart pounding in his chest.

"Oh crap!" he thought to himself. "Molly could've been attacked by a coyote or run over by a car. And she means so much to Stella. Oh, man. This could be bad!"

Brian was experiencing his primary emotion of fear. First, he was afraid for the dog's safety. Second, he was afraid of how this would affect his wife. And third, he was afraid of how this would affect his wife's feelings toward him. Now, that's a lot of fear and information going out in a split second, but you probably know from experience that this is how fast primary emotion works.

Think back to a time in which you forgot something really important, like Brian did. Let yourself re-imagine the situation unfolding. As you do, pay attention to your body. Where do you feel your emotion? Can you name your primary emotion? Share these experiences and feelings with your partner, and have your partner do the same with you.

Primary emotions are important because they tell you what's *really* going on for you. When you're receiving information from primary emotion, you're running on all cylinders. You're living more holistically. You're much more aware of "the moment." This is the largest part of what is called mindfulness — a recent recognition in many professional therapy circles. For more on this topic, check out *Mindfulness For Dummies,* by Shamash Alidina (Wiley).

What primary emotion says about you and your relationship

Primary emotion signals what is most important to you in the moment. The key is slowing down and making sense of the incoming new meaning. It's happening naturally for a reason: to inform you.

Bob had a knack for staying in tune with what his primary emotion was telling him — so much so that most people just loved the guy. Most of the time he was considerate and caring, and he listened. He just seemed grounded. Bob had a 20-year wedding anniversary approaching. But he had let time slip away without planning anything, and now he was worried that he might disappoint and hurt his wife, Betsy. While driving and thinking about the situation, Bob felt a heaviness in his chest. This signaled to him that something important needed more of his attention. He focused internally on the tightness in his chest and on his upcoming anniversary. He realized that he was sad. He stayed with that feeling, allowing himself to feel the sadness. He didn't try to push it away, or to think positively, or to cheer himself up. He trusted that his sadness was there for an important reason and that he needed to feel it and listen.

Within a few minutes, Bob became fully aware that the anniversary was a big day for Betsy and that he really didn't want to hurt her. He also remembered how special Betsy was to him and that this day was important to him as well. His emotions and thoughts came together powerfully to give him clarity. And get this: Bob was no longer sad. He could've easily ignored the feeling of heaviness in his chest. But instead, he slowed himself down, listened, and got the important message his primary emotion was sending. He was initially sad for a good reason. But listening to his primary emotion gave Bob clarity. What he received moved him into a strong feeling of happiness. His chest was no longer tight. In fact, he felt a sense of lightness inside.

That's how primary emotions work. When you allow yourself to fully experience your primary emotions, instead of cutting them off or pushing them away, they evolve into a different primary emotion. In the case of Bob, he went from sadness to happiness.

Primary emotions are there for a purpose. They're sending you important information. Start trying to slow down and notice when you're feeling soft emotions, like sadness, hurt, and fear. Where do you feel them in your body? If you aren't sure what the emotion is, try to tie your bodily sensations to an emotion. When you find the bodily sensation (for example, butterflies in your stomach, a sinking feeling in your stomach, and so forth) and/or emotion, let yourself feel it for a few minutes. Just slow down and focus on it. Consider what message or information it may be sending to you. Allow emotion to change emotion.

You may be saying to yourself, "I never pay attention to primary emotion. I'm not even sure I have primary emotions in the first place. This is over my head." If this wariness resonates with you, you're not alone. The good news is that we've seen people who initially feel this way catch on and love it. It opens up a whole new world they never knew existed! What we're talking about is a skill and a resource you can use.

How your own primary emotion impacts your partner

Your primary emotion not only has a lot to give you, but also has a lot to give your relationship. The key is to learn to listen to it, and then learn to share it with your partner. Say you notice that you miss your partner, for example, because the two of you haven't spent time alone in a while. Sharing this feeling directly with your partner from a vulnerable place — rather than a blaming place — can often be very rewarding for a partner to hear.

Your partner will likely enjoy hearing that he or she matters this much to you, and the fact that you're sharing your feeling directly with your partner will often pull him or her to offer you care and concern.

For example, Diana began to notice that when she went away for short business trips, she felt tenseness in her shoulders and heaviness in her chest. She also realized that she often fought with her partner, Lisa, before leaving on these short trips. For the first time, she began putting the tension in her shoulder and the heaviness in her chest together with the fighting with Lisa. Diana was starting to listen to her emotions on a whole new level.

On her next business trip, Diana sat down in her hotel room alone. She located the feelings of tightness and heaviness inside her. She simply focused her attention inside herself. After a minute, she silently asked herself, "What's going on with these feelings and me traveling?"

Then she just listened to her breathing and felt the tenseness. It did feel a little strange, but she stayed with it.

Then a sense of guilt came into her awareness. She felt this in her body but also located it in her thinking. "Hmm," she thought. "That's new." So she simply allowed herself to stay with her guilt. She didn't allow her mind to race, or to try to "figure it out." Diana just patiently and quietly sat there. She listened, breathed, paid attention to her shoulders and chest, and then slowly asked herself, "What's up with this guilt? What is it I need to uncover?"

It was then that a sense of fear washed over her. It was powerful, and it was clear. She felt a clear shift in her body to a lighter feeling. One thing became clear to her: "I'm afraid that I'm disregarding my family when I travel."

On the one hand, she *knew* that this wasn't very logical or reasonable. She and Lisa made sure their kids were fine while Diana was away. And she didn't travel excessively anyway.

But on the other hand there were these feelings of fear and guilt. She could no longer deny them, and she no longer *wanted* to deny them. By slowing down and experiencing her fear, Diana was confident in the message she was getting. She was afraid that she was letting down her family when she traveled.

To Diana's credit, she didn't try to cut off her emotional experience. This often happens when you dismiss a primary emotion. Here are some common ways that people dismiss their primary emotions:

- ✔ **By forcing themselves to think about something else:** Often, people feel a little of their primary emotions and then get scared. They quickly distract themselves with other thoughts, shutting down the primary emotions and missing out on the information the primary emotions could've given them.

- ✔ **By downplaying the importance of emotion:** Beware of disregarding your emotional experience. It's there to guide you, if you allow it to.

- ✔ **By changing the way you're looking at the situation:** Some self-help gurus today tell people to simply change their attitude and all else will follow. But your emotions are there to help guide you and inform you. If you pull the "ejection cord" and try to change your attitude by bypassing those emotions, you run the risk of cutting yourself off from your emotions. And by doing that, you cut off their information. The key is to listen to your built-in emotional positioning system (EPS; see Chapter 3), not to turn it off.

- ✔ **By cheering yourself up too soon:** There is a time to cheer yourself up, but that time is not before you've allowed your primary emotion to inform you in the moment.

- ✔ **By making a list that *rationally counters* why you shouldn't feel what you're feeling:** This is a classic cognitive behavioral intervention. But it isn't helpful before you allow your primary emotion to work itself through and give you some understanding of what's bothering you.

- ✔ **By pouring yourself a stiff drink (or going shopping or eating or engaging in any other activity that numbs you from what you're feeling):** One of the main reasons people drink is to cover up their emotional experiences. You may not be used to integrating your primary emotional experience into your daily life, but stuffing this world by drinking is not the answer.

Not everyone turns to alcohol — some people shop or eat to excess, other people gamble, others do drugs. Whatever it is that you're using to avoid facing your emotions, even if it isn't on the surface "unhealthy," is something that's keeping you from receiving the messages your primary emotions impart.

✔ **By getting angry and looking for someone else to blame:** This is one of the most common actions people take. But it leads nowhere. Getting angry often stuffs your primary emotion and robs you of the vital information being carried by it. Anger is most often a reactive, secondary emotion (see the next section).

Cutting off of your emotional experience before it naturally evolves to an ending point — a point at which you're sure of its message to you — is the common theme running through the preceding list. That kind of thinking stems from an outdated understanding of emotion and what it brings. In fact, we now know that suppressing your emotions is unhealthy. When you suppress your emotions, you're cutting off a natural part of what it means to be human.

Diana's guilt and fear were real and powerful. These emotions had been there in Diana for a while, but just outside her awareness. Because these emotions remained outside Diana's awareness, she wasn't able to hear their message. Instead of connecting with her primary emotion, Diana had a habit of barking at Lisa, being short with her, which in turn started a painful cycle of fighting between them. Neither Diana nor Lisa was aware of what was really happening emotionally at a primary level for Diana.

When Diana returned from her trip, she sat down alone with Lisa. "I think I've learned something new about myself and us," she shared. "I've become aware that deep down inside me, I have a real sense of guilt about going out of town on business. I'm afraid that I'm not being a good mom to our kids when I travel." Diana began to softly cry when she said this. "That's why I get so uptight and bark at you before going on these business trips."

Lisa had rarely seen this part of Diana. As she heard Diana's vulnerable emotions of fear and guilt, it moved Lisa to compassion for Diana. "I'm sorry, honey," she said. "I can see that it's hard on you. It's okay. We'll handle this together." Lisa then reached for Diana's hand and held her.

When you share your primary emotion with your partner from a place of caring and vulnerability, it has the potential to greatly impact your partner. When Diana opened up and shared her primary emotion with Lisa, for example, Lisa naturally, in turn, reached for Diana's hand because she was moved to comfort her. Primary emotions have that kind of a powerful relational impact. They cause people to move and be moved by emotion.

Primary emotions are powerful in relationships because they

✔ **Inform you of exactly how you're authentically feeling in the moment.** It became clear to Diana that she was afraid she was hurting her family by traveling too much. She was feeling guilty because of it.

✔ **Guide you toward what you need.** Diana needed to resolve these feelings — to do something about her possibly hurting her family, assuage her guilt, and be certain that she was being the kind of mother and partner that she wanted to be.

✔ **Move you toward others for help.** When Diana became fully aware of her emotions' message to her, she was moved to address it with Lisa. Emotions are relational in nature — they move you to seek resolution with those close to you.

✔ **Have a direct positive impact on your partner.** When you share your primary emotions in an open, vulnerable way, they often have a great pull on significant others to comfort and reassure you. Lisa, for example, was moved to hold Diana as she cried, and to assure her that together they would handle this. She reassured Diana that she wasn't alone.

Read the following two examples:

"I'm worried that we're growing apart," Sonya said with concern. "We used to spend so much time together. And we actually talked. I miss that."

"I'm worried that we're growing apart!" Sonya said loudly. "We used to spend so much time together. And back then we actually talked, and you actually listened!"

Put yourself in the place of Sonya's partner as Sonya shares her sense of sadness. In the first example, she shares from a place of vulnerability within herself; in the second example, she doesn't. Feel the difference? Share your emotional experiences of each example with your partner. Which one drew a sense of compassion from you? How did the other example feel to you? Which one of these styles is currently most like yours?

In the first example, Sonya took a risk and opened herself up emotionally as she spoke. This carried with it a sense of vulnerability, which invites empathy and compassion. In the second example, Sonya's frustration and anger led the way, and Sonya's vulnerability remained hidden. Chances are, you felt blamed when you read that. The tone of a message carries a lot of weight.

Primary emotion moves you (see Chapter 3) to act, to reach out to your partner for resolution. By identifying your own primary emotion and receiving its message, and then sharing those things with your partner from a soft place, you're directly seeking authentic emotional connection with your partner.

How to use your primary emotion

This section is about "zeroing in" on your primary emotion more effectively. This is a very important part of emotionally focused therapy (EFT). It's vital that you and your partner are both able to recognize your primary emotions and begin practicing understanding their messages.

When you give a little kid a basketball, she can't even dribble it. Once she has learned to dribble, walking and dribbling at the same time is a tall order. As hard as it may be to believe now, even Michael Jordan couldn't run and dribble the first time he touched a basketball. But in time and with practice, dribbling, shooting layups, passing — all these things become second nature. An athlete doesn't even consciously think about them.

The same is true of learning to recognize and use your own primary emotion in your life. At first, it may seem awkward and difficult. But in time and with practice, you can master this process. Just as the athlete commits aspects of the game to "muscle memory" and doesn't have to think about them, with practice you'll do the same by integrating your emotions naturally into your life. But right now, practice is important.

Primary emotions are your initial bodily felt signals stemming from your immediate situation. These are the softer and more vulnerable emotions. They happen rapidly — before you can even think. In fact, they set the mood for thoughts. Here are some examples of how you might feel primary emotion in your body:

- ✔ Sweaty palms
- ✔ Butterflies in your stomach
- ✔ A throbbing heart
- ✔ Tightness or aching in the back of your neck
- ✔ A sinking feeling in the pit of your stomach
- ✔ Heaviness in your chest or shoulders
- ✔ An aching heart

With your partner, think back to a recent argument you had with each other. Find a mild to moderate argument — not a doozy! It could've happened this morning, yesterday, last week, or last month. It doesn't matter when it happened, as long as you both remember it.

Now, together, re-create the steps of the argument. For example, "I walked in the door and you were watching TV. I got pissed right away because I knew how much work needed to be done in the house. I told you to get off your butt!" The other partner responds, "Then I got angry. I asked you, 'What's your problem?!'" Talk through the argument, re-creating the steps until it ended.

Each of you take a moment alone and try to locate what your primary emotion was as the argument was unfolding. Also, try to find the trigger. The trigger is often what pierces you, resulting in your primary emotion. Your primary emotion was most likely not spoken outwardly during the argument. You probably weren't aware of it. Imagine yourself back in the argument. Remember it. Replay it. When you find the primary emotion, stay with it and try to locate where you felt it in your body.

Often when you replay an argument vividly enough, you'll feel your primary emotion in your body all over again, similar to how you felt it during the initial argument itself. This is a very common occurrence in EFT. So, if you can't find your primary emotion, you most likely haven't detailed and re-created the argument closely enough to the real action. You may need to go back together and re-create the argument a bit more realistically.

"I was so mad at you," Erika shared with Jack. "At the time, that's all I was aware of. But now as I reflect, I realize that there was more in me. The trigger was seeing you sitting there, watching TV. My primary emotion was hurt. I was hurt that you weren't working on the house because we had so much to do. It was so important to me. I thought it was important to both of us."

Share with each other what your primary emotion was during that argument. Write it down, like Erika's response, if you need to. After you share what each of your primary emotions were, share with each other where you felt them in your bodies and what the trigger was.

Secondary Emotion: What You Feel after Your Gut Reacts

When most people talk about emotion, it's usually about secondary emotions, which follow primary emotions. Secondary emotions are the ones that you're most aware of in your life. They're the second layer of emotional experiencing. Whereas primary emotion fires immediately and gives you helpful guidance, secondary emotions are a *reaction* to your primary emotions.

Typical secondary emotions include anger, frustration, guilt, and defensiveness.

Ramiro, for example, recoils as his partner, Cara, accuses him. "I'm sick and tired of this!" Cara says loudly. "All you care about is watching football! You'd rather watch stupid football games than do something with me!"

Ramiro quickly gets angry. "I just want to see this one, big game!" he responds, matching Cara's level of intensity and volume. "I spent all day with you yesterday. And we went to dinner and had a great night. Then we had breakfast this morning. Get off of my back already."

Anger is Ramiro's secondary emotion. At first glance, it appears that anger was his initial response, but it wasn't. On another level, in an instant, it initially hurt Ramiro that Cara was so upset with him. If you could slow down Ramiro's emotional process even more, you might see that he's somewhat afraid, too.

But in the blink of an eye, without even thinking, Ramiro *reacts* to his primary emotion of hurt (and possibly fear) and responds in anger (the secondary emotion) toward Cara. He isn't even aware of bypassing his hurt and fear — it happens so quickly.

When couples argue, it's almost always from a circular loop of secondary, reactive emotion, as each partner hurls insults or criticism at the other. Although this strategy usually results in arguments, it does make sense. Often, anger feels much more comfortable and safer than the underlying, vulnerable emotions. Revealing your hurt on the heels of being criticized can feel threatening.

Anger: Primary or secondary emotion?

Anger is both a primary emotion and a secondary emotion, depending on the situation. Anger at being used, violated, or abused for example, is most often primary. When you're intruded upon, your anger is healthy. It's there to help you assert your boundaries and protect yourself. Lisa, for example, spoke about how hurt and angry she was when she discovered her partner's affair. Both the hurt and anger were primary emotions.

The difference between anger as a primary emotion and anger as a secondary emotion can be in how the anger is expressed. When Lisa shared her primary anger, for example, she was asserting how she felt at a deep or primary level. Even though it was anger, it invited compassion from her partner. "I can't believe that you had an affair," she said to Bill. "I'm so angry at you for doing this to us. I didn't deserve this."

When anger is secondary, it has a destructive effect on the relationship. It doesn't protect you or move your partner to come closer to you or help you. "I hate you!" Steve says to his partner, Meg. "I can't stand the way you talk, or the way you look at me. You're disgusting." This is secondary emotional expression.

Secondary anger is meant to attack and hurt your partner. Primary anger, on the other hand, explains being wronged, that it wasn't deserved. Primary anger often leads to the sharing of how painful something was.

Uncovering your own secondary emotional reactions

Do you know what secondary emotions arise in you most regularly? Most people have a few secondary emotional reactions that have become habitual over the years. Without realizing it, these reactions are familiar and somewhat comfortable.

Think back to a recent time when you got upset with your partner, or even with a co-worker, a friend, or another relative. Remember what happened that made you upset. Replay it a few times in your head. Let yourself re-enter those upset feelings. Now, how did you respond? What did you say in return? Finally, how did it all end? Did you and the other person work it out between the two of you?

"My friend told me I was 'too dramatic,'" Sharon said. "I got really angry fast. I told her, 'Dramatic? Do you know how many times I hold back what I'm really feeling?'" The rest of the evening, Sharon pulled away from her friend, feeling angry at her most of the night. "I don't think she knows me as well as I thought," she told herself.

Sharon's secondary emotion was anger, and her reaction was mainly defensiveness in return. She then went quiet and turned inward for the rest of the evening. She didn't approach her friend again to work it out between them. This was how Sharon reacted to most situations in which she found herself angry. She got angry inside at a secondary level, and then she defended herself.

Katrina, on the other hand, had a different way of handling such stressful situations. When her partner, James, said to her, "Honey, why haven't you cleaned up the kitchen?" she found herself boiling inside. "Why haven't *you* cleaned up the kitchen?!" she said loudly. "It isn't just *my* job you know! You hardly ever help anyway. And when was the last time you cleaned the bathrooms? You promised to do those, too, remember?"

Katrina's secondary emotion was usually anger, and her reactive behavior was usually to attack back even harder. For as long as she can remember, this is how she has responded when she has felt attacked. She can't remember a time when she went back to the person who made her angry to work it out together.

You may not fit into either of these descriptions. You may just go quiet. Or you may find yourself trying to lighten the mood by cracking a few jokes. You may even act is if you didn't hear anything in the first place. What's helpful right now is looking back on what some of your go-to secondary emotions and reactions are and identifying them.

Identifying how secondary emotion pushes your partner away

When primary emotions are revealed from a place of vulnerability, they usually draw others to aid and comfort you. But secondary emotions usually push others away. When you show your secondary anger at your partner, for example, your partner usually moves away and doesn't say much to you. Secondary emotion doesn't provide a safe environment.

Dan was frustrated. He had worked on a recipe all day, and it still didn't taste good. "I can't get this stupid dish to taste right no matter what I do," he fumed. "I make it over and over again, and it still sucks!" Claire decided to stay in the other room and kept quiet until Dan's frustration blew over.

If you share primary emotion tinged with secondary emotions of anger or frustration, it gets drowned out. You have to share primary emotion from a place of vulnerability within yourself. If you don't, the other person will most likely feel blamed and put down rather than empathic toward you.

Instrumental Emotion: What You Show But Don't Feel

Instrumental emotions are used to manipulate or control others. You may have heard them referred to as "crocodile tears." We often see instrumental emotions in children, but make no mistake: Couples overdo emotional responses to win arguments, too.

Couples can get caught in a trap in which they misuse emotion to make the other person feel badly or to get their way. It's one thing to be genuinely hurt, but it's quite another to feign being hurt in order to punish your partner or to get your way. Feigning hurt to get back at your partner is an example of instrumental emotion.

Consider the following example in which Sam turned a naturally occurring situation into one of manipulation. Sam took a nasty fall while working in the backyard on a Saturday afternoon. He stepped in a hole, badly turned his ankle, and a neighbor had to help him get back into his house. His wife, Katie, was supposed to be home at four o'clock. When she didn't return until six o'clock, Sam used the incident to lay into her. He was lying on the couch with an ice pack on his ankle when Katie returned home.

"Where have you been?" Sam asked.

"I've been running errands," Katie said. "It took me longer than I thought. What's wrong with you?"

"I stepped in a hole in the backyard," Sam said. "I've really hurt my ankle badly."

"Gosh, I'm sorry," Katie said. "Is there something I can do?"

Sam began to use emotion to manipulate Katie. "I'm hurt so badly," he said, piling it on and making it sound much worse than it was. "I'm in a lot of pain. If you cared, you would've been here on time. I've had to sit here in pain all alone. It's been awful. Why can't you be home when you *say* you will be?!"

Sure, Sam was in pain. But he was using the situation to make Katie feel awful. And it worked: For the rest of the night, Katie felt terrible, and Sam made sure she waited on him hand and foot.

Couples can use emotion to try to win arguments, to try to get their way, to try to persuade their partners to do all sorts of things. But eventually most people figure this out and no longer stand for it. Sam may have gotten his way in the short term, but his behavior will wreak havoc in the relationship long term. No one likes to be manipulated.

Part II

Emotionally Focused Therapy in Action: Moving from Problems to Patterns

The 5th Wave   By Rich Tennant

"Sometimes I think you enjoy pulling my triggers."

In this part . . .

In this part, we help you to see the common struggles in your relationship in a new way. You renew the strengths and power of positive emotion by looking back on the early days of your relationship. You discover common ways you argue and respond to conflict, as a couple. We help you understand how your individual relationship histories shape your expectations about love and emotions.

Throughout this part, you find examples of couples discovering their conflict styles and ways they can hang on through the inevitable challenges of making life together. In these examples and exercises, you begin to see your relationship differently, especially when you can face the patterns that so often run underneath the surface of your problems.

Chapter 5

Finding Common Patterns of Conflict

*O*ver the past 25 years, research has taught us a lot about how couples argue, the predictable roles they fall into, and what elements of arguments or fights are most destructive to relationships. Researcher John Gottman interviewed couples, and based on that one brief interview, was able to predict which couples would divorce at a stunning 94 percent accuracy. These predictions were based on the presence of certain characteristics that Gottman had previously found to be the most destructive in relationships.

This chapter explains many of these relationship factors and helps you assess how prominent they are in your relationship. We help you begin to eradicate the destructive ones right now. But before spotlighting patterns of conflict, it's important to first remember what drew you to each other in the first place. Remembering the early days helps many couples reconnect with their positive roots.

Remembering the Early Days of Your Relationship

You can get so caught up with life — taking care of work and the kids — that you run the risk of forgetting about what your early days together felt like. As therapists, we see this all the time. The negativity and day-to-day chores of the relationship can seem to take over. But that person that each of you fell in love with is still there. She may be buried in paperwork and spaghetti stains at the moment, but she's still there.

It's very easy to forget how you felt when you were first getting to know each other. But those times were the building blocks for your relationship. There was something special when you two were together back then. You can't go back to those days now, of course, but you *can* remember what those days were like — and doing so is helpful and important. Some couples only think negatively about their partners and their relationships today. But being able to remember times when the battle lines weren't yet drawn can be quite the relief. You may have forgotten some wonderful times.

REAL WORLD EXAMPLE

Stu hadn't thought back to how special it felt to be around Jenny in the early days of their relationship in so long that he wasn't sure if he'd ever even tried. "Man, that was 25 years ago," he said. "I have no idea how I felt."

One of your authors, Brent, explained to him that remembering these things together could be beneficial. "It helps you connect with a time when you weren't fighting or arguing nearly as much with each other. And these were often times when you couldn't wait to be together."

"I know, I thought about him all the time," Jenny said. "If I was at work, I was thinking about him. If I was at the store, I was thinking about him. Didn't matter where I was — I was thinking about him!" she said, smiling.

"I notice that you're smiling as you're saying this," Brent said to Jenny. "That's the first time I've seen this. What was it like when you were together then? What was the mood?"

"Almost like fantasy," Jenny said. "You idealize each other so much — you don't even see the negatives."

"That's true," Brent said. "In the early days, couples tend to see only the positives. But my sense is that you and Stu have been mainly seeing the negatives for so long that remembering some of the positives would be helpful. Do me a favor and stay with this. Go back and remember what the mood between you was like. What was it like waiting to get to spend time with him? Let yourself go back."

Brent noticed Stu perking up a bit, sitting up in his seat, and sneaking a peak over at Jenny. . . .

"Intoxicating," Jenny said. "It was intoxicating. I couldn't wait to be with him. And when I was with him, I felt so safe. I felt so heard. I felt so . . . alive."

Now Stu was downright glued to Jenny's every word. Brent had Jenny turn and share with Stu directly. He could tell it meant the world to Stu to hear this. After Jenny finished sharing with Stu, Brent said, "Stu, what is it like to hear Jenny share these things right now?"

"It's really nice," Stu said. "At first, I thought it was corny. And I guess it still is. But when she said that directly to me, I'll be honest, it was nice to hear."

"It's been a long time since you've heard nice things about you from Jenny?" Brent asked.

"Oh, man, yes," Stu said. "I haven't been saying nice things to her either though. But it feels nice to hear it." Brent then had Stu turn and share this directly with Jenny. Something powerful happens when you share directly with your partner.

Thinking about when you first met

Remembering your early days often stirs positive emotions in each of you (see Chapter 2). The therapy field is beginning to realize how powerful it is for couples to rediscover positive emotions, and not focus just on negative ones. If you aren't careful, you'll fall into a trap of only identifying the negative emotions in your relationship.

Remembering when you fell for each other can be a powerful exercise that positively impacts your relationship. Those were very meaningful times for the two of you. Being with each other really mattered. When you were together alone there was an emotional climate that was nice for each of you. You may be tempted to downplay remembering these times, but try not to.

There are plenty of negative emotions that probably pull you and your relationship down. And unfortunately the positive emotions are usually few and far between. Having Stu and Jenny take a moment to feel their positive emotions after they shared with each other helped them to focus on the positive feelings rather than the usual negative ones.

"Stu," Brent said, "what's it like inside emotionally for you right now as you two remember and share these things from the early days?"

"I feel kind of light inside," he said. "It's like being on a roller coaster, I guess — but in a good way, not a scary way. It's like a burden has been lifted. I realize we haven't 'solved' anything, but right now it feels really nice between us."

"You feel sort of light inside?" Brent asked. Stu nodded yes. "This feels good to you?"

"Very good," Stu said.

"Right. Stay with that just a moment," Brent said. "Stay with that 'light' and 'good' feeling. Let yourself enjoy it just a bit."

Brent then had Stu share directly with Jenny. "This is nice," Stu said. "I do feel light inside. I like it. I feel closer to you. It's been a while since I've felt closer to you this purely."

This activity was powerful for Jenny and Stu. It didn't solve their current problems, and they still were angry with each other and hurt by each other. But still, it was a nice moment that they shared, and those moments had been happening far too rarely for them.

In the following activity, you and your partner will remember back on your first meeting:

1. **Take three to five minutes to consider the first time you met your partner.**

   Think about where you were, and what was going on at the time. Then recall your first date or the first time you spent quality time together. This might not have been an official "date." It may have been a group event, for example, in which you ended up talking together for a while and getting to know each other. It may have even been time together mixed with phone calls or online meetings.

2. **When you have a clear picture and a feel for that time, briefly answer the following questions on a separate sheet of paper:**

   • Where were you when you first saw and/or met your partner?

   • What were a few things that attracted you to your partner?

   • What was the mood like when you were together?

3. **After answering these questions, take turns sharing your responses.**

   Do this one person at a time, and follow the suggested outline that follows:

   • When I hear you sharing that what first attracted you to me were _____ (list what your partner said), I feel _____.

   • As I listened to you sharing these things, I felt my emotions in my _____ (stomach, shoulders, neck, and so on).

   • It feels good to hear positives from you about me. Thank you.

4. **When you've both had a chance to respond, take a minute to check inside yourselves for your current positive emotional state.**

   Ask yourselves, "What is it like inside right now as a result of the activity?" Look for your immediate, primary emotions in the moment, the ones occurring after finishing the activity.

Share with your partner the positive emotions you're feeling as a result of this activity — no matter how small they may be.

The key is to allow yourselves to begin to tap into these emotional arenas that you most likely aren't used to paying attention to. You usually just quickly feel them and keep them to yourself. Then you move on to something else. There is power in noticing and feeling them more deeply with your partner, even when you're just beginning to notice these positive emotions.

Remembering and sharing positive emotions with each other, and then going further and talking to each other about what it's like to feel the positive emotions, is helpful in reducing distress in relationships. It may seem small to you, but it's needed and powerful.

Considering your partner's positives

When was the last time you thought about the positive characteristics that drew you to your partner? For many couples, there really is no answer to this question because they can't remember *ever* doing it. But when you think about it, your partner must have had positive characteristics that you admired when you first met.

Some of those initial positive characteristics, interestingly enough, may be some of the very things that now bother you about your partner. For example, you might have loved her free spiritedness, but today you're irritated and see it as being "flighty." Even if you're now annoyed by those characteristics, think about the characteristics that you liked about your partner in the early days of your relationship.

Brent asked Stu and Jenny to think back and remember the most positive characteristics of each other in the early days of their relationship.

"I know I liked how independent she was," Stu said. "Other girls just hung all over me when we were dating, but she didn't. She was sure about her major in school. She knew what she wanted to accomplish in college. She was sure of her abilities, and pretty much sure of herself. I loved this about her."

"You liked these things about Jenny?" Brent asked Stu.

"Yes," he said. "Very much. She had it together, if you know what I mean. I could be me, and she could be herself, and we were good with that."

Jenny being independent was a top positive characteristic for Stu. Brent asked Stu to tell him more. Stu talked about how confident Jenny was and how at ease that made him feel around her. Then Brent had Stu turn and share these things directly with Jenny. Yes, it was a bit uncomfortable, a bit forced, and even a bit odd when he started sharing with Jenny. But as Stu spoke, they loosened up, and the words came out more naturally. The remembering and sharing created a very nice atmosphere for both of them.

Jenny had no idea that Stu saw these as her top positive characteristics. "I'd heard bits and pieces of it before," she shared. "But I'd forgotten that. It feels really nice to hear this. It makes me remember back to a time when we weren't enemies. That seems so far away, and yet as he shares this with me now it feels good inside to hear it. Maybe it's not as far away as I thought."

As Jenny remembered Stu's early positive characteristics, what stood out in her memory was how easy he was to talk to and how well he listened to her. "He listened to me talk about my day," she said. "That's not the most important or interesting dialog, but he always listened. And I could tell that he always cared." She also said Stu's sense of humor was a big positive. She loved how they laughed together.

Your partner may not know what you most liked about him or her initially in the relationship. And you probably don't know what your partner saw as your top positive characteristics either. Sharing them with each other is a start to better communication and treatment of each other. Even if you aren't sure that you still see things in the same way, it feels good for each of you to hear.

Revisiting why you fell in love

The stress of life has a way of stealing away joy, to the point where you forget why you fell in love in the first place. During the early days of many relationships, partners relate to each other from an overall sense of warmth, acceptance, and love. Things just seem "right" when you're together. You see your partner as special, and it feels like the world is a happier place than it was before you found each other. You look forward to seeing each other every day. When you're apart, you hold a special place in the other person's mind and heart.

Sometimes people look back on those times as being silly or unrealistic. But that doesn't have to be the case. Those times and those emotions were very real and anything but silly. As couples who've had many years of distress in their relationship start to grow closer in therapy, they often start to describe their current relationship as feeling a lot like it did 10, 20, 30 years ago. "We feel like we did when we were just dating," they typically report.

As they begin to feel closer to each other emotionally, they remember why they fell in love in the first place. And as they see and feel those positives again, they begin to describe their relationship in terms of a sense of warmth, acceptance, and love — again. But now it's a more mature love and a more mature emotional connection. Now they can even more deeply appreciate what they have together because life's experiences have taught them how special it is and how lonely life can be without it.

Do you remember why you fell in love with your partner? It may have been a long time since you asked yourself that question. There were some special reasons you were attracted to each other. And while you and your partner have likely changed since then, you may be surprised to find that those initial reasons and attractions are still important. Many of them are still there.

You may be taking each other for granted, or maybe you've somehow fallen into a pattern of not complimenting each other. You may have fallen into a trap of arguing, fighting, and hurting each other. When you contrast how it was early on to how it is today, what happens inside you? As you're being asked to remember and take a kind of inventory of the closeness in your relationship then as compared to today, you may feel sad. As you read this, you may feel an emotion somewhere inside right now — a tinge, a sinking feeling. Do you? If so, what do you think your primary emotion could be trying to tell you?

Primary emotion is there for a reason. It informs and guides you. It moves you to action — if you pay attention to it, and don't ignore or push it away (see Chapter 4).

Something about you really mattered to your partner in the early days of your relationship. And something about your partner greatly mattered to you. Earlier in this chapter, we have you list several key things that drew you to your partner. But you haven't yet addressed what *attracted* you to your partner. Some of these reasons are interchangeable. Stu, for example, when speaking of his early attraction to Jenny, said that he liked the way Jenny dressed and the way she took pride in her appearance. He especially remembered how her eyes and her hair drove him nuts! Stu also talked about Jenny's faith and how it attracted him to her as well.

Couples give many different reasons for initially being attracted to each other. Here are some reasons couples often give:

- ✔ He listened to me.
- ✔ She had beautiful eyes.
- ✔ He had a great sense of humor.
- ✔ She was hot.
- ✔ He was kind.
- ✔ She was caring.
- ✔ He was sexy.
- ✔ She had beautiful hair.
- ✔ He was smart.
- ✔ She was genuine.
- ✔ He was a great kisser.
- ✔ She was honest.
- ✔ He had a great smile.

  ✔ She was wise.

  ✔ He had values similar to mine.

  ✔ She was a great lover.

  ✔ He shared my faith.

  ✔ She was happy.

  ✔ He was confident.

  ✔ She was independent.

  ✔ He was trustworthy.

This list is in no way complete (and we alternate the gender pronouns to be equal, but they could just as easily be reversed), but the list should help in stimulating your memory. Hopefully, you can find an item or two from this list that fits for you, but don't be limited by this list. Attractions can be unique. The goal here is for you to recall whatever it was that attracted you to your partner.

Take a minute to remember the things that attracted you to your partner early in the relationship. Each of you write down two or three of these items on separate sheets of paper. When you're finished, share your lists with each other.

The reasons for why you fell in love with your partner include

  ✔ How you felt when you were together initially

  ✔ The emotions that were coursing through your veins

  ✔ The positive characteristics you admired about your partner

  ✔ The things that attracted you to your partner

These aren't *all* the elements that go into why you fell in love, but they are powerful ones. Remembering and sharing them with each other helps you once again feel what initially played a vital role in your falling in love. This information and the activities are very important. The idea is that in remembering and sharing with each other, some of those early but special emotions and feelings begin to rekindle — just a tad.

Understanding How Couples Argue in Predictable Ways

John Gottman, a psychologist at the University of Washington, studied more than 2,000 married couples over two decades. During that time, he discovered patterns of ways that couples relate to each other, and he was able to use these patterns to predict which marriages would succeed or fail.

For years, Gottman was a leading proponent of teaching couples proper communication skills. He and many other scholars put the teaching of communication skills (listening, speaking one at a time, using "I" statements, repeating back what was said) at the core of their treatment plans. If couples could learn to use these techniques and learn healthy ways of communicating, they thought, they could resolve issues, be happy, and not divorce. This seems to make perfect sense.

Ironically, it turns out that Gottman's own meticulous research proved this belief to be false. He found that distressed couples actually communicate very well. They're very clear in communicating what they feel and mean. To make matters worse, Gottman found that his "master couples" — those that remain well adjusted and happy through the years and don't divorce — don't even use the communication skills that so many therapists (including Gottman) have been teaching for so long. They don't, for example, use "I" statements. And they don't use "reflective listening." They do argue and fight, however.

This research powerfully points out that negative emotion has a consistent destructive effect on your relationship. Negative emotions rip at how you feel about yourself, your partner, and your relationship. Gottman's "disaster couples" — those who ended up divorcing — regularly employed negative emotion. Happy couples still argue and fight, but they don't get caught in the trap of tossing painful personal attacks back and forth at each other. It's the "getting personal" over time that hurts relationships so much.

Seeing the impact of negative emotions

Gottman found that four concrete behaviors emerge over time when couples form habits of putting each other down personally. He refers to these ways of arguing as "The Four Horseman of the Apocalypse." Put simply, they're danger signs. Couples who consistently use "The Four Horsemen" in their relationships are headed down the road toward divorce.

Following are descriptions of each horseman, followed with a brief explanation of how master couples deal with them differently from disaster couples. As you read these descriptions, ask yourself whether you and your partner are more akin to masters or disasters and which of these horsemen you're using in your relationship.

- ✔ **Criticism:** Stating a problem in the relationship as a defect in the partner. Attacking your partner's personality or character, usually with the intent of making someone right and someone wrong. For example, "You always . . ." or "You never . . ." or "You're just like your mother. . . ."

- Disasters: When conflict arises, disaster couples are critical. They have a sense of diagnosing each other's personality defects. For example, "I can't believe you did that. You always do that. There's something wrong with you — I swear there is."

- Masters: Master couples are gentler with one another. When they raise issues, it's as if they're playing around with an invisible ball, in that they both take responsibility and pitch it back and forth. For example: "It sucks that this happened. I've done the same thing before, though."

✔ **Contempt:** Contempt is the *best* predictor of relationship breakup. It's basically any statement made to your partner from a superior place. Attacking your partner's sense of self with the intention to insult or psychologically abuse.

- Disasters: Disaster couples use hostile humor, sarcasm, or mockery. Their tone of voice can be especially demeaning. They also sneer, roll their eyes, and curl their upper lips – which are nonverbal communicators. Furthermore, they may use destructive and hurtful words such as *bitch, bastard, wimp, fat, stupid, ugly, slob,* or *lazy.*

- Masters: Master couples hardly ever do this. They're low in contempt.

✔ **Defensiveness:** Warding off a potential attack. Seeing oneself as the victim. Defenders often raise a kind of counterattack, whine, or present themselves as innocent victims.

- Disasters: Disaster couples become defensive. For example: "I can't help it. I always end up being talked at like this. Doesn't matter what I do. I'm always on the losing end."

- Masters: Master couples do just the opposite of defending. They enter into the conversation to learn and to clear things up for the better of both partners. For example: "That's an interesting point. Tell me more of how you see our problem and how I contribute to it."

✔ **Stonewalling:** Withdrawing from the relationship as a way to avoid conflict. Interestingly, Gottman found people who stonewall have a dramatic increase in heart rate while doing so. These partners may seem disinterested, but physiologically their bodies are going haywire (which obviously isn't healthy).

- Disaster: In disaster couples, one partner yells, while the other partner is silent. For example: "Dammit, Erika!" Scott says. "How come you just sit there and don't answer back?!" Erika simply shrugs her shoulders. She's stonewalling.

- Masters: Master couples still stonewall at times, but they're able to self-soothe themselves physiologically so that their heart rates don't skyrocket and they don't totally shut down or walk away. For example: "I hear what you're saying. It's not easy, though, when you get loud."

Assessing for "The Four Horsemen" in your relationship is a great way to pin-point actions that are a sign of dangerous distress levels in your relationship. These predictable actions are rooted in professional research and borne out in our years of doing therapy as well.

If there are no horsemen in your relationship, we suggest skipping ahead to the section called "Discovering the Three Fighting Styles."

"The Four Horsemen" can be unsaddled! They aren't personality defects that you were born with. As you work through the activities in this book, you'll move away from relating in these ways. For now, it's good to begin to recognize them and the degree of their destructiveness in your relationship.

Many people believe that anger is the root cause of unhappy relationships. Gottman found that conflict itself is not the problem. A problem can arise based on how we handle anger with each other. For example, speaking about anger constructively can clear the air and start to get a relationship back in balance. However, anger and conflict do become problems when they're accompanied by the presence of "The Four Horsemen."

After reading about "The Four Horsemen," Olivia and Becker immediately knew that a few of them were stampeding on their relationship, and they were scared. But they also knew somewhere inside that recognizing some things that had gone wrong in their relationship was long overdue. Instead of arguing about it or downplaying it, they decided to accept it and go to work remedying the situation.

Becker was the first to step up. "I know for a fact that I get defensive and stonewall," he said in front of Olivia in a therapy session. "When I do something wrong, or forget something, and she gets upset with me, I quickly get defensive."

We talked about when this usually happens and around what circumstances. A key stumbling block for them was Becker not being on time. He was usually late in getting home from work. They both worked, and Becker was responsible for picking up their daughter from daycare. This was the plan that Becker himself agreed to — Olivia taking their daughter to school in the mornings allowed Becker to get to work early, which he liked. In turn, it was his responsibility to pick her up and get home at a decent hour.

But that was the problem: He was habitually late, and they argued about it almost every day. This put Olivia in the horseman role of habitual criticizer. "I know I need to do better," Becker said. "I hate it when I'm late."

"And yet you continue to be late at least once or twice a week," Olivia chimed in. "If you hated it so much, you'd think you'd be able to leave a little bit earlier from work."

"So, this is how it goes?" Brent asked. They both nodded.

We spent several sessions getting to know when the horsemen appeared, and how those fights unfolded. We came to the conclusion that Olivia took on the role of criticizer, but not any of the other horsemen. Becker took on the two horseman roles of defensiveness and stonewalling. Olivia was able to talk about it without getting angry or accusing, and Becker was able to resist getting defensive or shutting down. We also discussed the primary emotions around these horseman roles — how it felt for each of them to play the role of horseman, and what it was like for the other when they were on the receiving end of this behavior.

Separately, take five to ten minutes to consider the presence of each horseman in your relationship. For each horseman, ask yourself, "Do I employ this horseman?" Then consider, "Does my partner?" Jot down brief notes so that you can remember your thoughts. If clear examples come to mind, be sure to make note of them.

When you're both finished, go through each horseman together, and use what you jotted down to start the conversation. This isn't the time to argue. Instead, it's simply a time to assess which horsemen are present and with whom. Consider the following:

- Do I take on the actions of that horseman?
- If yes, when are the most likely times I act like this?
- When I act like this horseman, what is the topic usually around (for example, work, chores, money, sex, children, and so forth)?
- When I act like this horseman, how do I feel?
- When my partner acts like this horseman, how do I feel?

Take the time needed to discuss these questions with your partner. Recognizing who does what, when, and how it affects both of you emotionally is a step toward being able to stop it.

If there are horsemen in your relationship, they didn't appear overnight. Before there were horsemen in your relationship, there were less-severe cycles of negative emotion present in your arguing. The level of distress and amount of time for simple disagreements to morph into negative emotional interactions and then on to horsemen is unique to each couple. But the presence of horsemen is usually the result of escalating negativity and unresolved arguing over a period of time.

Repeating cycles of negative emotion

Most likely, there was a time when your relationship had none of "The Four Horsemen" (see the preceding section). Remembering how you argued before you allowed "The Four Horsemen" into your relationship helps you see that things weren't always the way they are now. At one point, you got caught in a cycle of negative emotion when arguing or fighting, but you didn't personally attack. This is important because Gottman found that master couples do, indeed, argue and get angry, and this scenario repeats itself. But what they *don't* do is personally attack each other in their anger.

Do you remember how you argued earlier in your relationship? Were you able to stop the escalation of negative emotion before personally attacking each other? Many couples say they didn't used to attack each other personally, but they can't remember how they didn't or how they resolved the arguing before it got to "The Four Horsemen" level.

For example, Becker and Olivia reported that they never argued as "nasty" as they do now. They used to be able to manage their negative emotion before it spiraled into horsemen terrain. But over time, as negativity built up, they could no longer hold off the horsemen.

So, Brent gave them a homework assignment to sit together during the week and think back to earlier in their relationship. They were supposed to help each other remember how they argued without getting so negative and personal. What was different then that enabled them to hold off "The Four Horsemen"? They came back a week later with very insightful stories.

"We both found it interesting how difficult it was for us to remember how we argued without fighting the way we do now," Olivia said. "We had never really thought about our fighting being more intense and personal now. I think we just assumed that we always fought like this because we've been doing it for so long — the only difference is that we fight more now."

They said that, earlier on, when Olivia got angry with Becker, she would tell him more "lightly" that it bothered her sometimes when he was late. Olivia recalled, "I'd say, 'Honey, I know you're busy at work, but when you're really late, I miss you.' And I'd give him a hug."

Gottman found that the woman's level of critical "start-up" heading into discussions over topics often ending in arguments plays a significant role in determining how personal the argument typically gets.

"How did that go for you?" Brent asked them.

"It was much better," Olivia said. "We realized this week that his being late really didn't begin bothering me until we had a child. Before then, we had all night together anyway. So, while I didn't like it, it got much worse when our daughter was born and our time alone together became much more limited."

Becker and Olivia realized that early on they could argue over Becker being late, but their way of going about it was more easygoing and less critical. And this worked, as Becker changed his pattern of lateness. But when a baby came into the picture, the stress level rose, and Olivia found herself being more angry when Becker would come home later than expected. And who can blame her? Unlike before, now there was a child who had to be fed, taken care of, and put down to bed — all on top of the normal evening responsibilities. Olivia simply depended on Becker's help at night now more than before.

Becker noted how, over time, Olivia's anger at him played a role in his pulling back, staying at work longer, and even avoiding her. "I got so tired of being the bad guy," he said. "I'm late sometimes. But who wants to come home to mean looks and angry attacks? It's no wonder that I stay later at work. At least no one is disappointed in me there."

What they took home from this exercise was that when one of them got negative, the hurtful exchanges quickly picked up momentum and they both got hurt. Earlier on in the relationship, they spoke from more vulnerable places, which helped hold the negative emotional cycles at bay. This allowed them to hear each other better. Becker lost sight that Olivia missed and needed him when he was late, and Olivia had forgotten that her anger made Becker feel like a disappointment.

Discovering the Three Fighting Styles

Couples typically assume one of three fighting styles, but they often aren't aware of how they fight. Identifying how you fight is important. Conflict is inevitable for most couples, so gaining an understanding of what you do and how when arguing takes away some of the mystery of it. When something is mysterious, it can seem untouchable and out of reach of repair. But by taking away some of the mystery of your fighting styles and cycles of negative emotion, you're taking away some of the power associated with them.

Some couples mistake the negative impact of their arguing with the quality of their relationship. In emotionally focused therapy (EFT), we find that these negative emotional experiences tend to push out the positive intentions that couples bring when fighting for their relationship. Yes, the fights can get bad, but they aren't always the best indicator of what's really going on in the relationship. When you understand the fight, you can better see what it's really all about.

In this section, we spell out the three styles of fighting, with explanations and examples of each. As you read through this section, try to figure out which style best fits the pattern you and your partner are in. You may have more than one style, but usually one is predominant.

As you read about fighting styles, keep in mind the following:

✔ **You take on fighting styles for very good reasons.** You may not even be aware of it, but you have very good reasons for assuming the fighting style that you have. Granted, it probably isn't working well for either of you, but fighting styles aren't character defects, and they aren't permanent.

✔ **All styles are created equal.** Sometimes people can get down on themselves, for example, because they may be more attacking in times of distress. Other people beat themselves up because they "wilt" in the face of attack. They defend, which leaves them feeling weak. But the reality is, one style isn't better or worse than another.

✔ **You aren't your fighting style.** Your fighting style describes what you *do*, not who you *are*. The fighting styles aren't measures of your self-worth. They're simply ways that you deal with your emotions in times of disagreement with your partner. They carry no value or moral judgments.

✔ **No fighting style leads to resolution.** You just keep fighting. Sure, you eventually stop, but the issue rarely has been resolved.

✔ **Fighting styles are servants to secondary emotion.** In EFT terms, fighting styles are the ways that partners act when they're responding from their secondary, reactive emotions (see Chapter 4). If you stay in your secondary emotion, you'll stay in conflict and inflict damage on each other and yourself.

Attack/attack

When disagreements occur in attack/attack couples, neither partner wants to give an inch. Both partners are making their points, and there is rarely any time to hear each other. It's like they're on a battlefield, and the other person is the enemy. Back and forth they go, often getting louder. You've probably seen couples like this — they stand out, whether in a grocery store, at a restaurant, or around friends.

In EFT language, both partners are lost in the secondary, reactive emotions. They've totally blocked out any primary emotions and their messages. Secondary emotion does the opposite of attracting others — it repels them. It sends a message of preparing yourself for battle, because an aggressor has arrived. So, while one partner attacks, the other instantly gets a message to protect himself.

For couples who do this often, this style of emotion shows up in their bodies. They're ready at a moment's notice to defend, to go on the attack. Living in this pattern can keep you on edge, tense, and aggressive.

David and Hannah fell squarely into the attack/attack fighting style.

"Where are my keys?" David asked Hannah loudly.

"I don't have your keys," Hannah shot back. "Every time you lose your keys, you blame me!"

"That's because most of the time I lose my keys, it's because you took them and left them somewhere else," David said.

"Oh, bologna," Hannah said. "Quit blaming everyone but yourself."

In seconds, you can see their negative cycle. No doubt, it's attack/attack.

Attack/defend

Attack/defend couples find themselves in a tit-for-tat similar to the attack/attack style, but in this case one partner defends himself or herself instead of attacking back. As the attacking partner gets agitated, the other partner begins to defend himself or herself. This makes the more-attacking partner more agitated, and he or she does more of the same, except stronger — attack! And as he or she attacks more, the other partner continues to defend. The defending partner is put on his or her heels. It's another vicious cycle.

Blake and Trisha fell into the attack/defend style. Trisha was the attacker, and Blake was the defender. "Blake," Trisha said, "did you pick up the dog food last night? I just went in to feed the dogs and there's no food!"

"Ah, man," Blake said. "I totally forgot."

"How could you forget?" Trisha asked. "I texted you before you left work!"

"I was in a hurry because I knew we were going to eat pizza at seven o'clock," he said. "I was so concentrated on getting home on time that I forgot."

"I don't get it," Trisha said. "I even texted you!"

The more Blake defends, the more angry Trisha gets. The more angry Trisha gets, the more Blake defends. Once again, in EFT language, this style finds couples remaining in their secondary, reactive emotions. Secondary emotion reacts off itself, spiraling out of control.

Silent/silent

Most of the time, couples who find themselves in the silent/silent fighting style were previously operating under one of the other styles. Over time, couples in the prior two styles can move farther away from each other and move into the silent/silent style. But this isn't always the case — some couples are so concerned with conflict that they avoid it at all costs, right from the start.

When we see silent/silent couples in therapy, they've usually worn each other out with their previous fighting style. The attacking partner just got tired of attacking and gave up. The defending partner had been withdrawing in defense for some time, so he was already distant. Or, they never fight, always avoid conflict, and over time lose a sense of connection in their relationship.

Luke and Grace had fallen into the silent/silent style after eight years of marriage. Luke came from a family that argued a lot. He described his childhood as one in which "I did everything possible to keep away from my parents when they were fighting, and keep away from them at other times so they wouldn't get angry with me." Luke learned from an early age to avoid conflict at any cost. If his parents got angry with him, "there was hell to pay." It's no wonder that in his married life he avoids conflict.

Grace came from a family that, as far as she knew, never fought. "I can't recall seeing my parents fight or raise their voices at each other once," she said. "Not even once." It's no wonder that when conflict arises between Grace and Luke, the only way Grace knows how to handle it is to go silent. That's basically all that was modeled for her and all she really knows.

Grace and Luke reported handling conflict as follows: Person A gets frustrated and asks Person B about the conflict. Person B responds in a non-specific manner, the topic is buried, and nothing gets resolved. For greater clarity, Brent asked them to think of and describe a recent example.

Luke described an incident in the previous week in which he couldn't locate a bill that needed paying. He really struggles with Grace "losing bills that I place in a safe place." Grace didn't respond to this (note her silence). "I asked her if she had seen the bill that I thought I'd put on the desk," Luke said. "She said she hadn't seen it. I later found it in my drawer in our bedroom. I guess she moved it there when straightening up." That's where Luke stopped.

"So, what happened when you found it?" Brent asked. "What did you say to her?"

"I didn't say anything," Luke said. In a previous session, Luke had told Brent that it drove him crazy when Grace moved his things around. But he never talks to her about it — he goes silent, and Grace does, too. But over time, stuffed frustration grows into resentment, which neither partner ever expresses.

Looking At What's Going On Underneath

EFT is almost always focused on what's going on emotionally underneath. That's one of the things that make the approach unique. In this chapter, we introduce you to "The Four Horsemen" and the three fighting styles. In this section, we move into the *reasons* you act in these ways with your partner in the first place.

These reasons for your style usually remain hidden — not only from your partner, but also from yourself. When you start to understand what's going on underneath, your negative emotional cycles begin to make sense. Your anger or your defensiveness, for example, begins to fall into place when you learn what's happening underneath.

Barbara was always kind of a puzzle to Stan. He loved her, and they were a happy couple, but sometimes she got really quiet around him and he never understood why. After an argument, Stan would wonder if Barbara was really okay. After so many years, this bothered Stan. He felt a distance between them that he didn't like. They came to see Brent for therapy. One of the things they worked on was Stan better understanding what was going on underneath for Barbara. In a nutshell, when Stan got upset with Barbara, her internal emotional response was very different from what he could've known.

We discovered that Barbara was extremely sensitive to Stan's frustration. When he started to get upset, even a little, Barbara started to freeze up and go quiet. This happened so quickly that even she was unsure what was going on inside. It turns out that Stan's signals of frustration hit a deep-seated fear in Barbara. This fear told her that Stan might find out that she wasn't very smart and that she was too common. She worried that, in time, he would leave her.

Stan had no idea this was how Barbara felt! But once he was able to see and understand what was really going on for her, it made sense to him. The last thing Stan wanted to do was play a role in Barbara feeling afraid that she wasn't who he wanted or that he would leave her. "Nothing could be farther from the truth," Stan said to Barbara. "You're the last person I would ever want to hurt. And I would never leave you."

Barbara wasn't yet able to go to Stan and ask for his reassurance when these fears popped up, so their work together in therapy wasn't over. But Barbara gained an understanding of herself, and Stan gained an understanding of Barbara, and that combined to give them a much clearer picture of what she went through in their relationship. They both reported feeling closer to each other as a result.

Acting defensive for a reason

When partners find themselves responding defensively, they have very good reasons for this. Although it may appear rude and uncaring, there's a *lot* going on inside the defensive person during disagreements. When you discover what these things are, it greatly helps you understand the defensive person's responses better.

If you're the *non*-defensive partner, try to recognize and share what you see when your partner is in defensive mode. These are the signals that often make you frustrated or angry. Together, think about how things go when you're in your negative emotional cycle. If you're the *non*-defensive partner, locate yourself in your mind just as the argument is starting. (We'll assume that you most often approach your partner with something that needs to be resolved.)

This activity is for the non-defensive partner. Here's a list of behaviors that are often present when your partner is acting defensively:

- ✔ My partner makes excuses.
- ✔ My partner turns away from me.
- ✔ My partner's eyes look away.
- ✔ My partner's eyes look down.
- ✔ My partner's eyes say that he or she is _____.
- ✔ My partner's eyes say that he or she feels _____ about me.
- ✔ My partner is avoiding me.
- ✔ My partner is angry.
- ✔ My partner disapproves of me.
- ✔ My partner is afraid.
- ✔ My partner is sad.
- ✔ When my partner is acting defensively, I see or hear _____.

Write down which of these items you see in your partner when the two of you are caught in your negative emotional cycle. Feel free to add other things not on this list.

The preceding list evokes emotional responses in you. You may not even be aware of them, but it's time to start recognizing what happens inside you when the signs of defensiveness appear in your partner. Say to yourself, "When I see the things listed above, it makes me fear that you might deep down _____" (write down the ones that apply):

- ✔ Be tired of me
- ✔ Be angry with me
- ✔ Be fed up with me
- ✔ Not be sure you still love me
- ✔ Wish you were with someone else
- ✔ Be frustrated with me

> ✔ Be thinking of leaving me
>
> ✔ Other: _____

When you're finished, sit down with your partner and share your answers. This list may be more difficult for you to share than the first one was. That's normal — but you can do it.

This may be brand new to your partner's ears. Your partner may not be aware that these feelings stir in you when you see his or her defensiveness. Chances are, you don't often show them.

A note for the defensive partner: Try not to be defensive while your partner is sharing his or her answers for this activity. It may be most helpful to simply tell your partner which ones stick out to you — but not in a defensive manner. For example, after hearing his partner's two lists, Stu shared in response, "For the first list, I wasn't so much aware I did some of those things, but it sounds right." He added, "For the second list, I wasn't at all aware that you were afraid that I might be fed up with you or leave you. Wow. I had no idea." Stu didn't try to make excuses, get angry, or defend. He realized this activity was more about his partner and less about him.

When you're caught in your negative emotional cycle, you're unable to really hear the other person. And you certainly don't come anywhere near understanding what's happening inside each other at a much deeper level. In fairness to each of you, neither of you is able to show what's happening inside *yourselves* during these arguments. So, how could either of you know what's happening inside your partner?

This activity is for the defensive partner. The goal of this activity is for both of you to start becoming more aware of what's happening inside the defensive partner during your negative emotional cycle. Take the time you need to think about a recent argument in which you fell into your cycle. Let yourself feel what goes on inside you as the argument proceeds. When you're ready, answer the following question in your own notebook:

> When we're into our negative cycle and you're (angry, blaming, upset, and so on), deep down I feel _____ (write down the ones that apply):
>
> • Like I just want to get out of there
>
> • Like I'm failing
>
> • Afraid you'll reject me
>
> • Overwhelmed
>
> • Weak
>
> • Stupid
>
> • Like I've disappointed you again

- Like I can never get this right

- Like I screwed up again

- Like a child

- Other: _____

When you're finished, sit down with your partner, and share your answers. This list may be difficult for you to share — that's normal. You're beginning to delve into your primary emotional world in response to your relationship. You can do it!

This may be brand new to your partner's ears. Your partner may not be aware that these feelings stir in you. Chances are, you don't often show them.

Finally, take one or two minutes to share with each other what it was like for each of you to do these last two activities together. Consider this with each other. "When we talk to each other about what's going on underneath emotionally for both of us, I feel _____." Don't go back into the specifics of the activities — just share how it feels to talk about these emotions with each other. In therapy terms, this is called *meta-processing,* and it's an important step.

Sounding the alarm

Partners who find themselves in the position of attacking have very good reasons for it. Although it may often appear mean spirited and aggressive to others, there's a *lot* going on inside the attacking person during disagreements that remains unseen. When you both realize what's going on inside the attacking person, it helps you understand those angry responses better.

Desiree often found herself in the attacking fighting style. While she hated being aggressive, her anger got the best of her. It just seemed like there was no way out, no other way for her to handle herself during arguments. "I try so hard to not get angry," she said. "But it gets the best of me almost every time. I can only hold it back for so long!"

It's helpful for the defensive partner to recognize and share what you see when your partner is in attacking mode. These are the signals that often make you defend yourself. Think about how things go when you're in your negative emotional cycle. Locate yourself in your mind just as the argument is starting.

This activity is for the defensive partner. Here's a list of behaviors that are often present when your partner is acting from within the attacking fighting style:

- ✔ A face of anger
- ✔ Eyes that say about me _____
- ✔ A voice getting louder
- ✔ A voice tone that says to me _____
- ✔ A voice tone that says about me _____
- ✔ Pointing of fingers at me
- ✔ Body language that says to me _____
- ✔ Body language that says about me _____

Write down the things you see in your partner when the two of you are caught in your negative emotional cycle. Feel free to add other things not on this list.

The next question is about your feelings in response to what you noted in the preceding list. The preceding list evokes emotional responses within you. You may not even be aware of them, but it's time to start recognizing what happens inside you when the signs of attack or anger are directed toward you.

Say to yourself, "When I see the things listed above, it makes me fear that you might deep down _____" (write down the ones that apply):

- ✔ Be tired of me
- ✔ Be angry with me
- ✔ Be fed up with me
- ✔ Be unsure that you still love me
- ✔ Wish you were with someone else
- ✔ Be frustrated with me
- ✔ Be thinking of leaving me
- ✔ Other: _____

When you're finished, sit down with your partner and share your answers to both of the above questions. The second list may be more difficult for you to share. That's normal. But you can do it!

This may be brand new to your partner's ears. Your partner may not be aware that these feelings stir in you because you may mostly only show defensiveness.

*A **note for the attacking partner:*** Try not to get upset or show disapproval while your partner is sharing answers for this activity. It may be most helpful to simply tell your partner which ones stick out to you — but not in an aggressive manner. For example, after hearing her partner's two lists, Hannah shared in response, "For the first list, I wasn't so much aware I did some of those things. But I can see it." She then added, "For the second list, I wasn't aware that you were afraid that I might be fed up with you or leave you. That must be scary for you." Hannah didn't try to make excuses, get angry, or attack.

When you're caught in your negative emotional cycle, you're unable to really hear the other person. And you certainly don't come anywhere near understanding what's happening inside each other at a much deeper level. In fairness to each of you, neither of you is able to show what's happening inside *yourselves* during these arguments. So, how could either of you know what's happening inside your partner?

The goal of this activity is for both of you to start becoming more aware of what's happening inside the attacking partner during your negative emotional cycle. A note for the attacking partner: Take the time you need to think about a recent argument in which you fell into your cycle. Let yourself feel what goes on inside you as the argument proceeds. When you're ready, answer the following question in your own notebook:

> When we're into our negative cycle and you're (defending, making excuses, avoiding, and so on), deep down underneath I feel _____ (write down the ones that apply):
>
> • Afraid that you don't really care about us
>
> • Like I'm the bad person, always nagging you
>
> • Afraid that you don't really care about me anymore
>
> • Afraid that you'll leave me
>
> • Other: _____

When you're finished, sit down together and share your answers. This list may be difficult for you to share — that's normal. You're beginning to delve into your primary emotional world in response to your relationship. You can do it!

This may be brand new to your partner's ears. Your partner may not be aware that these feelings stir in you. You may not have been aware either. Chances are, you don't often show them.

Take a few minutes to share with each other what it was like for each of you to do the last two activities together. Consider this with each other: "When we talk to each other about what's going on underneath emotionally for both of us, I feel _____." Don't go back into the specifics of the activities; just share how it feels to talk about these emotions with each other. In therapy terms, this is called *meta-processing,* and it's an important step.

What we don't talk about

Most couples don't talk about the primary emotions going on underneath — and for good reason. Beginning to open up and share from such vulnerable places can be difficult. Staying in your secondary emotional responses is safer and easier. Unfortunately, these secondary responses don't attract your partner to you — they propel you away from each other.

When one of you shows anger, for example, it's difficult for your partner to hang in there with you, much less see the hurt underneath. But the hurt underneath "pulls" your partner to comfort you. Consider the effect of the following two statements as you read them:

> I'm so angry right now! *(Loud)* I can't believe that you did that again! I've told you a million times to please not do that. It makes me so upset!

> I'm so angry right now. *(Soft)* I can't believe this happened again. Sometimes I get afraid that you don't care for me anymore. *(Softer)* It scares me.

The first statement comes right out of secondary emotions, and it stays there. It pushes you away as you read it. That's what anger is there for — to assert boundaries. But at the wrong time, asserting boundaries isn't the best idea. When you're trying to resolve a problem with your partner, you're not wanting to establish boundaries. You're wanting to come together to solve a problem.

The second statement starts in secondary emotion, but with less volume. And it moves down to primary. Did you feel the difference? As the voice got softer, and the emotions of *afraid* and *scared* were genuinely felt and shared, it showed a vulnerability that has a real possibility of eliciting care and comfort from your partner. Because it's honestly felt and shared in the moment, it allows emotion to "move" both you and your partner. This is healthfully *using* emotion as it's supposed to be used. That's why it's there!

The second statement could be used in a manipulative way that wasn't genuine, yet *sounded* genuine. In other words, the primary emotion could be faked. Doing so would be an example of an instrumental emotional response (see Chapter 4). Be on guard not to do this — it'll only come back to wreak havoc on your relationship by killing trust. A major factor in EFT is being honest and genuine with each other. It's okay to be angry, for example — anger can be understood and worked through. But faking emotions to manipulate — that can greatly impede any progress.

You may not be used to talking about your primary emotions. Maybe this is new to you. That's okay — it's new to most of the couples we see in therapy. But that's changing now for you. You're changing, taking some risks, putting yourself out there and on the line in front of your partner. You could get hurt. You could get rejected. Even so, you're committed to staying the course. You can do this! You're on the road to a much closer, more intimate relationship. Trust the process of EFT. It works!

Chapter 6

Finding Common Roles in Conflict

. . . .

In This Chapter

▶ Exploring your history of important relationships

▶ Understanding the role of the pursuer

▶ Uncovering the role of the withdrawer

. . . .

You and your partner have your own relationship histories — with your parents, family, friends, and other past romantic partners — and those relationship histories shape your actions and expectations today. In fact, your past relationships have a huge impact on the roles you take with each other today. Your history of close relationships has a lot to do with how you share intimacy and happy times, as well as how you argue. What your parents or caregivers modeled for you as you were growing up helped shape who you are today.

But more important than the modeling your parents did is the emotional climate. This emotional climate plays a vital role in how close you allow your partner to get to you, and how close you allow yourself to get to your partner. If you were consistently taken care of and attended to when you got hurt and cried as a child, for example, you'll typically respond similarly to vulnerable emotions as an adult. If you get angry when you hear someone crying, you probably had parents who taught you to have a stiff upper lip and not complain. Your parents' level of emotional connection or disconnection with your emotions as you were growing up greatly impacts you today. This chapter helps you gain clarity into how your past relationships are affecting your present one.

Over time, most couples find themselves in predictable roles of conflict. These roles are shaped by fighting style (see the preceding chapter) and relationship history. Many couples get lost in what they fight *about* — in other words, the content. Content is the topic, like arguing over whose turn it is to take out the trash, or why one of you forgot to pick up the kids from school. But the content doesn't matter as much as the roles you play.

Conflicts, especially major ones, cause emotional distress. Over time, each of you develops typical ways of coping with this distress. Some partners increasingly turn *toward* their partners in these moments; others turn away. We call these roles pursuing and withdrawing, respectively.

One helpful way to decrease conflict in relationships is to figure out *how* you fight — meaning who does what and when. In your relationship, who most often pushes the intensity or pace of the fight (pursuing)? What does this person do to kick it up a notch? Or do both of you kick it up a notch? Who tends to shut it down first, or go quiet first, and look to move away from the scene of the crime (withdrawing)? In this chapter, we help you start to understand the roles you and your partner play in conflict, which helps you get a grip on your arguing. And getting a grip helps you begin to gain some control over it.

Delving into Your Relationship Histories

You and your partner have different pasts when it comes to relationships. Everyone has a mother, for example, but no one had a mother exactly like yours. Research on attachment theory (see Chapter 2) has taught us that even brothers and sisters with the same parents can have different relationship styles with each parent. And two sisters can have very different relationships or attachment styles with the same mom. So, as you and your partner learn about each other's pasts, realize that each of you has a very different story to tell.

In this section, we walk the two of you through those histories, together.

Looking at what your parents taught you about relationships

What went on in your home has direct consequences for who you are today. Some people don't want to hear that, and that's understandable. Maybe you came from a home that wasn't so great, and you're determined to be different. Good for you! The good news is that you *can,* most certainly, be different. But even so, your past has an effect on you. Trying to deny your past can lead to repeating it. But recognizing your past and sharing it with your partner is the surest route to defeating old, bad behaviors, *together*.

The way your parents interacted with each other can have an effect on your present relationship. If you watched a bad marriage unravel over time, possibly leading to divorce, it probably taught a lot of what you currently believe about intimate relationships. Although this is logical, it can have a negative impact on you and your partner. You may have beliefs about relationships that your partner doesn't know about, and vice versa. We see this all the time in therapy.

Elise and Chris came from very different families. Elise's family was always on the move. Her mom had a different man in her life every year. "You can't trust any man," Elise's mom instilled in her. "They all lie and all they want is sex." Elise was less than excited about boys growing up. In her mind, they only grew up into monsters anyway. Not surprisingly, today she finds it very difficult to trust that Chris really loves her. Her great fear is that if he really knew her, he wouldn't love her. She's certain that if he had the chance, Chris would realize his mistake and leave her.

Chris loves Elise dearly, and he tells her this often. But Elise simply can't let that in — not really. She just can't believe him. "I know what he says is true for him," she said. "It's just not true for me. I can't believe that he loves me for who I am."

As Chris learned about Elise's past, it all began to make much more sense to him. He could see Elise's upbringing all over their relationship. "It's like I'm not just fighting with Elise to prove myself and make this relationship work," he said. "I'm fighting all the things that her mom taught her, with her words and her example, long before she even met me."

Chris, on the other hand, grew up in a home with parents who never spoke of divorce. But they really didn't speak about much of anything emotional with each other either. He described his parents as "basically getting along, but not close."

Chris now finds himself in a marriage feeling "like a roommate." He says that this isn't what he wants, but he and Elise have been like this for 13 years. Chris wasn't really aware of it, but his present relationship was normal to him. It's what he was used to. It fit well with what he learned about intimate relationships growing up.

Adults who lived through their parents' painful divorces as children can carry a real sense of fear into current relationships. Some partners are very sensitive to possible warning signs of incoming danger for the relationship. A forgotten call from work saying she would be late in arriving home suddenly becomes evidence that there really is an affair. An argument over socks in the morning when running late can spiral into a belief that they're no longer compatible. Little, insignificant events can quickly trigger catastrophe based on people's backgrounds.

Consider Karen and Dwight, for example. They came to therapy after 15 years of marriage. Karen vowed as an adolescent that she would never put her future children through a divorce. "That was so hard on me as a child," she said in tears. "I swore that I would never do that to my children. Now I'm so afraid that it may happen."

Karen's fears of divorce had taken a toll on their marriage. Dwight didn't understand Karen's fear. What he did understand, though, was her intense worry. "I've lost her to worry and fear," Dwight said. "We used to be carefree — some of the time anyway. Now I walk on eggshells, so careful not to set her off." Dwight bit his tongue rather than expressing his real feelings to Karen because it so often led to "her fear basically sending her into a depression."

With guidance, Karen and Dwight learned to listen to each other's relationship histories. Dwight finally "got" how afraid Karen was, and why. Karen "got" how powerful her childhood memories were, and how they were impacting Dwight, her family, and herself in ways that weren't necessary. In time, they were able to better separate out the past from the reality of the present.

Karen learned how to recognize when fear crept in, and how to go to Dwight and tell him that her fear was getting the best of her. She learned to ask him to reassure her that their relationship was theirs — not her parents'.

Because Dwight better understood Karen's fears and where they came from, he could place the fear in a proper context and keep himself more calm and centered on behalf of Karen. "I learned that most of the time only 50 percent of what's happening for Karen is actually about me," Dwight said. His increased sense of calmness within the storm is what Karen needed, too.

There's just something profound about handling old false beliefs and fears *together*.

Ask yourself what beliefs about intimate relationships you likely carry with you based on your past. Think about past relationships that impacted you the most as a child, adolescent, or even young adult. You may hit upon some things that you'd never considered before. For example, you may have just accepted certain things to be "true" because that's all you really knew at the time, which is common. Fill out the following, either in this book or on a separate sheet of paper:

Three beliefs based on past intimate relationships that I likely carry with me are (for example, "Women don't like sex," "You can't trust men/ women," "Men always cheat"):

_____

_____

_____

Several fears associated with these past beliefs creep into my present relationship as (for example, "I'm afraid that I'm not a good enough lover," "I'm afraid that you sneak around with other women," "I'm afraid to get angry or I feel guilty when I get angry"):

_____

_____

_____

Recognizing how past beliefs are, in fact, things of the past and not relevant in your current relationship helps you to take back the power they may have over you. When you start to see that your fear is misplaced — it's not really about you and your partner today — it allows you to step out of your fear, rather than be consumed by it. And most important, confiding in your partner when these old, misplaced fears and beliefs show up allows the two of you to take control of them as a team.

Remembering who was there for you

Your relationship past plays a key role in how you respond to your partner in the present. Significant early relationship interactions are imprinted on your brain. Even when you were an infant, before you had real thoughts and long before you had words, you had constant emotionally laden exchanges with your parents or caregivers. The degree to which your cries were heard and responded to, the degree to which moods are matched, smiles are shared, eye gazes connected . . . these combine to create a template for how you view yourself and others today (see Chapters 8 and 9 for more on this subject).

One of the important questions we ask early on in emotionally focused therapy (EFT) involves your past. It's helpful to understand who was there for you in times of distress when you were very young. The question typically goes like this:

> Think back to when you were a child, say 7 or 8 years old. When you were afraid, or hurt, or had a bad day. Think about a time when the world seemed against you. You felt alone and maybe were in tears.

> Now, think about who you went to for comfort in those times. Who would listen with care, maybe put you on his or her knee or lap, and hold you? Who did you go to for understanding and comfort that would understand your emotional state? Not just a person who was there, but someone who would empathize with you.

Dwight thought about this question for a minute or two. "My mom," Dwight said. "That's easy. My mom. She would listen and hold me. She would take care of me. I can't remember what she would say, but I know I felt better. I know she felt my pain in the moment." Like Dwight, many people can't remember what a caregiver would say to them in these times of distress, but they can vividly remember how they felt *emotionally* during those times. Dwight knew he felt safe when he went to his mom. By confiding in her, he knew he'd feel better.

In EFT terms, Dwight most likely had a *secure* emotional bond with his mom. *Secure* means that he could count on her to be there for him in times of fear and distress when he went to her, and that he could count on her to be emotionally available and safe to share and be vulnerable with. He knew she would care for him, and hold him. He knew she would treasure hearing his fears and primary, vulnerable emotions.

In Dwight's marriage, he felt the emotional bond with Karen was lacking. He wanted to be closer to her, to have sex more often, to just hold each other more often, to be more intimate — both emotionally and physically. Karen sometimes felt a bit suffocated by Dwight. He wanted so much emotion from her! "He wants to sit and hold hands," she said. "Of course, like most men, he wants to have sex, too. I understand that. But I can't do it. It's too much closeness."

Brent asked Karen who *she* went to when she was young and afraid. Who comforted her? Who connected with her painful emotion? "No one," she said. "There was no one. I was too busy being there for my mom. There was no time to worry about my own fears. I had to take care of her." Karen described a home life of ups and downs, depending on the swinging moods of her mother. Karen had what is referred to in EFT as an *insecure* emotional bond with her mom. It was never safe to go to her mom. Karen learned to stuff her own emotions, as if they weren't there.

Emotions are unknown and dangerous to Karen. She goes to great lengths to keep herself from feeling intense vulnerable emotions. "I won't go to sad movies," she said, "because I'm afraid I won't be able to stop crying." When Dwight wants to get close, Karen tries, but before long, she retreats. The closeness overwhelms her. It's an emotional cat-and-mouse game with them. He craves closeness; she wants distance. They rarely argue or fight.

You can see how both Dwight and Karen's pasts are impacting their present relationship. This isn't good or bad — it just *is*. The key is recognizing your past and possible associated tendencies today based on it. Getting a handle on these tendencies and using them to your mutual advantage in your current relationship can help bring about greater understanding, empathy, and happiness.

In time, Karen, for example, faced her fear of emotion and allowed Dwight to slowly comfort her and reassure her when her old beliefs and fears resurfaced. And they often resurfaced. This was hard work for them. It took a dedicated commitment to be aware and diligent. At times, they lost the fight against their pasts, but overall they came together and put the past in its place more often than not.

Recognizing your past and sharing it with your partner is the surest route to defeating old, bad behaviors *together*. Consider what Karen learned: "Before learning about how past histories affect us today, I was at times able to talk to myself about my own fear," Karen said. "And that helped some. But then we learned to *confide in each other* when these fears and false beliefs pop up . . . and really, that's where the magic is. It's just *so* much more helpful when we face it together. When Dwight hears it from me, and accepts me and reassures me anyway," she says, shaking her head and smiling, "that's when I fall in love with him all over again."

Talking about your histories

You can find healing when you share your relationship history with your partner. It's funny how that works. Whether you're proud or ashamed of your past, having your partner hear it, understand it, and accept you regardless of it is a powerful gift that you can give each other. In fact, your partner may be relieved to find out your past because it puts some of your current behavior into context that makes sense.

For example, Dwight jumped and got angry at Karen every time she shut the door loudly, whether at home or in the car.

"Why did you holler?" Karen said to Dwight after she shut the door. "You scared me!"

"Scared you?" Dwight said. "You slammed that door so hard I almost jumped out of my own skin!"

"That doesn't make sense," Karen said. "I didn't shut the door that loudly. Why do you overreact so much?"

Dwight shared that his parents often slammed doors when they were fighting. As a child, he used to sit down on the floor in a corner of his room, gather his toys, and try to be "small and quiet" to escape the sense of fear and anxiety he felt while his parents were fighting. When he heard doors slamming nearby, he got more afraid because that meant someone was near his bedroom. When his door would sharply open, usually one of his parents would address him angrily. He always jumped as a child when that happened. Now, as an adult, he couldn't help it.

"My body just jumps and tenses up," he said. "My heart races, like it's going to burst. I start breathing fast. I sweat. I tense up like I'm ready to fight an intruder. At this point in my life, it's just built in I guess. I can't help it."

Karen had no idea about Dwight's history. As we talked about it, she began to feel empathy for Dwight around this like never before. "I'm so sorry, honey," she said. "I didn't know. I can just see you as a child, sitting there afraid. I'll be more careful. I promise."

These kinds of turnarounds are not uncommon when couples take the time to think about their histories, and about how what they experienced growing up affects their current relationship. And it's not only their experiences as young children that can have lasting effects. Partners have experiences as elementary-school kids and adolescents that play a role in how they interact in adult love relationships, too.

You aren't affected only by past *negative* experiences. Maybe you had a teacher or coach who showed an interest in you like no one before, and this adult's interest sparked a part of your character that makes you a much better partner because of it. One of Brent's clients fondly remembered her cross-country coach telling her how caring she was, and how she was the quintessential "team player" that every great team desperately needs. This translated into her partner telling her that her coach was right, that he had always loved the way she cared not just for him, but for the well-being of others as well.

Carefully consider the following question, and write your answers in a notebook: Think back to when you were a child. Think about when you were afraid, or hurt, or had been through an especially tough day emotionally. Think about a time when the world seemed against you. You felt hurt and alone. Take as long as you need to locate a memory. Who did you go to? Who would listen with care, maybe put you on his or her knee or lap, and hold or console you? Who did you go to for understanding and comfort?

When both you and your partner are finished answering, take some time and share your responses with each other. As you listen to your partner, try to imagine your partner as a child in a time of distress, seeking an adult for comfort. Try to imagine seeing your partner doing what he or she describes. Ask yourself, "What emotions does this stir in me toward my partner right now?"

Making Sense of Pursuing

Pursuers respond to distress by trying to maintain contact with their partners. An argument or disappointment can trigger a pursuing person to look for reassurance and support. This is how a pursuer copes with the insecurity he feels when there is distress in the relationship.

Imagine a person learning to ice skate. As she begins to lose her balance, she reaches out for the walls surrounding the rink or to another person to regain her balance. Similarly, a moment of relational distress can knock a pursuer off-balance, and in those moments she'll reach out to her partner to regain stability.

When you pursue for connection, you're looking for a response or an acknowledgment — some evidence that you matter in your partner's world. You hope that being seen and comforted will calm the swirl of negative emotion swirling up inside you. The negative emotion was triggered by initial, rapid feelings of disconnection and uncertainty.

Ironically, pursuing often has the opposite effect of what was intended. This easily occurs because the negative emotions that are common in conflict often build walls of defensiveness between partners. These barriers get in the way of being able to reach and respond. When a pursuer relies on making emotional contact, and this emotional contact is blocked, she tries even harder to get through, with more desperation. This is often perceived as an attack rather than an attempt for connection.

Inside, the pursuer's emotional world is churning, often with fear. Over time, this leads to desperation. As this situation unfolds between partners, the emotional messages seeking comfort or contact are garbled by other emotional responses like frustration, anger, fear, and hurt. The panic and confused messages often push the other partner to increase his or her distance or attack back to gain space from the pursuing partner's anxious distress. This, of course, makes the fears and worries of the pursuing partner even greater.

For example, Emma worried when Sam failed to call at their arranged time. When Sam was out of town on business, he made a priority of calling home to connect, but this night he was delayed by a late meeting. His cellphone died, and he missed a series of text messages from Emma. Sam knew Emma worried when he was away and sometimes struggled with his work travel. She had divorced her first husband after discovering that he cheated on her while away on business. Sam was exhausted when he plugged in his phone and called. He gripped the phone firmly as he prepared for the call, fearing Emma's response to his absence.

Sam began the call. "Hi, honey. I'm so sorry I'm late. I called—"

"Yes, and it's been hours since you told me you would call," Emma interrupted. Her voice mixed with relief and frustration.

"I know. I would've called sooner, but my phone was dead and the meeting went through dinner," Sam stammered.

"And I was waiting. No word from you. No text. Just waiting for hours. Do you have any idea what that was like for me?" Emma demanded.

"No, I guess not." Sam said meekly.

"I called the office, then the hotel, and your cell. No response. What was I supposed to do?" Emma fired back.

"I don't know," Sam said cautiously. He began to emotionally withdraw, his voice getting smaller.

"You should've known. This scared me to death! You should've known." Emma responded, her protest loud and clear.

Now resigned, Sam tries his apology again in hopes of putting an end to the issue. "Like I said, I'm sorry. I get it. I'm sorry," Sam said. His impatience started to show.

"I don't think you do get it. I needed you!" Emma said, angrily. "And you didn't call. You could've done something more. But you didn't," Emma said, continuing to plead her case.

The conversation went on for some time, with Emma expressing her frustration and concern and Sam repeatedly trying to turn down her anger. But both of their attempts to manage this distress took them farther away from the peace that each of them was looking for.

From the outside, Emma's response to Sam's delayed call seems harsh and unrelenting. Even with his apology, Emma continues to press her point, claiming that he failed her, even though all he did was call later than expected. As Emma's voice and words get stronger, her negative emotions in full display, Sam backs farther and farther away from the heat and intensity of Emma's anger. As he backs off, her fears only increase — she feels like he doesn't care about her desperate concern.

Inside the world of pursuing, Emma's response makes sense. Her angry protest is her attempt to make clear to Sam how important he is to her, how much she relies on his care and presence in her life. Unfortunately, her anger and contempt send a mixed message about her need for reassurance and comfort. Emma's relationship history with a former husband loads her fear and how she experiences Sam's delay. When this fear kicks in, her anxious response takes over, and this is exactly what Sam was anticipating when he picked up the phone to call.

Sam has fears of his own: He fears Emma's anger, as well as the helpless feeling of being stuck and not able to make things better for their relationship.

Emma's fear and despair create an overwhelming emotional experience. In this place, her emotions move to the extremes. She feels vulnerable, afraid that she may lose him, and angry that he has let her down. When she reaches out for him, her fear and anger get mixed in an intense way. She feels desperate, and as she reaches to Sam, she comes off as intense, angry, and controlling. Emma wants Sam to know that he's important to her, but what come across are frustration, accusation, and blame. She's feeling overwhelmed by her fears, and Sam is feeling bewildered by her.

The goal of pursuing is to gain a response from your partner. In a distressing situation, pursuing provides a way to stay connected either positively or negatively. Even though the pursuer *wants* positive responses, negative responses will do — *any* response is better than no response, better than feeling you're all on your own.

In times of relationship distress, those who pursue often say to themselves:

- ✔ I'm invisible. My needs mean nothing.
- ✔ I can never get through.
- ✔ No matter what, it's up to me.
- ✔ My feelings don't matter.
- ✔ No matter how hard I try, I can't get close to my partner.
- ✔ When we're together, I still feel all alone.
- ✔ I know I push and prod, but how else will I get a response?

The logic of pursuers

The goal of pursuing is to maintain an emotional connection. This connection provides a way of relieving unwanted emotion felt about oneself or one's partner. Pursuing is a powerful response to fears of being left alone, rejected, or abandoned. These fears become powerful organizing forces that motivate the pursuer to relentlessly seek care or contact in response to a distressing experience.

The logic of pursuit is straightforward: If I can connect to you, I'll feel better. Because I feel distress in my relationship with you, I'll do what I can to make this better and I need you to respond to me. If I give up, I'm afraid you may leave me alone, which is the fear that keeps me pursuing. In pursuit mode, a person says to himself, "If I can just get close, if I can just be acknowledged and know I matter, I'll be okay."

Connecting your past and present emotional reactions

Thomas complains that Marc is absorbed in his work. Marc works long hours and most weekends. Over the past few months, they've spent less and less time together. Marc has reassured Thomas on a number of occasions that his busyness was temporary, but as the months passed, Thomas feared that Marc's reassurance was just words — nothing he could really count on.

The couple had been seeing Alicia, an emotionally focused therapist. In a recent session, Thomas complained that Alicia didn't really understand what it was like for him and he was frustrated that they weren't making progress. Alicia suggested that she take some time with Thomas alone at their next session, to really understand his concern.

At the next session, Alicia met with Thomas, hoping to better understand his frustrations. About midway through the session, Thomas threw down his notebook in disgust. Here's how Alicia remembered the session: "I had just told Thomas that his worries about Marc made sense and that they were 'normal.' Something about that word set him off," Alicia said.

"Normal? Really? I have been waiting months for things to change, and you're saying that my feelings are normal," Thomas said, with frustration.

"Okay, so I'm missing something important here. Help me understand. It sounds like *normal* is not the right word. Not a word you would use to talk about what's going on with you and Marc," Alicia said, tracking Thomas's experience.

"Exactly!" Thomas responded intensely. "Is it *normal* not to spend time with someone you care about? Is it *normal* to have him blow you off when you want to talk to him about it? If it *is* normal, then why do I feel so bad inside? You tell me!" Thomas fired off. His face turned red.

"Right, that's what happens. He isn't there. This is serious and there is no way to talk about it. That is not normal. That is serious," Alicia responded. "Okay, I think I'm getting you now."

"*Normal* is not a word I use," Thomas started slowly. "I pretty much hate it. Who decides what normal is? My parents don't think I'm normal. They pretty much hide the fact that I have a relationship with Marc. He seems okay with that, but it matters to me. That bothers me, too. You know, you try to connect on something like that, something that's so important, and then Marc is casual about the whole thing. It makes me wonder—," Thomas pulled back.

"Can we stay here a minute?" Alicia asked. "Saying something is normal misses something important for you. Just like those moments when Marc seems to miss how hard it is for you that your family doesn't really see you or accept you. Yes?" Thomas looked away as tears filled his eyes.

"It makes me wonder if I matter," Thomas said softly. "You know. Like do I matter to him? And when he ignores me I feel horrible." Alicia invited Thomas to share his sadness and hurt from family experiences of rejection.

"I know I'm wound tight about this," Thomas admitted. "I mean Marc says something in a joking way when we're talking about his schedule, and I flip into this place, where I keep pressing him to see what he really means. He gets defensive after a while, and I don't let up. I've got to have an answer. I guess I can see how that would be annoying."

"Do you ever talk with Marc about this sadness you feel sometimes?" Alicia responded. "That feeling of hurt and rejection can be a heavy thing. You know, like what you were feeling earlier."

"No I pretty much hide that side of me," Thomas admitted. "In the moment, I probably don't even realize that the sadness is there. I'm pretty much a 'deer in the headlights,' afraid Marc is moving on."

Alicia helped Thomas slow down his pursuing role to connect to the other emotions he's feeling in moments of uncertainty with Marc. For Thomas, his fear makes sense not just because of Marc but also because of his family. The word *normal* was a trigger that hit his very real vulnerability around acceptance and rejection. Tuning into his sadness opens new ways for Thomas to connect with his own experience and, over time, with Marc. He may not need his "pursuit mode" when he's able to be more open with his own hurts from his family.

Common actions of pursuit

When you find yourself pursuing, there are usually two layers of emotion going on inside at the same time:

- ✔ At the more obvious, secondary layer (see Chapter 4), you're most often feeling angry, frustrated, or anxious. You're trying to get an answer, for example. "Why won't this person answer me?!" The more you try to get an answer or solution to the problem at hand, the louder your voice tends to get.

  In response, the other person tends to get quieter and withdraw. This, in turn, amps up your frustration and anxiety. It takes two to tango, and when you look at it in this way, it becomes obvious that there are two people responsible for pursuing actions.

- ✔ On the primary emotional level (see Chapter 4), however, a pursuer is really pursuing for closeness. This may seem hard to believe because the pursuer usually demonstrates frustration or anger. But your understanding of primary and secondary emotion really helps you here. Recognizing that there are more vulnerable, primary emotions behind the secondary reactive emotions can help you both in seeing through or beyond the anger. As one client said about his pursuing partner, "When she gets angry at me now I don't react like I used to. I can see through it to the hurt she's experiencing behind it." Because he understood the difference between secondary and primary emotion, he was able to, in his words, "weather the storm."

Stemming from his or her secondary emotions, a pursuing partner mainly displays the following behaviors:

- ✔ Requests and appeals for answers
- ✔ Demands
- ✔ An increasingly louder voice

> ✔ Blame
>
> ✔ Finger pointing
>
> ✔ Physically following the partner
>
> ✔ Criticism

The pursuing partner's *intent* is to get on the same emotional page with his or her partner, to feel connected and close. **Remember:** It's like he or she is on skates and starting to fall. The pursuing partner is reaching out to try to reestablish equilibrium. Equilibrium in intimate relationships occurs when partners feel emotionally connected and supported by each other.

Unfortunately, while the pursuing partner's intent is good, the *impact* of his or her behavior usually guarantees distance and disconnection — the exact opposite of what he or she wants and needs.

Getting Familiar with Withdrawing

In times of relationship distress, partners who withdraw look for ways to exit the distress. These self-protective coping responses include a number of strategies to turn off the alarms (fears, anger, shame) of distress. So, if an argument heats up, the more withdrawing partner is likely to move away from the conflict or in some way try to shut down the emotions happening in the moment.

If you use withdrawing as a way of coping, your approach to distress tends to be more independent and self-reliant. You tend to turn away from your partner in times of distress and prefer to manage your emotions on your own.

Joanne sees this all the time with Doug. She calls it his "shutdown mode." Joanne said, "It's like I say something and a switch gets flipped for him. He goes into hiding. If I ask him about it, he just says he needs time and wants to think it out. The last thing he wants from me in that moment is a conversation. He's got to sort this out on his own."

Withdrawal involves cognitive and emotional distance. Here, a withdrawing partner responds to emotional situations with logic and reason. It's assumed that being more rational or "neutral" is necessary to solve problems, so these withdrawing partners try to remain emotionally detached from a distressing situation.

Beth, as an emergency room doctor, functions well in a crisis. She prides herself on remaining cool under fire. "I'm able to think things through quickly and make a decision in the moment. I just have to put my emotions aside." This works well at the hospital but not so well when she's dealing with Eric's frustrations about her schedule. "He says I don't understand, but I do. It's more that I don't agree with his point of view." Beth explained how she feels put down by Eric: "He makes it seem like I prefer work over him, but that's not what this is about. We just have to get through these next few years, and things will be better."

Beth doesn't back away from these conversations with Eric. She just doesn't approach the issues in the same way. When Eric complains that she doesn't seem to care and doesn't prioritize their relationship, Beth responds to him rationally, using a somewhat detached tone. She's careful — just as she is with her patients — not to make things worse. Beth just wants to solve the problem. If she's being honest, Beth also hopes Eric will be more mature about their scheduling issues instead of always taking things so personally. From Eric's perspective, Beth never lets her guard down and never lets him in.

Signs of emotional or cognitive withdrawal include the following:

- ✔ A strict reliance on logic
- ✔ A distrust of emotion
- ✔ A strict emphasis on objectivity
- ✔ A focus on facts exclusively

The process of withdrawing involves suppressing emotional thoughts and experiences. Partners who withdraw tend to dampen and muffle their emotional responses, particularly in times of distress. The process of shutting down other people's naturally occurring emotional responses can be quite demanding. It takes a toll on you both physically and emotionally.

Research studies have linked strategies for avoiding emotional distress with negative physical and psychological effects. These strategies don't lead to resolution of the problems that are the source of the distress. As a result, the ongoing distress may increase negative feelings toward the relationship, including more hostility and greater likelihood of emotional detachment.

Partners who withdraw often rely on thought suppression as a primary means of creating emotional distance. This can be an effective strategy in the short term, but over time, the suppressing of emotion can have a rebound effect. A withdrawing partner may become overwhelmed and respond with an outburst of hostility, when he or she is no longer able to dampen intensifying emotion. The effects of emotional suppression may also show up in other ways, including impulsive actions or bingeing behavior.

Chuck and Lori came to therapy after Lori found out about Chuck's habit of visiting online pornography sites. Chuck dismissed Lori's concern: "It wasn't a habit," Chuck said. "It's just something I use to deal with the pressures of my job." Lori described Chuck as someone "always under pressure, always keeping his feelings to himself."

Typically, Chuck responded to Lori's concern and fears by trying to reassure her that things would be okay and that he would change. He said in session: "I want Lori to know that this isn't about her. It's just my way of coping with stress. I'll stop and find another outlet."

Lori expressed exasperation at Chuck's attempts to reassure her. She responded in a furious tone: "He has no idea how serious this is. He has no clue. The only thing he seems to get is his job and his porn."

When partners like Chuck turn inward and shut down emotionally, they become less aware of their own needs and their impact on their partner. In many ways, Chuck is out of touch with his emotional needs when it comes to Lori. So, when he tries to reassure her about his faithfulness to her, his responses are hollow and baseless. He's out of touch with his own experience and his relationship with Lori. Sadly, she knows it, but he doesn't.

Managing emotions by withdrawing suppresses both negative *and* positive emotions. As a result, withdrawing partners have less emotion to work with in their relationships. Keeping their emotions at a distance reduces the resources they need not only to communicate but also to connect at a romantic level. A withdrawing partner may be able to manage his emotions in the moment, but over time, he becomes less and less in touch with what matters most in a relationship of trust and closeness.

The logic of withdrawal

Partners who withdraw are often trying to keep the peace of a relationship by deactivating distress through emotional and physical distance. Common responses may involve "giving in" or "going along" with the other partner's complaints, just to reduce the likelihood of a fight. Other forms of withdrawal involve moving away from negative emotions through silence, logic, or physical distance. Though the actions of a withdrawing partner may seem uncaring or indifferent, withdrawal is ironically a coping response intended to minimize conflict and restore peace and well-being to the relationship.

Although a withdrawer would seldom say it, inside she's thinking:

- ✓ If you could just calm down, I could come closer.
- ✓ I feel like I'm a failure as a partner.
- ✓ Even when I take a step toward you, it's never enough.
- ✓ I'm always failing in your eyes.

Common experiences of a withdrawer include the following:

> ✔ I never get it right.
>
> ✔ I'm not what you want.
>
> ✔ I have no feelings.
>
> ✔ I'd rather be left alone than feel this much pain.

Partners who withdraw have often gotten the message to dismiss or avoid their emotions. Parents may have coached them to "toughen up" or "be a man." Both are indirect ways of saying, "Don't show your feelings." They may withdraw not only when their partners are critical and angry, but also when their partners seek to confide in them about intimacy. They may feel anxious and afraid when their partners try to address the relationship itself, or other more intimacy-related concerns. This may be because they haven't learned how to navigate through their emotional world, because they've been taught to suppress their emotions. Not only do withdrawing partners not know how to address their fears, but they're afraid to address them in the first place (see Chapter 8).

Some parents feel uncomfortable with a child's negative emotions. The child's unhappiness makes the parent anxious, so the parent tries to distract the child from what's bothering him.

For example, Paul had a difficult childhood. He's committed to his kids having a different experience. When his 6-year-old daughter, Lucy, is upset, Paul tries to "cheer her up" by being lighthearted, telling jokes, and being silly. He tries to pull her out of her sadness or upset place.

When you have parents who aren't comfortable with your negative emotions, you don't learn how to "work through" or "manage" your negative feelings in constructive ways. Instead, you learn to dismiss or distract in order to get the attention off them. Later, you practice these coping responses as adults in romantic relationships.

These withdrawing strategies are limited. They don't get to the source of the negative emotion. And in a romantic relationship, the source is often impor-tant to the other partner.

Cameron learned to "live above his unhappiness." "Life is too short to dwell on negative things," Cameron said in therapy. "I try to find the bright side and move on."

"And that's what you offer Shelly when things aren't going well?" Brent said, assuming he used the same strategy in his adult relationships.

"Well, I try to be positive," Cameron said, his voice quivering as he became more guarded.

"And how's that working for you?" Shelly mocked.

Shelly felt embittered by Cameron's tendency to dismiss her loneliness and concerns in the relationship. He seldom showed empathy for Shelly's pain, in part because he seldom allowed himself to feel his own pain.

Fear is a primary reason to withdraw in a relationship. Fear is part of the fight-or-flight sequence (see Chapter 3). It's part instinctual and part learned. You learn to withdraw from showing vulnerability because in the past you got hurt for it. Withdrawing out of a fear of pain is a self-protective response that, when practiced enough, becomes part of your emotional "muscle memory." In other words, you don't even have to think about withdrawing — it's just something you've learned to do when the cues for vulnerability arise.

For example, Lisa avoids conflict like the plague. Her parents fought unrelentingly when she was a kid. She often withdrew to the safety of her room so she could filter out the distress that filled the home. She relied on music and video games to steel herself against the pain.

Marie remembers her first fight with Lisa after the relationship had gotten serious. When she raised her voice in frustration, Lisa got an ashen look in her face and went quiet. Within a few minutes, she was out of the door for a long walk — and she was gone for hours. Marie felt that, in many ways, Lisa had never fully come back from that walk. "It's like I lost a part of her when she walked out that door way back then," she said. "Like a part of our innocence was gone. I want that back. I miss that in her."

Lisa is committed to Marie, but she has no stomach for arguing. As a child, she watched her parents rage at each other. "It was awful," she said. "They fought all the time. It was loud, and it was mean. I told myself early on: 'I will not be in a relationship like this.'" At the slightest hint of anger from Marie, she's off to her office, which is her safe place as an adult. The growing emotional distance in their relationship led Marie to seek therapy for them.

The cost of withdrawing can be significant. Withdrawing partners often feel criticized and unworthy. They may be aware of their withdrawing tendencies, often because of their partner's protests, and have a strong sense of shame. The loneliness that can result from keeping a distance in intimate relationships can leave a withdrawing partner feeling alone and ineffective.

The emotional causes of distress are not addressed by withdrawing. They're only managed. The pain is still present and active.

Common actions of withdrawal

The signs of withdrawal are often physical. You can spot withdrawal in a person's body posture. Like a turtle going into its shell, a withdrawing partner pulls in to hide from the intensity of the moment. Here are some behaviors you may notice:

- ✔ Not listening
- ✔ Not responding
- ✔ Avoiding eye contact
- ✔ Crossing legs
- ✔ Folding arms
- ✔ Turning the body away
- ✔ Exiting the room
- ✔ Exiting the location

Any combination of these signals can send the following message:

- ✔ Leave me alone.
- ✔ I'm not available.
- ✔ I need space.
- ✔ Now is not the time.

Joanne recognizes these signs and knows that if she pushes the conversation further, Doug will physically leave. "It's like he gets to a point where he can't handle it anymore, and he walks away," Joanne said. "He not only shuts down, but he's gone."

Partners can also withdraw when the conversation switches to discussions that involve vulnerable emotions, such as discussions about intimacy in the relationship. By "intimacy," we're talking not just about sex, but also about how the relationship is going when it comes to emotional closeness.

"If I want to talk to him about how we're doing as a couple, such as spending enough time together talking or sharing about how we're doing relationally in terms of feeling close," Joanne said, "forget about it." She went on to say that Doug avoids these conversations "like the plague." "And if I bring them up," she said, "it goes nowhere fast."

Doug experiences immense emotional distress when Joanne brings up issues around intimacy. So, he responds to them as he does other emotionally distressful situations — he avoids them and withdraws. Joanne doesn't experience these issues as distressful, and she doesn't understand that Doug does. He gets overwhelmed in his anxiety, and he can't sufficiently communicate to Joanne what's going on for him.

Sometimes Doug will attack back at Joanne. This is done to "throw her off" so that he can end the conflict faster. This is another form of withdrawing.

The key is understanding that partners withdraw when they feel emotional distress, emotionally overwhelmed, or simply emotionally unprepared for what's coming next. It's not that they don't care — it's that they're afraid of the unknown. And as we illustrate in this chapter, it's usually for a good reason, anchored in the past.

Take a minute to discuss a recent disagreement or argument. Discuss who pursued and who withdrew. Who wanted to "get to the bottom of it" (pursue) and who wanted to "move on to something else" (withdraw)? If you need more help in determining which roles you assume, think about what happens when you talk about intimacy-related issues, such as how happy each of you is in your relationship, or how your sex life is going. In those situations, who usually invites discussion and who would rather not talk about it or keep the talk brief? Considering both of these situations should help you define who tends to withdraw and who tends to pursue in your relationship.

When you've determined which role each of you assumes, discuss with each other to what extent this chapter successfully captures your logic, secondary and primary emotions, and actions as a pursuer and withdrawer in your relationship.

Chapter 7

Working Toward Fighting Less and Feeling Better

*W*hen couples are able to see the roles they take and the pattern they follow in a conflict, they find new resources for facing their distress in new ways. The familiarity and intensity of couple conflict often blocks your ability to step back and see the predictable nature of a fight.

These patterns are common when couples get stuck in negative emotion. These patterns can easily become like emotional quicksand. When you're stuck, you start to sink farther and farther into hurt, pain, and fear, which gets expressed as anger, control, shame, and distance.

In this chapter we help you slow these patterns and find your way through them as a couple. You see more clearly the role you play in your pattern. Understanding these roles also gives you a new awareness of the vulnerable emotions that are present in these patterns. Working with your partner, you can use this understanding to stand together against the isolating power of these negative patterns.

Staying Aware of Patterns and Roles

As you grow more aware of the patterns and roles you take on in your relationship, you can more easily step back and see the habitual ways in which you and your partner emotionally disconnect from each other. For many couples, the *way* they argue and emotionally disconnect is something they just "do," but not something that they're able to recognize and label as having a life of its own.

Similarly, you probably weren't aware that one of you usually takes more of a pursuing role, while the other ends up taking a withdrawing role (see Chapter 6). Maybe you hadn't recognized your fighting styles, in which one of you ends up being more critical, while the other is more placating or defensive (see Chapter 5).

None of these patterns or roles is more correct or better than the other. You aren't "good" or "bad" based on the role you usually take. Roles and patterns are neutral in that regard. You both have very good reasons for the roles and patterns (and the fighting styles that make up the patterns) in which you find yourselves. As of right now, those reasons probably remain hidden, mixed with primary emotion (see Chapter 4), and mostly out of your awareness. When each of you understands those reasons and the vulnerable, underlying emotions in more depth, it'll be easier for you to empathize with your partner, begin breaking your old negative patterns, and start new positive ones.

Sometimes partners feel guilty because they find themselves naturally taking a role that they think is more negative or worse than another. Demetrius, for example, felt bad because he most often ended up defending himself and withdrawing when he and Chloe disagreed with intensity. "I'm a man," he said. "I'm weak — all I do is end up giving in."

Repeating patterns of fighting are two-way streets — you and your partner both equally participate and sustain their existence. Finding fault in one over the other is useless. If your partner didn't withdraw, for example, you would have no reason to pursue. If you didn't pursue, your partner would have no reason to withdraw. Trying to assign blame doesn't help. The key is recognizing that when you get caught going back and forth in these roles and patterns, you end up emotionally disconnecting from each other. And that's what's not good.

Identifying your pattern and the role you play

Although they overlap somewhat, there is a difference between patterns and roles. You and your partner both have "go-to" roles — the role you most naturally and most often assume. You usually find yourself either pursuing or withdrawing (see Chapter 6), whether you're in conflict or you're dealing with vulnerable relationship issues.

In addition to these roles, you have patterns that you fall into during conflict (see Chapter 5); for example, you may both go on the attack by criticizing. You both get angry at times, but that anger is an emotion, not a role. You both experience a myriad of emotions — primary and secondary (see Chapter 4). However, you fall more into one of the roles of withdrawing or pursuing regularly with your partner.

Exploring Ways to Stay Connected When Facing Conflicts

Both of you play a part in how you argue and disconnect from each other emotionally, and both of you play a part in maintaining your sense of connection, too. You're in this together. If you're going to overcome your past pattern of arguing, you need to take a stand together.

The way to beat your negative pattern is by teaming up together against it. If your negative pattern gets between the two of you, and you allow it to pit you against each other again, the negative pattern will win every time. It's that powerful.

Chloe and Demetrius came together and worked hard to understand and recognize their pattern. Then they teamed up against it. "We used to go at it," Chloe said. "Neither of us had any idea that our arguing was a pattern, or that it was something that had a familiar pattern to it, or anything like that. But when we starting helping each other see it, and see our roles in it, I think that was the start of our turning the tide back toward the positive."

There's no better time than the present to make a commitment to come together to fight off your old negative pattern of arguing. You can start this by employing some of the strategies we offer in this section.

Hitting the brakes

Ready to start noticing your negative pattern and fighting back against it? One way is to negotiate together how you'll "hit the brakes" and take a quick exit off Interstate Fight before you escalate negative emotions and someone gets hurt. At this point, you're both very familiar with each other's fighting styles, go-to roles, and overall negative patterns. (If you're not, be sure to work through Chapters 5, 6, and 7 before you continue here.) If you notice yourself starting to defend against your partner, for example, both of you can agree that it's good for you to say something like this:

> I'm starting to defend right now. Something's happening here. Let's hit the brakes and stop this before we escalate by falling into the trap of our old pattern.

The following examples are meant to help **pursuing partners** begin to "hit the brakes" in the heat of the moment. These are simple suggestions to help you begin to be aware, vocalize, and together fight the enemy by slowing down and exiting:

- ✔ I'm starting to get frustrated. Has our pattern started?

- ✔ I'm getting angry. Can you tell?

- ✔ I feel like you're not listening, and I don't want to chase you. Am I already doing that?

- ✔ I want to be critical right now. Help me not be critical.

- ✔ I think we're starting our old negative pattern. What do you notice? Who's doing what?

- ✔ I think if we argue right now, it means our old pattern gets a victory. What can we do that's different to get us through this right now?

The following examples are meant to help **withdrawing partners** begin to "hit the brakes" in the heat of the moment. These are simple suggestions to help you begin to be aware, vocalize, and together fight the enemy by slowing down and exiting:

- ✔ I think I'm starting to feel overwhelmed. Can we agree to shelf this for now before our old pattern kicks in?

- ✔ I'm wanting to withdraw. What can we do differently to help me not do that right now?

- ✔ I think we're starting our old negative pattern. What do you notice? Who's doing what?

- ✔ I think if I defend my actions or myself right now it means our old pattern gets a victory. What can we do that's different to get us through this right now?

- ✔ I don't want to just give in to you right now and let our old pattern win. Help me not do that.

Chloe and Demetrius found coming together to intentionally fight the old pattern kind of fun. "I enjoyed that," Demetrius said. "Just noticing when the old ways started appearing. That was exciting to me. It was new." He went on to describe how they recognized their pattern in the strangest of places. "I remember, early on, we caught ourselves beginning to get loud at each other while driving out of town on vacation and stopped at a gas station! Here we were on the road, not even sure of the town, and we're starting to fight over snacks for the kids. It hit me that I was starting to get anxious because Chloe had this demanding tone. I said something like, 'Hey, I don't want to admit this really, but I'm getting anxious here over this. Can we regroup?'"

Apparently that's all it took, too. "It really brought it home," Chloe shared. "I knew when he said it that he was right. We were escalating and I was falling into our old trap. When he said that, I just 'rebooted' like a computer. There was no way I was going to let that pattern get us that easily."

They agreed to calm down right there in the snack aisle of the gas station, which gave them perspective. They were able to come together and even joked about it on the way to the car after paying for the snacks.

When you make a commitment to start noticing your pattern and coming together to exit from it, you're on your way to having much greater control over it. The two of you against the pattern gives you the advantage. Be on your toes, though — it typically rises up when you're tired, short on time, lost, running late, hungry, busy, agitated, and so on. That's why it's *so* important that you commit to fighting it together.

Looking inside for understanding

Your partner is a teammate in helping you slow down and recognize your negative pattern before it gets out of control, but your own body is an excellent tool, too. In Chapter 4, we explain how to begin looking inside and listening to your body. Now it's time to add onto that skill and use *yourself* to help you and your partner work together to decrease arguing and increase connection. The more you both learn to listen to your internal compasses, the clearer you'll become at recognizing what's happening between you in the moment.

Your internal emotional state gives you clear signals as to what's happening between you and helps you recognize what you want and need. When you feel close, for example, your internal feelings will be felt in your body. Some partners report feeling "warm" when they connect emotionally with their partner. They feel "heard," "understood," and "in sync." Checking inside and pinpointing where you feel these emotions in your body helps you to feel it more vividly, and to live in the moment.

Listening to your body

Your emotions operate with your nervous system, and you feel them in your body. The signals your emotions send are immediate. Many people have been taught to ignore their emotions, but when you ignore them, you shut off a healthy source of information. (Turn to Chapter 4 for more on the different types of emotion.)

As we explain in Chapter 2, emotions fire in the brain and send their signals throughout your nervous system much faster than thoughts. When you have to move fast, the answer lies in listening to your primary emotion. Later, when you have time to think and reflect, you integrate your primary emotions with your thoughts, which is ideal. But when you start to get into emotionally charged negative patterns with your partner, your emotion often overruns your thoughts. Research on couples shows that the negative emotional pattern takes over when couples argue. Your ability to have calm, rational thoughts flies out the door. Couples try to maintain calm, but too often the secondary, reactive emotions just take over.

A key to stopping this runaway train is learning to feel the warning signs in your body, and beginning to separate out your primary from your secondary emotion. Your secondary, reactive emotions are what get you into trouble, not your more vulnerable, primary emotions. And it's your primary emotions that are signaling to you in your body. Unfortunately, many people quickly push aside their more vulnerable emotions and act out of their secondary emotions, such as anger, frustration, and irritation.

Where in your body do you feel your primary emotions most vividly? Some people say they feel emotions most in their chests; others, in their heads or even specific parts of their heads (like the back, the front, and so forth). Some people talk about feeling emotions in their stomachs and in their shoulders. You really have to slow yourself down internally in the moment to allow your primary emotional signals to get through to you and bring their meaning. If your partner lets you down, for example, and if you don't slow down, you run the risk of organizing around the secondary anger that usually comes rushing in. And if you do, you'll respond with anger, and you'll push your partner away. That's the old pattern.

But if you try to heed the feeling under the anger, or the primary emotions that occur in you *before* the anger, and organize around that instead, the outcome is often very different. If your partner lets you down, for example, and instead of responding from your anger you allow your primary emotion of despair in, it can make a big difference.

Consider the following two examples:

> ✔ Demetrius is under a tight deadline at work, and he's trying to get a project finished at home. Chloe walks into his office and says, "Your car won't start." He knows right away that Chloe was the last one to use his car the night before. Apparently, she left a light on or didn't shut a door entirely, which drained the battery overnight. She's done this before.

Demetrius was already feeling stressed about this project's deadline, and now this. He feels his anger rise in him. "What did you do this time?" he said loudly. "I didn't do anything," Chloe responded. "Well, we both know you used the car last night!" he shot back.

✔ Demetrius is under a tight deadline at work, and he's trying to get a project finished at home. Chloe walks into his office and says, "Your car won't start." Demetrius feels his anger rise in him. But instead of giving a loud, knee-jerk reaction based on his secondary emotion (anger or frustration), he makes himself stop and not say a word. He thinks to himself, "When I respond quickly from my anger, I almost always regret it." He lets himself feel his frustration. "Yes," he says to himself, "I'm angry and frustrated. But that's not all."

"That sucks," he says to Chloe. "Can I do some more work before we take care of that with the jumper cables?"

"Sure," Chloe says.

Demetrius knew there were primary emotions under his frustration, but in the moment, he steeled himself from lashing out at Chloe, responded well to the problem at hand, and needed to get his work completed. There would be plenty of other times to delve into his primary emotion. Now was not that time.

In the first scenario, Demetrius let his secondary, reactive emotion get the better of him. He wasn't able to contain it or get underneath it. These kinds of responses water the seeds of a larger negative interactional pattern.

In the second scenario, Demetrius used his emotional system well. He recognized his secondary emotion of anger or frustration and refused to respond from it. He was able to control it. Furthermore, he was able to talk to himself about what was going on for him. This "self-soothing" is very helpful. Note that Demetrius didn't delve into his primary emotion around this issue. Considering the situation (his deadline at work), this was fine. You don't always have the time to examine your primary emotion. Had he had the time, Demetrius may have realized that he was under pressure and on edge. The tense situation for him set him up to "blow" if faced with another frustration. And that's a part of life.

The goal is to become more in tune with and act from your primary emotion, but you can't always do that. Sometimes life just determines that we do our best and move on. And that's okay. Being able to keep your secondary emotions in check, and not respond from anger or frustration — that alone is a big step forward.

Tuning in to hurt and comfort

As you pay more attention to the feelings occurring in your body, you'll become increasingly aware of when your partner hurts you. Whereas before, you may have quickly pushed away your immediate hurt, and instead organized around secondary anger or anxiety, now you're paying attention to your primary hurt. And with that comes new, more authentic information. Your partner needs to know when you're hurt. That helps him or her stop — and it helps your partner want to stop, too, because he or she doesn't want to hurt you.

As you become more aware of your primary emotion, you'll also notice yourself being impacted more strongly when you see your partner experiencing primary emotion.

Chloe, for example, noticed how often she felt a push to go over and give Demetrius a hug or put her head on his shoulder. "As I plug into my core emotions more," she said, "I'm moved by *his* emotions because he's doing the same things. When I see his fear, I want to go to his side. When I see him hurt, I want it to stop. So, I go over to him and try to comfort him. It's like a new world is opening up for us."

Remember: Your primary emotions are there to inform and move you toward what you need in any immediate situation. You can feel them in your body right smack in the middle of a heated argument, during romantic times, during sexual intimacy — you name it, and your emotions are there to give you meaning. Primary emotions enrich your experience of positive times, tell you what you need and what's important to you in uncertain times, and nudge you to act toward meeting those needs when it's time to move out of your anxiety. They consistently tell you when something is healthy or not, when you need more of something, need something else altogether, or need to get the heck out of the room! They happen instantaneously, and when you pay attention to them, they combine with your thoughts for the best guidance you can get.

These kinds of reflections are common for the couples we see in therapy. They've had these internal, vulnerable emotions there to guide them all along, but they just hadn't been cued in to them. As they start feeling them and taking in their meaning, they find themselves acting with much more sensitivity toward each other. And that's good — that's what you want. That means you're making progress.

Finding Exits Before It's Too Late

Conflict patterns can take on a life of their own. The patterns can be perpetual, with each negative response reinforcing the next one to come. You may be like some couples who spar over personality differences and playfully tease, but once conflict patterns take hold, even these innocent attempts at teasing can trigger an avalanche of negative emotions. Now that you have a close-up look at your fighting style, go-to role, and personal responses, we walk you through ways you can face these patterns together.

Stopping in time

Finding ways to exit a conflict pattern before your fight becomes destructive protects your relationship. A couple who is more aware of these destructive forces is better able to assess the cost of escalating a conflict. You can endure many arguments and disagreements as a couple, but over time the more negative these exchanges become, the more likely these negative emotion-filled patterns will erode your relationship. It's important to recognize when a conflict has gone too far.

Once the escalation takes over, destructive forces can envelop the relationship. As we illustrate in Chapter 5, "The Four Horsemen" ride into the relationship and can carry away every last vestige of positive emotion, leaving you awash in negative emotion. Contempt and stonewalling can be powerful forces that can erode a couple's positive emotions and lock them in a defensive struggle (see Chapter 3).

Here are some indicators of destructive conflict:

- ✔ Going days or weeks without talking after a fight
- ✔ Using personal attacks, including harsh language and name calling, during a fight
- ✔ Being physical aggressive, feeling unsafe, or feeling out of control during a fight
- ✔ Threatening divorce during a conflict

Escalating negative emotion can create an absorbing state, almost like relational quicksand. Couples get lost in a vortex of negativity and pull each other under. Over time, partners disengage and their conflicts cease, but so does the vitality of their relationship.

Charles and Priscilla don't argue anymore. A steely cold distance defines their relationship. Priscilla knows the "hot topics" that trigger Charles's rage. She walks on eggshells, afraid of his anger that can erupt without warning. Charles manages his frustration by remaining cool and rational. Their decisions are negotiated in a businesslike manner to detour around past hurts and unresolved issues. "I think of it like a DMZ, a demilitarized zone," Charles said. "No one's getting shot anymore, but that doesn't mean it's safe." Their fighting style is avoid/avoid (see Chapter 5). It offers stability but not intimacy. Both Charles and Priscilla are coping on their own. They no longer turn to each other in times of disappointment or difficulty. They go it alone.

Emotional disengagement results when conflict patterns have gone on too long without being addressed. Here are some warning signs that things have gone too far and disengagement may be setting in:

- Actively trying to avoid your partner
- Not sharing with your partner how you feel
- Keeping to yourself
- Being more withdrawn from your partner
- Often agreeing just to get along

Finding ways to exit a destructive conflict pattern is crucial. Seeing your conflict pattern is a crucial first step in finding a way out. If you can see the pattern, you can work together to find a way out.

Calling out the pattern

When you and your partner recognize your patterns, you can call them as you see them. Now that you've looked carefully at your fighting style and go-to position, you're better able to catch the pattern as it's taking hold. Both of you can use this awareness to slow down the escalation by drawing attention to the pattern itself and facing it together.

Keep in mind that your ability to see your pattern is enhanced by listening to what's happening in your body and paying attention to your primary emotions. Your increased awareness will also help you be more aware of your partner's experience. You may see her turn to her go-to role, which is a sign that the pattern is underway.

When a couple shares an awareness of their fighting style and go-to roles, they can hit the brakes and then let each other know that the pattern is taking hold. In John Gottman's research on couple conflict, he found that couples who were able to make these observations and exit their patterns were better off. Gottman called these actions *repair attempts* because couples work actively to respond to and repair their negative experiences. Other repair attempts include

- Slowing down and being intentional in listening to your partner
- Sharing and responding to a partner's more vulnerable emotions
- Using distractions like humor to release emotional tension

Keith and Samantha were looking for tools to help them deal with what they called a "communication problem." Changes in Keith's job were putting pressure on the couple's ability to manage their day-to-day schedules. Their fighting style was attack/defend. Samantha's go-to role was pursuit, and Keith handled most conflicts by either waiting out her complaints or simply giving in. When this didn't work, he headed to the garage to work on restoring a vintage car. He could be gone for hours. He defended by withdrawing.

After weeks of talking through their stuck pattern in therapy, Keith walked in grinning, quite a change from his typical low-key, under-the-radar approach to their relationship.

"We did it!" Keith said emphatically. "We used the tools."

"Really!" Jim said, surprised. "Okay, so let's hear about this."

"Well, we started to get into it." Still smiling, Keith was clearly proud of his efforts. "It was getting heated and I could see things going from bad to worse. You know the 'same things' and 'same complaints.' After a few minutes, I reached for the back door to get away and then I stopped. I could see it. Our pattern was starting to happen."

Keith went on to explain how he had remembered their pattern, which they had discussed in their last session. When he reached for his go-to role, he saw what was happening. "So, I stopped, looked at Samantha, and said 'Sam, we don't have to do this. Let's sit down and talk. I don't want to do this. I don't want to ruin our evening.'"

"Hard to believe, but that is what happened," said Samantha. "He stayed and talked, and the fight stopped. I hardly knew what to say."

Keith and Samantha found a way out of their pattern. When Keith saw himself moving to his withdrawing position, he recognized his go-to role and he called out the pattern. Withdrawing was practically an automatic response for Keith. Over the years, he failed to understand why Samantha's anger fumed when he took off for the garage. Often, he was simply flooded by her intense anger and frustration. Once he could see his go-to response, he was able to reverse his actions.

Calling it out means that you're ready to exit the escalating conflict pattern. Helping your partner know that you're both entering your conflict pattern gives you both a chance to step back, slow down, and stop the escalation.

Listening for hurt

Primary emotions help couples stay connected, especially in times of distress. When you see your partner tear up in response to something you just said, her primary emotion is giving you a signal. Just like a GPS calling out "Recalculating . . ." after making a wrong turn. Primary emotions provide relational cues that help couples stay in touch, particularly when it matters most.

Conflict patterns often emerge when there is misunderstanding, disappointment, or fear. As defensiveness takes over in a relationship, partners can do and say things that hurt each other. These reactions are often almost automatic. They're emotional survival skills you learn in life that keep you safe and protected. For couples, these strategies often undermine the security of the relationship.

Listening for hurt is a way for partners to work together against their patterns. Often, the fight or the pattern does damage, even though the person's intent wasn't to cause harm but just to stay safe or return the relationship to a better place.

You can listen for hurt in a variety of ways:

- **Tracking hurt with secondary emotion:** If your partner's go-to role is withdrawing, you may have seen her recoil in silence to a harsh remark made in an argument. Her still and quiet response is like a turtle withdrawing into its shell. When you know your fighting style as a couple and your partner's go-to pattern, you can follow a secondary response (for example, withdrawing) back to a possible primary emotion (for example, fear).

Travis pulled back when he saw Lynn look away. He could feel her pulling away as he ran through the list of concerns he had about their finances. He was anxious and intense. He probably went on too long about his worries and need for a better system of managing it. Lynn had just returned from the store with a recent purchase that she was delighted about. He caught her cue. "Hey Lynn, hang on. Are you okay? I'm wound up about this, and I think I did something here. You okay?" Travis saw Lynn move to her go-to role and he used this awareness to avert their typical pattern of attack/defend. Instead he used her secondary emotion as a cue to help him slow down and check in. Her reaction to what was said was a clue to her underlying emotion.

- **Tracking hurt with bodily responses:** Signs of hurt may be most obvious in a partner's face. A sad look, tears, a quivering lip may all be markers for an underlying hurt. You may also see your partner sigh, look away, or take a deep breath. All may be signs of a primary emotion.

When you see these signs, you can change your focus from what's being said to what's being felt.

Marcia was struggling to be heard. Intently, she said, "Shawn, how can you not understand? You should have known. This was important to me."

Shawn looked down, sighed deeply, and then was silent. Marcia, caught off-guard, felt the immediacy of his pain. She softened her voice, "This is important. You are, too. Can we talk about this?"

Marcia felt some of Shawn's primary emotion yet to be fully shared. She slowed down and softened in response to the sign of his hurt.

✔ **Tracking hurt with relationship history:** When you understand your partner's relationship history (see Chapter 6), you have greater awareness for the ways hurt can be triggered in a fight. Past experiences can play prominent roles in conflict patterns. When you know your partner's history, you can better anticipate themes and situations that can trigger fear and hurt from the past.

Becky grew up under the critical eye of her father. "You're a disappointment" was the message that came through loud and clear. Randy often felt that Becky was "too sensitive" and that she didn't appreciate his sarcastic, teasing sense of humor. In therapy, Randy saw firsthand the lingering effects of his father-in-law's harsh expectations. Moved to tears, Randy could see more clearly how his efforts to get Becky to "lighten up" underscored a deeper sense that she was unacceptable. Randy had a deeper understanding of Becky's experience both as a child and wife. He interrupted a recent conflict saying, "That probably sounds a lot like your father. I'm sorry — that isn't what I meant." Understanding Becky's relationship history gave Randy greater empathy not only for her past but also for her present.

Listening for hurt means giving attention to the signs and cues of underlying emotion. If your conflict pattern is heating up, it's often a sign that the emotional threat level is also going up. Tuning into secondary emotions, bodily responses, and relationship history can give you a way out of an escalating conflict, by simply acknowledging hurt.

Tuning into your partner's pain is a powerful resource for healing. When partners are able to look at each other face-to-face in these moments, they have access to powerful empathy resources at a neurological level that can facilitate healing at a profound emotional level.

Think about where your partner would most likely see your hurt in an argument. It may help to think of an argument where you know you felt hurt. If you say, "I never show hurt when we argue," then you probably show your pain through your secondary emotions. Check inside your experience. How do you guard your pain? If you say, "I'm not sure I feel hurt when we argue," then where would the hurt show up in your body? You may not say it or see it, but where would you *feel* it? Finally, how may your relationship history show up in an argument, especially if you felt hurt? What memories have you had about the past when having an argument with your partner?

Now turn to your partner and take turns talking about where hurt shows up in your pattern. Check in and see what it would be like for your partner if you asked him or her about his or her hurt in an argument. What would make that go well? What would make that blow up?

Talking about your hurts with each other is a risk. If you need more resources, read the following section.

Talking about the pattern

A major turning point in EFT occurs when a couple is able to put together their conflict pattern and talk about it together. When you see the pattern for what it is, you can see it as an obstacle in your relationship and an opportunity to join sides against it. Couples who can see their pattern in the moment and talk about what's happening are able to redirect their reactive emotional responses toward greater understanding and support.

Miranda and Liam looked for help when they could no longer talk without fighting about Liam's career plans. The two were divided on Liam's hopes to return to graduate school and the impact that this would have on Miranda's career choices and family planning. In therapy, the couple identified their fighting style as attack/defend. Miranda moved to attack mode when she felt dismissed. Miranda said, "I can't stand it when he looks at me like I'm a child or too emotional. If he puts me off, I won't let that go until I know he has heard my point."

Liam saw clearly how he resisted Miranda's emotional intensity and tended to try to quickly shut down arguments. Liam admitted, "I try to listen, but after a while, it's too much. I do what I can to end the conversation — anything to shut it down."

Jim walked them through their feelings and actions as this typical fight unfolded. When Miranda felt dismissed, she turned up her anger, trying to get Liam to see her side of things. She also felt hurt that he didn't seem to care, though this hurt was indistinguishable from her anger. Miranda acknowledged that in their pattern, she was almost always angry. She summarized her experience by saying, "I don't give up on things that really matter, but there comes a point where we aren't fighting about the job. I'm fighting because we're fighting."

Similarly, Liam felt overwhelmed and tried to manage their heated discussions by trying to cool things off, choosing logic and physical distance to keep Miranda at bay. He often felt defeated in these moments but never let on about how bad he felt disappointing Miranda. Privately, he feared that they wouldn't be able to resolve their differences. Liam said, "It gets to the point where she's disgusted with me and I have to get away. I feel powerless to change things at this point. There is nothing I can do."

Couples who can see their pattern clearly can take steps to change. These steps often don't reach the underlying issues that propel a pattern, but they do help the couple begin to step out of their escalated pattern. In EFT, we call this *de-escalation* because the fights decrease in frequency and intensity. There is more shared understanding of what the fight is about and what's going on under the surface. Partners gain understanding about the impact of their actions in the pattern and experience more empathy for each other as well.

Speaking for yourself

Understanding your pattern begins with your own experience. We start this chapter by asking you to take a deeper look at key components of your conflict pattern including your fighting style, go-to role, and emotional experience. With this understanding you're better able to share with your partner what your experience is like.

Often, especially in high-conflict relationships, partners have two very different experiences of the same relationship. So, don't assume that your partner will understand your experience or even be able to anticipate what it's like for you. Keep in mind that although your partner may disagree with you about the relationship, he or she may be having a different experience of the relationship.

Reluctantly, Liam shared that their fights often got the best of him. He explained to Jim that he often felt frozen at the intensity of Miranda's angry approach. Even though she pursued his opinion, he often felt criticized and, as a result, hesitant to make his feelings known. He felt sick to his stomach and usually left the room at that point. Jim asked Liam what this feeling in his stomach was like, and he said, "I feel sick to death. Like there's no hope for us. Like there's nothing that can be done."

Miranda reacted, "Of course, there are things you can do. Like listen to me. Hear my side of things for a change."

Jim helped Miranda find the pain underneath her angry protest. "You also feel alone in this relationship. How desperate is it when you can't find a new way to reconnect?" Jim asked, as Miranda nodded in agreement, fighting back tears.

Jim focused on Miranda's vulnerability, which was becoming clear. "You may be lonely and angry, but he never sees the lonely part, the painful part. Do you ever show him?"

"No, not really, I just figured he knew," Miranda said. She struggled to take in the thought that Liam may not really understand what the past few months have been like for her.

The emotionally focused therapist helps partners look inside their own experience of the conflict pattern they share. Talking for yourself helps you see your experience more clearly and helps your partner begin to see beyond the pattern into your experience.

A couple can have two very different experiences of the same conflict. Partners often try to correct or assume that they know the experience of the other. In other cases, one partner may dismiss or invalidate the experience of the other. The first step to changing an emotional experience is accepting what you're feeling. This acceptance opens space for more feelings to be felt and more understanding to occur.

Opening up to vulnerability

As couples pay more attention to the underlying emotions in their relationship, they can take a step back from the negative impact of conflict in their relationship. If you can see and acknowledge your partner's pain, you've moved away from a possible escalating of conflict. Empathy and compassion can stand in place of other more negative emotions, inviting new possibilities of more positive experiences.

Taking this one step further involves sharing more about how you're affected by your fighting styles and common roles. Opening up about these experiences means you're willing to share directly about your primary emotions that often shape the common roles of withdrawal and pursuit.

Partners who take the pursuing role often feel

- ✔ Alone or abandoned
- ✔ Hurt
- ✔ Desperate
- ✔ Unappreciated
- ✔ Invisible
- ✔ Isolated

Partners who take the withdrawing role often feel

- ✔ Rejected or unwanted
- ✔ Inadequate
- ✔ Afraid of failure
- ✔ Numb or frozen
- ✔ Overwhelmed
- ✔ Judged

Liam and Miranda were better able to talk about their fights and Liam's tendency to disappear from conversations that got intense. Replaying a recent argument, Jim pointed out Liam's tendency to wall off Miranda's anger and not show any impact from her anger. Liam described his wall as his "last defense." He said, "Look, I know Miranda sees my wall as a sign that I don't care. She can throw all kinds of things at it in a fight. But on the inside, on my side, the wall is crumbling." Liam looked down as he confessed his vulnerability.

Jim picked up on his pain. "You mean you're crumbling?"

Liam went on to describe how his wall of protection kept him stuck in fear that Miranda might one day give up on him. His inadequacy was pervasive. Jim wondered aloud if he had ever told Miranda about his life behind this wall. "No, I've always kept her out. I don't like to dwell on these feelings, and why give her one more reason to be disappointed in me?" Liam said, acknowledging his underlying fear of rejection.

Meanwhile, Miranda was quiet. Both curious and feeling more compassionate, she responded, "I'm not disappointed in you. That's not what this is about for me. It's just hard for me when I feel so alone, like I can't reach you when I need you."

Jim helped Miranda explore her loneliness and fears of being unwanted. The more she opened up about these feelings, the more Liam came forward in his responses. He felt safer as she shared these things.

Talking about the pattern is more than talking about fighting styles and go-to roles. It also involves opening up about the emotions underneath these protective responses. Partners share more openly about their experiences during a fight and the wounds and fears that keep these protective responses in place. As you're able to take risks to share and to acknowledge the pain the pattern has caused, you're better able to stand together against the reactive responses that can drive you apart.

Take a moment and review the underlying feelings listed earlier in this section. Think about a recent argument and your go-to role. Think about what feelings best describe what it's like when you feel stuck in your pattern. Imagine having a conversation with your partner about this feeling. What would you need from him or her for this conversation to go well?

Now discuss with your partner what you would both need in order to have a conversation where more vulnerable feelings could be shared and explored. Keep in mind that a safe, trusting conversation — even if it's about what you need for sharing more vulnerably — will help you move toward de-escalating your pattern.

Moving Away from Fighting and Toward Each Other

The more you're able to recognize your pattern, the better you're able to work together against it. Arguments can stay fixed on differences that come between the two of you in ways that seem unchangeable. Seeing clearly the defensiveness and self-protection that drive your pattern opens a different way of experiencing your problem. In this section, we explore some ways you and your partner can move away from your pattern.

Naming your pattern

Some couples give their pattern a name. They refer to their pattern as "the enemy," "a fear dance," "vicious cycle," or "runaway train." These "code names" act as a kind of signal to the couple when the pattern is underway. This can help them stop and pay attention to the escalation that is happening between them. Other couples compose a drawing that illustrates the pattern of escalation that happens between them.

Invite your partner to take a moment to help you draw out your pattern. Take a piece of paper and draw a line down the middle. One side is for you to map your side of the pattern, and the other side is for your partner to do the same.

Now, think about a typical argument you have. Focus on what you typically do — do this as if you're watching a movie, as opposed to focusing on what you're arguing about.

1. **Map your go-to role.**

Divide a piece of paper into two columns. At the top of the left column, write down *your* go-to role. Here, you want to focus on what you do and what your partner sees when your conflict pattern is up and running. Think about what you do and how you respond to your partner as your go-to roles take over.

Think of the beginning, middle, and end of an argument to get a full sense of your pattern. As you think about this, begin to write down examples of what you typically do. Give at least two examples for each beginning, middle, and end. How do your actions change over the entire conflict?

Keep in mind that you're writing down your own responses. It's important that you speak for yourself in describing your experience. Actively resist filling in your partner's side of the page.

As you do this, you may want to take turns. This will enable you to look at your partner's list and think about what you do in response to his or her actions. If she withdraws by going silent, how do you respond? Think of this as an unfolding dance, and you're choreographing each step in the dance.

At the bottom of the page, make sure you describe what actions signal the end of the pattern and how you each respond to this signal.

Review this with your partner. Have you captured the essence of your pattern? Does this seem familiar to you? Are there any important actions missing?

2. **Map your underlying emotions.**

   Divide a new piece of paper into two columns. Write *your* go-to role at the top of the left column. List what's going on inside you during an escalating conflict pattern.

   Look at the page from Step 1, with the actions listed for the three stages of your conflict. Then fill out the following statements:

   - When I'm _____, inside I'm feeling _____. (For example, "When I'm <u>talking loudly</u>, inside I'm feeling <u>afraid</u>.")

   - When I'm _____ (use the action and feeling listed above), I find myself thinking that _____. (For example, "When I'm <u>talking loudly and feeling afraid</u>, I find myself thinking that <u>I don't matter to you</u>.")

   Now think about your partner's actions. Choose one that is distressing and complete the following statements:

   - When my partner is _____ (name the action), inside I'm feeling _____. (For example, "When my partner is <u>getting quiet and withdrawing</u>, inside I'm feeling <u>uncertain and anxious</u>.")

- When I see my partner _____ (use the action listed above), I find myself thinking that _____. (For example, "When I see my partner <u>getting quiet and withdrawing</u>, I find myself thinking that <u>he doesn't care what I'm saying and may not care about me</u>.")

Write down examples of your feelings and thoughts across the beginning, middle, and end of your conflict.

Keep in mind that your feelings may be secondary or primary emotions. If you identify a secondary emotion, it's helpful if you can also identify the primary emotion that underlies it. For example, if you write down "frustration," ask yourself what you're feeling inside in those moments (for example, hurt). If you aren't sure, make a place for your primary emotions by writing in a few question marks. You can always fill this in later when you have a better sense of your experience.

Review this with your partner. Have you captured the essence of your pattern? Does this seem familiar to you? There should be some responses that aren't obvious to you or your partner. If there aren't, you may want to look over the sheet and ask yourself, "Where do my more vulnerable emotions get triggered in our conflicts? What are these emotions?"

3. **Name your pattern.**

Look over the two pages in front of you. The actions page (Step 1) is what you both typically see when your conflict pattern is underway. The feelings/thoughts page (Step 2) is often what is *not* seen or heard. You may want to take time to ask questions about your partner's experience. It's normal not to understand why your partner reacts, feels, or thinks a certain way.

Keep in mind that the line down the middle of the page tells an important lesson. Couples can have different experiences in the same relationship. These experiences aren't right or wrong. They make sense in the distress and uncertainty of a conflict pattern.

Now talk together about a name for this pattern. The name provides you with a way of talking about this dynamic that comes between you. You can use this as a signal when you see signs of the pattern starting.

When you can *see* your pattern together, you can *face* your pattern together.

Making it two against the pattern

One way to work against your pattern is to understand its function. Keep in mind that the secondary responses you use are coping responses to help you navigate your needs in times of insecurity in the relationship. If you're able to see the emotional logic that shapes your coping responses, you can see, acknowledge, and understand your partner's actions, your responses, and the pattern as a whole.

In EFT, we want to help couples see their pattern as a common enemy — an enemy that keeps them from what they both want, which is a sense of well-being and security in their relationship where important needs are able to be met. This also gives the couple a way of fighting together against a pattern that neither partner wants.

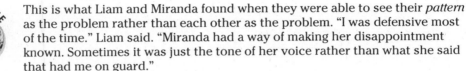

This is what Liam and Miranda found when they were able to see their *pattern* as the problem rather than each other as the problem. "I was defensive most of the time." Liam said. "Miranda had a way of making her disappointment known. Sometimes it was just the tone of her voice rather than what she said that had me on guard."

"Yeah, I felt that, too." Miranda acknowledged. "Liam seemed tense but would never admit it. He kept his distance, and the more I tried to get him more involved, the farther and farther he went away. I took it personally. But when we started seeing this as something we do together, like 'pursue and withdraw,' that made it easier to talk about what we wanted because we were in this together."

An emotionally focused therapist helps a couple find their pattern's emotional logic by viewing this pattern in attachment terms. Typically, at some level, your responses are organized by emotional triggers that cue you to a lack of security in your relationship. These alarms warn you that you may not get what you need from your partner. When you move to your go-to role, you're responding to these warning signs of uncertainty or insecurity.

Here are some good reasons partners pursue or withdraw:

- **To move to safety:** Here a partner's move to withdraw is a response to protect himself or herself from what's experienced as dangerous or unsafe. Moving to safety enables this partner to better navigate the issues after things have calmed down. This move is all about protecting yourself. The hope of the withdrawing partner is to gain some distance from all the intensity and tension.

- **To keep things from getting worse:** A withdrawing partner's efforts to pull away from conflict are an attempt to stabilize the relationship. Moving away can create more space for the couple to calm down and reconnect. This move is to help the relationship. The hope of the withdrawer is to turn down the heat and keep matters from deteriorating further.

- **To sound the alarm:** The pursuing partner often protests the loss of emotional contact. Intensifying emotional signals draw attention to the problem and often are a cry for help or a protest response. If your partner isn't responding, you just need to ring the bell louder. The hope of the pursuing partner is to gain the attention of a partner who has turned away.

✔ **To fight for connection:** Pursuing partners often reach for their partners in desperation. Their attempt to connect is a specific response to feeling isolated and alone. Their pursuing is an appeal for contact. Over time, these efforts can be filled with anxious desperation. The hope of the pursuer is to find contact with his or her partner, who doesn't appear available.

The secondary emotional reactions that make up a couple's conflict pattern are normal responses to distress. People suffer this distress because their partners are people they trust and rely on, especially in times of concern and uncertainty (see Chapter 2). The desire and intent to rely on your partner is often lost in the swirl of negative emotions that define your pattern.

In distress, you may turn to secondary strategies in hopes that your needs will be met. The pattern is evidence that these needs aren't getting met, but the intent and hope is that someday these needs *will* get met. You may not like what your partner is doing in these moments of distress, but when you understand the purpose behind the pursuit and the wisdom behind the withdrawal, you can honor your partner's intent to try to make things better.

Researcher Ed Tronick demonstrated clearly the natural tendencies of these coping responses in his "still face" experiment. Tronick demonstrates the range of responses an infant makes to regain contact with a caregiver who is nonresponsive (that is, has a still face). In this experiment the engaged parent turns away and then returns to the child with a blank face. The lack of response from the parent illustrates clearly how a child's positive and negative emotional cues are used to try to correct the parent's failure to respond.

Adult attachment researchers Phillip Shaver and Mario Mikulincer suggest that adults use similar positive and negative cues as responses to the experience of emotional withdrawal adult relationships. These behaviors make sense as a way of trying to stay connected in a relationship that is of highest importance but also of great discomfort.

Noticing when things go well

Couples who are able to talk about their patterns and see what underlies them are better able to find more positive emotions in their relationship. When you can see your pattern as the enemy, there is less need to see your partner as the enemy. Consequently, there is less need for defensiveness and reactive responses that come when you're registering the uncertainty and threats of distress. When you can move away from these problem patterns together, you open new opportunities for negative experiences to be replaced with positive ones.

Looking back, Miranda and Liam laugh now at how their pattern got the best of them. Now that they have a better sense of the futility of Miranda's attempts to reach Liam behind his wall, and Liam's attempts to calm Miranda's intense protests, their pattern makes sense. This awareness has helped them slow their escalation and exit their pattern.

"It feels good to know we can get out of it," Liam admitted.

"We still have issues, but it feels like we're in this together, and that changes things for me," said Miranda smiling.

"This is what you're looking for, right?" Jim asked. "You guys have been fighting this battle alone in many ways, and now you're finding ways of seeing this as something you want to do differently, as a couple."

"Right, and I think we are," Liam said, looking at Miranda and smiling with a renewed sense of confidence. "We aren't out of the woods, but we're in this together."

An emotionally focused therapist helps couples explore these positive moments. As couples find new experiences and shift their focus to positive emotions of joy, peace, and happiness, the therapist continues to help couples track their emotional experiences and use these positive emotions in their relationships.

As couples move away from these reactive patterns, they're better able to respond to each other. Positive emotions can organize new experiences for the couple and, as researcher Barbara Fredrickson noted (see Chapter 2), couples are better able to "broaden and build" more resources in response.

At this point, couples have found a way to say to each other, "We're in this together." You now have a way out of your stuck pattern. You also have a better understanding of your partner's go-to role and fighting style. This way of seeing your relationship helps to bring you together. You have to work with the needs and vulnerabilities that you've found in the context of your problem pattern.

Part III
Finding Intimacy in New Ways

The 5th Wave   By Rich Tennant

"I heard it was good to use humor when you're having an argument."

In this part . . .

*H*ere, we dig deeper into the heart of your relationship, looking closely at typical ways couples deal with their fears and vulnerabilities. You see more clearly how your partner's actions — especially those that cause confusion and hurt — make sense. Through the examples of other couples, you see how to work through the emotional blocks that keep you from strengthening the very heart of your relationship. You also find exercises that invite you to risk more deeply with your partner as you gain greater confidence in your relationship.

This part also tackles where couples get stuck in deepening their trust and intimacy. You find examples of couples working through times of broken trust. We show you how partners can renew trust in the face of infidelity and regain a more resilient relationship through emotional healing. We show you ways to remove the shadow of shame from blocking the closeness needed to be valued deeply by your partner.

This part isn't for the faint of heart. We challenge you to take risks in your relationship and face the fears that can so easily keep you from the promise of what your relationship could be. But taking these risks as a couple makes sense when you understand and face your fears together.

Chapter 8

Seeing through Withdrawing Eyes

. . . .

In This Chapter

▶ Uncovering what's happening internally when you withdraw

▶ Identifying the fears that shut you down

. . . .

*T*he most common relationship pattern forms around the roles of pursuing and withdrawing (see Chapter 6). In this chapter, we take you behind the scenes of the world of withdrawing. Regardless of who withdraws and who pursues in your relationship, this chapter helps the two of you uncover what's going on inside emotionally that's driving the withdrawing that happens when your pattern is running.

If you're the withdrawing partner, the information in this chapter allows you to access your emotions and see new ways you can respond to them. Withdrawing can be an instant response — it happens without your thinking about it. Often, you're withdrawing from emotions you're experiencing at the same time you're withdrawing from your partner. Here, we give you a better understanding of these emotions.

If you're the pursuing partner, beginning to understand what's happening inside emotionally for your partner often opens up a new world of insight and empathy. You begin to see the reasons behind the withdrawing, which helps break the negative arguing cycles that often result.

Looking Under the Hood: Why Withdrawing Makes Sense

If your car's engine stopped running, you might pull over and look under the hood, but chances are, unless you're mechanically inclined, you'll be challenged to get the car going again. Couples can feel just as helpless when withdrawing shuts down their relationship. No matter how hard you try, you can't make sense of withdrawing, and it seems like there's no way to get your relationship running again. In this section, we give some insight into what's going on in withdrawing.

In Chapter 6, you identify who tends to withdraw and who tends to pursue in your relationship. You realize there are different contexts for withdrawing and pursuing. But you're probably not yet aware of the emotions stirring in the withdrawing partner during times of emotional intensity.

Often, withdrawing is an attempt to tone down intensifying emotions in an argument. But it can also be a self-protective strategy that helps partners who are feeling overwhelmed pull back and begin to identify their experience at a cognitive level.

Partners who turn away in moments of conflict can feel depleted, like they've run out of energy. Regardless of the reason, withdrawing tends to shut down the withdrawing partner's contact with his or her emotional experience.

Eric and Karen provide a good example of the ways withdrawing works and its consequences. They came to therapy arguing like cats and dogs. It was one of the most viscous negative cycles one of your authors, Brent, had seen. Karen was the partner who pursued Eric whenever they disagreed. Here's an example of an argument they might have and what happens afterward:

> "I don't understand why this keeps happening," Karen said. "I've asked you to let me know when we're low on milk!"
>
> "Why is that my responsibility?" Eric asked
>
> "Because you and the kids are the ones who drink the milk like it's water in the first place!" Karen yelled. "I don't drink it — I buy it! And you have to tell me when we're low or out! How hard is that?"
>
> "I can't always remember to tell you," Eric said.
>
> "Obviously not," Karen replied.
>
> Eric went quiet, withdrawing.
>
> "So, now what?" Karen, said, pursuing.
>
> Eric shrugged his shoulders, continuing to withdraw.
>
> Karen continued pursuing: "That's it?! Dammit, don't act so stupid! We have to have some way of knowing when we're almost out of milk!"

The primary emotions within Eric, combined with the continual pursuit from Karen, are causing him to respond by going quiet. His primary emotions are vulnerable, but Karen's current demeanor just about makes it impossible for Eric to approach her with what's really going on inside him.

So, although it's true that Eric withdraws, Karen plays a part in causing him to withdraw. Two people are caught up in a cycle together. They play off each other.

Consider what's going on inside emotionally for Eric right now. What's happening for him at this exact moment? Try being Eric for a moment. Put yourself in his shoes. Read through the argument again and put yourself in Eric's shoes for a few minutes. Then talk with your partner about what Eric might be feeling about himself and about Karen right now, deep down inside.

Eric was aware that he "froze" in the face of Karen's attacking and criticizing. Together, we slowed down the process, allowing his primary emotions to surface so that we could understand what was there and what he most needed to break the negative pattern. The arguing happens so fast. The secondary, more reactive emotions flood in so quickly, that you may not even realize that you have primary emotions inside of you during these times.

"Obviously, I don't like it when she gets upset and criticizes me," Eric said. "And I know I withdraw."

"You withdraw at some point," Brent said. "But let's try to focus on what happens inside you *before* you withdraw, or just as you *start* to withdraw. Can we please slow down and go back? You guys are in the kitchen. Karen is getting upset about the milk. She says something like, 'Hey! Why don't you ever tell me about the milk!' Later, she refers to you as 'acting stupid.' Can you slow down a bit, check inside yourself right now, and try to re-imagine what it's like during those moments for you?"

Eric talked about feeling it in the pit of his stomach. He reported an "emptiness" and a kind of "burning sensation." Brent asked him to stay with those feelings, to pay attention to them in the current moment. This led to his realizing that when Karen talked to him like that, he felt belittled and put down. "I feel talked down to," he said. "It makes me feel like I'm dumb."

We stayed with it longer, which led to Eric realizing how much he feared those situations. He actually tried to evade them by "getting out of Dodge" when a similar situation started. "I hate it," he said, tears welling up in his eyes. "It's awful. I feel like a child. Like a dumb, stupid child."

When you can actually feel the pain that your actions and words have on your partner, you're much better equipped to be able to stop it. In other words, when you have empathy for your partner for your own actions, it can have a powerful effect on you.

Karen had no idea that her words caused Eric to feel this much pain. "I can't believe I'm hurting him like this," Karen said.

Brent asked Karen to focus on her feelings for Eric rather than on her own guilt. "I don't want you to feel stupid," Karen said to Eric. "I want to hold you and reassure you that you're anything but stupid. I really am sorry that I said that. I had no idea."

It's very common for the pursuing partner not to realize how painful it is for the withdrawing spouse. It's very important that pursuing partners get a sense of that pain, however — and not so much in their heads but in their hearts. Partners have to learn to start feeling each other's pain as a sort of extension of themselves. You can do this, in part, because of the mirror neurons in your brain (see Chapter 2), and you can get better at it with practice.

When you hear your partner's pain, as Karen did, be sure not to focus on yourself, such as how you're the one who caused the hurt or you're the one to blame. Your focus needs to be on your hurting partner, not on yourself. When your partner is vulnerable and shows his or her primary emotion, you need to be there for your partner.

Getting clear on your own pain helps you to receive clear primary emotional signals about what's wrong, and what you need. Eric, for example, became clear that he no longer wanted to feel like a child with Karen. Nor did he want to feel stupid. He let Karen know in no uncertain terms, "I'm not going to take that from you anymore. I need you to stop criticizing me. It's not okay. I know we get frustrated with each other, but saying such hurtful things is no longer tolerable."

Eric didn't only withdraw in the face of attacks. He was also uncomfortable talking about emotional closeness and intimacy with Karen. For example, Karen had been feeling emotionally distant from Eric for a month or so. She summoned her courage to speak to him about it.

"I have to psych myself up some," Karen said. "I don't know exactly why, but it's difficult talking to him about these things. It's obvious that it makes him uncomfortable." Karen spoke of being in a bind of sorts because, while she wanted to be emotionally closer to Eric, she didn't want to push him farther away by hurting his feelings or scaring him. "I don't know what to do," she said. "Or how to do it."

Karen usually approached Eric about it in bed when the kids were down for the night:

> "Honey, can we talk about our relationship for a minute?" she asked, softly.

> "Oh, that's doesn't sound good," Eric said.

> "I need to talk to you. I feel we aren't really close right now," Karen explained.

> "Do we have to talk about this now?" Eric asked, withdrawing.

> "I don't know any other good times. It's quiet now and the kids are down for the night," Karen said, pursuing.

> "I'm tired right now, though," Eric said. "Can we just relax? I kind of feel like this came out of nowhere." He's withdrawing and starting to blame.

Many times the conversation would end right there. Karen would just drop it and go to sleep. Sometimes she might try to schedule another time to talk with Eric, but those times never seemed to work either. As time went on, and she felt more and more distant from Eric, she would push the issue more during these nighttime talks:

> "I think it's important and I need to talk about it," Karen said. "I don't think it has to take that long. I just feel kind of distant from you. I mean emotionally distant."
>
> "What does that mean?" Eric asked. "I think we're together most of the time."
>
> "We're around each other a lot, yes," Karen said. "But we don't talk about how we feel about each other. You never tell me how you feel about me. Do you love me?" she asked, pursuing.
>
> "Of course, I love you. I don't know what you want me to say," Eric said, in a slightly angry tone.
>
> "We don't have sex that often anymore. Is something wrong?" Karen asked, continuing to pursue.
>
> "No, nothing's wrong. I don't know what I'm supposed to say right now. I'll try harder. I'll be more proactive when it comes to sex. You can come to me for sex, too, you know!" Eric said.

Consider what's going on inside emotionally for Eric right now. Consider what's happening for him at this exact moment in the argument. Read over the argument again. Notice how it escalates. Try being Eric for a moment. Put yourself in his shoes, but don't let his secondary anger throw you off what's really happening inside of him emotionally at a primary, vulnerable level. Talk with your partner about what Eric might be feeling about himself and Karen right now, deep down inside.

Karen has a very good reason for pursuing — she misses closeness with her partner. But Eric has very good reasons for withdrawing, too. Be sure that each of you discusses what you think might be Eric's primary emotions — both about himself and about Karen in this specific context. These vulnerable emotions usually remain hidden inside Eric — neither he nor Karen is aware of them. Eric needs to pay attention to them more, hear their message, and then share that message with Karen. That's how you integrate emotion into your relationship. But right now in this context, Eric is unable to that.

He isn't really clear what's going on emotionally for him during these times. In other words, he knows that at the secondary emotional level he's uncomfortable, which leads to him pushing back with a little anger in the hopes of getting Karen off topic. He recognizes that he wants out of those conversations, that he wants to withdraw. He just isn't yet aware of his primary emotions and their message. You may find yourself in a similar situation. A lot of withdrawing partners do.

The take-charge withdrawer

You can be the more outgoing, talkative, social partner and still be a withdrawer.

For example, Eric was in charge of keeping the house running smoothly. If the kids needed to be picked up from school, he most often did it or organized it. "I run a tight ship," he said. "Garbage can needs to be on the street? I'm on it. We work as a team, but I'm the organizer and more the leader." Eric was speaking of the everyday business of life.

"But when it comes to addressing our relationship, intimacy, emotions, or issues around sex," Karen, his partner, said. "He doesn't bring it up. And he's uncomfortable when *I* bring it up. It makes it very difficult for me."

This is a common scenario with couples. One partner can be very outgoing or take-charge at work or in social situations. But when encountered with personal issues around intimacy, he can have a hard time opening up.

If this sounds familiar to you, you may never be able to speak about emotion and intimacy as easily as you talk at work or in social situations, but this isn't unusual at all. You can begin to recognize and deal with what gets in the way of your being able to open up more with your partner. And that's the key. Your partner can help you do this. As your partner understands more, and you understand more, together you can begin to handle these situations with more care.

"I have no idea what's happening emotionally inside of me during these times," Eric said.

"Can you think about that for a minute right now?" Brent asked. "Can you imagine a situation where Karen wants to talk about how she feels you guys aren't connected or she feels distant from you? Take a second to let yourself go there as if it were happening."

"I don't want to do that necessarily," Eric said with a smile. "But I will."

Brent helped Eric imagine being in that situation where Karen is saying she wants to talk about "us." Eric took a deep breath and looked off into the distance. After about a minute, he shook his head up and down.

"I got it," Eric said. "I can see her approaching me and wanting to talk about our sex life."

"Great," Brent said to him. "What do you see in her face?"

"I see a look of disappointment," Eric replied. "I can see it in her eyes. She's trying to be nice, but this isn't going to go down well for me."

Brent asked him to talk more about this, and what he was experiencing inside as he imagined this scenario. "I can't seem to please her," Eric said.

Brent asked him what it was like to be in a place with his partner where it seemed like he couldn't please her. "It's not good," Eric said. "I feel like I'm failing. I'm failing as a husband." And with that, Eric's head fell, and he wept.

Feeling like you're failing as a partner in a long-term committed relationship can be devastating. We've seen many strong men crumble into tears when it really hit them that they felt like failures as husbands or partners. Failing at jobs or tasks is bad enough, but failing at being a good husband or partner? That's another thing all together. Realizing this feeling of pain surrounding failure hits many men hard.

Listening to your primary emotion in these situations is hard. And it's scary to consider sharing that fear with your partner. Fear shuts you down. But even though fear can be paralyzing, it's most certainly real. And it has to be listened to and acted upon.

Finding Your Fears

One of your authors, Brent, remembers it like it was yesterday. His eighth-grade football team was playing a cross-town rival, on their field, in front of their fans. They had two running backs who had been written about in the morning paper. A couple of guys on their team were so talented that people were already talking about where they might attend and play at the college level.

Most of the players on Brent's team were afraid of their opponents before the game even started. They stepped out onto the field and went through the motions. But the other team ran all over them.

Fear — that's what got them. Fear made Brent's team slower than normal. Fear kept them tentative. Fear kept their heads out of the game and in a kind of numbness. They were physically present that day, but in a lot of ways their minds were somewhere else. They couldn't get off that field, onto the bus, and back home fast enough. Similarly, when fear hits a withdrawing partner, it sends him packing.

"I am afraid that if she really realizes what a failure I am, she'll get fed up and leave me," Eric said. He didn't dare sneak a peek at Karen when he said this. He kept his eyes either on Brent or straight ahead.

"Tell me about that fear," Brent said. "I need to better understand. Do you feel it right now?"

"Oh, yes," Eric said. "I can feel it now. It grips my heart," he said, making a fist near where his heart is. "I'm afraid that she'll see me as fundamentally lacking. She'll finally say 'Enough!' and go find someone else who is a better fit for her. Someone who better meets her needs. Someone who can make her happy."

Eric said that he keeps his fear to himself, and doesn't risk letting Karen know how he feels.

"Do you ever tell Karen about this fear?" Brent asked him.

"No way would I tell her about it," Eric said, with emphasis. He couldn't tell her about it because she might agree with it. She might honestly admit that his fears were based in reality. "If she were to confirm my fear," Eric said, "it would . . . there's just no way would I tell her."

He went on to describe how when things get emotionally intense between them, at some point his mind begins to go "numb" and he withdraws.

"You get lost in your fear?" Brent asked.

"Yep," Eric said. "I haven't thought of it this clearly before now, but that's what happens."

 A fear of failing as a partner — of not measuring up — lies at the heart of a lot of withdrawing behavior. This may be a familiar storyline for you. When the emotional intensity rises, fear begins to ripple through your body, the alarm bells begin ringing, and you know that you'd better get out of there or get the topic changed very fast. This could be the time your partner finally says "Enough!" in your relationship.

Seeing what the fear is about

Fears behind withdrawing behavior are usually centered on your partner and/ or on yourself. Some partners, for example, spend considerable time and energy keeping fears of their partner leaving them at a distance. However, a nasty comment or argument from a critical partner can quickly awaken these fears and bring them front and center. Similarly, fears about yourself, such as whether you measure up or whether you deserve the relationship, can also be present and painful. In this section, we walk you through both types of fears.

Fears about your partner

Sometimes withdrawing from emotional intensity has to do with fears about your partner. These fears may include

- Failing as a partner
- Being rejected by your partner
- Not measuring up
- Not being "emotional enough"
- Not providing enough financially

- ✓ Failing sexually
- ✓ Not being good enough
- ✓ Not being a good parent
- ✓ Not meeting expectations
- ✓ Being a poor communicator

The theme running through all these fears is how negatively your partner may see you. The fear is that you're so deficient in these areas that the relationship will never be what your partner really wants. You may fear that your negatives will pile up so high that your partner will "come to his or her senses" and decide to move on without you. Your partner will either live alone or find another partner to share his or her life with.

Those who withdraw are often surprised to hear that their partners don't know they have these fears. Your partner may be very surprised, even alarmed, to hear about this kind of fear. It makes good sense if you think about it: What your partner mainly sees is that during times of emotional intensity, you tend to go quiet and move away. You likely come across as someone who isn't really affected and probably doesn't care much about the relationship. But this is exactly the opposite of what's really happening.

A note for partners of withdrawers: When your partner withdraws, there is a lot going on inside emotionally that's often unseen. The more you realize that there are fears stirring inside your partner when he or she withdraws, the easier it will be for you to step out of your negative cycle and typical behaviors. You can more easily empathize and seek to understand what fears your partner is battling.

When emotional intimacy issues arose, Eric withdrew, and Karen didn't understand why. As she began to hear how afraid Eric was, how he feared not living up to what she really wanted, it helped Karen to see and respond to the situation differently. Instead of pursuing, or being hurt and responding with irritation, she was able to begin trying to understand Eric's fears in those moments.

"When I started to see that Eric loved me and wanted us to be close, but he was afraid to be vulnerable with me, it helped me understand," Karen said. "I realized that it wasn't that he didn't care — he actually cared a lot. He was just afraid he wouldn't be able to please me or meet my needs." This greatly helped Karen slow down, fend off potential hurt, and focus on Eric's needs along with her own. "It helped me begin to see that we're in this together," she said.

Fears about yourself

For some withdrawers, the fear isn't just that their partner will find them lacking, but that *anyone* would. In other words, they fear that they themselves are the problem — not their partners, not their relationship, but them.

Some of these folks have been told by significant people in their lives that they're no good, or that no one will ever love them, or that they're inherently flawed.

"My dad used to tell me that no woman would ever want me," Eric said. "Because I was just impossible to love, basically." Eric had grown up hearing this. It was like a cloud that hung over him, accusing him, reminding him that he was unlovable. "When things go wrong in our relationship," Eric said, "I sometimes go back to him saying that."

"You go to a place that says, 'I may be unlovable after all'?" Brent said.

"Yeah," Eric said. "I try not to, but sometimes I do."

Brent turned to Karen. "Did you know that Eric has this fear that he may be unlovable?"

"No," Karen said. "I didn't know that. It makes me sad."

Soon after this session, Eric began to let Karen see the part of him that sometimes was afraid that he wasn't good enough to deserve love. Before this, his fear propelled him to withdraw and hide from Karen. The shame around what his dad had told him, the fear that maybe it was true, had kept him from ever telling anyone about this fear.

Eric had spent most of his life reacting from his secondary emotion when his primary emotion and fear arose within him. He became defensive or simply just gave in and found the quickest way out of the room. Sometimes he would physically leave the room; other times he would mentally check out. Karen was aware of Eric mentally checking out and physically leaving the room, but she had no clue about the pain occurring at a primary level for Eric around his fear of perhaps being unlovable.

If you find yourself most often withdrawing during more emotionally intense times with your partner, you probably have some primary emotion stirring inside that you're not totally aware of. The goal is to *become* aware of it.

This activity is for the partner who withdraws. The goal is to recognize which primary emotions signal to you during emotionally intense times in your relationship. Over the next few days or a week, set aside alone time for yourself. During these times, imagine yourself "re-entering" situations with your partner in which you feel the urge to withdraw. When you start feeling it, ask yourself, "What fears do I have underneath?" Listen to your body. Listen to whatever comes up for you. You may be surprised to find that your fears make themselves known to you, if you give them time to come to the surface and you don't withdraw from feeling them. Check inside for fears about how your partner views you, as well as fears about yourself — such as being somehow deficient and perhaps unlovable. If necessary, write down these fears.

Finding your needs emerging from your fears

When you recognize and name the fears that arise within you during more emotionally intense times, you're ready to take the next step and get the message from those primary emotions — your core relationship needs. The problem is that fears often block you from getting to your needs.

Primary emotions tell you what's important to you. They prime you for action and tell you what you really need. Your fears, however, can block you from getting this message. Recognizing and naming your fears (see the previous section) allows you to move forward and receive the message of what you need from your primary emotion. When you listen to and heed your fears, and you don't push them away, you create room for the primary emotions behind the fears to emerge. These previously hidden primary emotions carry vital information about what you most need.

The key is not letting your fears lock you down. Think of FDR's famous words, "The only thing we have to fear is fear itself." When you step into your fears — rather than away from them — you begin to understand what you really need to quell those fears.

Eric had fears about his partner *and* himself. He feared that Karen would never be satisfied with him, and that he really didn't deserve her anyway. Eric had to be courageous to face his fears. In his words, he had "man up" and quit running from his fears. "I get so scared that I can't please her," he said. "I try everything. If nothing works, I try to appease her. If that doesn't work, I get out of there. And that's when the fear really sets in. I've failed her." Eric talked about the immense pain he felt around failing as a husband and his fear that he would never live up to her desires.

Brent asked Eric what he needed from Karen when he felt so inferior. What did he need to help him not withdraw when things got emotionally intense? "I need her to just slow down and tell me everything will be all right. Tell me that I'm the one for her. And I need her to hold off on the frustration and anger — that just scares me more."

Withdrawing partners typically need one or more of the following:

- Reassurance that their partners love them
- Reassurance that their partners won't leave them
- Understanding that they're dealing with fears
- Understanding that anger overwhelms them
- Appreciation for their hard work
- Appreciation for providing for the family

✔ Patience while they learn to integrate primary emotion without withdrawing

✔ Empathy

✔ Reassurance that they're good partners

✔ Reassurance that they're good parents

✔ Reminders that they aren't failing and aren't inadequate

As this list shows, partners of withdrawing people can help them rein in their withdrawing. If your partner is the one who withdraws, you can help him or her begin to fight against withdrawing.

This activity is for the partner who withdraws. What are your own needs? Take time to read over and reflect on the fears you identified in the previous activity, and the typical needs listed in this section. Often, needs become clear after you identify your fears. As you reflect on your fears, consider what your needs may be. Be sure to write down your needs.

You may identify with Eric. Facing your fears isn't easy work. As you face your fears and begin to find your needs, your partner begins to see your withdrawing for what it is — loaded with feeling overwhelmed and tinged with fear. This helps both of you team up to break your negative cycle and understand each other better.

Chapter 9

Seeing through Pursuing Eyes

*E*ach person in a relationship has a role to play. In most relationships, one person is the pursuer, and the other is the withdrawer (see Chapter 6). The preceding chapter was all about what makes the withdrawer tick; this chapter is focused on the pursuer.

If you're a pursuer, this chapter helps you understand why you pursue. You may be pursuing automatically, not even aware of the emotions stirring inside you. Learning to recognize and listen to these emotions is key to beginning to integrate and change old patterns.

If you're a withdrawer, this chapter helps you understand what's happening inside emotionally for your partner, which can open up a new understanding in you. You may begin to see the reasons behind your partner's pursuing and even see your partner in a new light. This can help to break your negative arguing cycle.

Looking Inside Pursuit

If you find yourself pursuing your withdrawing partner, it can be a miserable experience. Your partner sees an irritated or angry person coming toward him for answers, but he's often totally unaware of all the hurt and fear deep inside you. These feelings may be difficult for you to come to terms with as well, and you may have formed a habit of pushing them away.

"I hate being in this place of chasing him," Laura said. "Time and time again we get into some kind of disagreement, and he ends up turning away or going silent. I follow him, often angrily, looking for a response. It doesn't get resolved. I don't understand how he can just walk away like that." Laura was unsure of the emotions brewing within her, but she knew that she didn't like being so angry with her partner and put in a position of pursuing. One thing was for sure: Her partner, Joe, had no idea what was really happening for Laura. All Joe saw was her being upset and critical of him.

The way to stop pursuing and to take control of your part of the cycle lies in facing up to your internal hurts and fears, maybe in a way that you haven't considered before.

Making sense of pursuit

To understand pursuing, you have to look inside and listen to your body when it's in the middle of pursuit. Now, stopping in the middle of pursuit during a real conflict is difficult, especially if you're new to this. So, to help a couple get in that state, a therapist will often have them re-enact a recent disagreement.

One of your authors, Brent, had Laura and Joe go back to a recent disagreement that had gotten nasty. Joe hadn't moved Halloween decorations out of the kitchen, as he promised he would do. It was the middle of November, and the boxes were still stacked up.

"Joe," Laura said. "You promised to move the Halloween decorations out of the kitchen for us a week after Halloween. It's now been two weeks and the boxes are still there."

"I know," Joe said. "I've had more important things on my plate."

"Really?" Laura said. "In two weeks, you haven't been able to move a few boxes to the attic?"

Joe didn't respond.

"I find that hard to accept, Joe," Laura said, her voice getting louder and harsher. "In fact," she continued, "I don't believe it at all!"

Joe didn't respond. He didn't even look at Laura.

"Just as I figured," Laura said. "Just sit there and say nothing, like you always do. If it's going to get done, I'll have to do it! You couldn't care less about my needs."

This example shows how a disagreement about everyday life (a chore around the house) can quickly shift into being about the emotions in your relationship. It also demonstrates how withdrawing and pursuing are central roles when emotions get heated.

"Laura," Brent said, "I want you to close your eyes and try to put yourself back into that argument. See yourself there in the kitchen, so frustrated that this was happening yet again."

As Laura "re-entered" the argument, she was able to locate where inside her body she was feeling her emotions. "My stomach is almost nauseous," she said. "I feel sick. Almost like crying, too."

"Pay attention to that in your body," Brent said. "Give it space and time. Just attend to it. Listen to it. Tell me about what comes up when you're ready."

As Laura stayed in tune with how her body was feeling, she was able to get clarity on her emotions in a new way. She was able to "drop down" below her secondary anger and frustration, which is where she stayed most of the time. (That's what Joe was used to seeing from her.) But as she stayed with it, she began to access her primary, more vulnerable emotions.

In emotionally focused therapy (EFT), it's the primary emotions — the vulnerable emotional states — that so often remain unheeded and unseen. Primary emotions have the power to create powerfully fast and long-lasting change. It's not about "naming" the primary emotion. It's about fully experiencing the primary emotional *state* so that you can receive not only its message or meaning but also its push for healthy action.

Laura began describing an emotional state of "cascading aloneness and sadness": "I feel like I'm in this alone," she said. "When I sense Joe withdrawing, I kind of panic. I can feel it building in me. It's like I'm sort of drowning. I reach and reach for him. I know what comes next — feeling alone."

Identifying common emotional states of pursuers

When you and your partner argue or disagree, and your partner pulls away and begins withdrawing from you, underneath your frustration and anger, you're likely feeling one or more of the following:

- ✔ Abandoned
- ✔ Alone
- ✔ Deficient
- ✔ Incomplete
- ✔ Invalidated
- ✔ Like a failure

- ✔ Panicky
- ✔ Sad
- ✔ Stupid
- ✔ Ugly
- ✔ Unimportant
- ✔ Unlovable

Recognizing your own primary emotional states when you're pursuing and your partner is withdrawing is key. This allows you to slow down and face what's really happening deep inside. Secondary emotions — such as anger and frustration — often fuel negative reactions and behaviors. They only push your partner away.

REMEMBER

Secondary emotions are secondary because they aren't the initial or primary responses to any situation. The primary emotional response is what's healthy and reliable in guiding you.

ACTIVITY

This activity is for the pursuing partner. Take a minute to reflect on the list earlier in this section. Think about a recent disagreement or argument you had with your partner, one that's typical of your cycle. Allow yourself to re-enter your emotional state. Close your eyes and re-enter your experience of pursuing and your partner withdrawing. It's not the words that matter so much or what you're thinking — it's more about what you're experiencing in your body as the cycle unfolds. Focus on your internal feelings. Where do you feel them? What do you think they may be saying to you? Give those feelings time and space to speak to you. Be patient. As it becomes clearer to you, write down your findings. You may have a few emotional states that aren't on the preceding list.

Engaging the hurt within

As you look over your primary emotional states (uncovered in the activity in the preceding section), you begin to get a deeper perspective and understanding of yourself. We often see this with pursuing partners in therapy. When their primary emotions around being in the pursuer's role become clearer to them, they begin to understand how painful it is to be in that position in the first place. It may be a pain that you've never consciously felt. It may be a hurt that you sometimes feel but quickly push away. Regardless, now is the time to fully experience and make sense of it.

REMEMBER

You have to fully arrive at a destination before you can fully leave that destination. In other words, you have to fully experience the hurt and pain of being in a pursuing role before you can defeat the negative cycle and take on a new and more productive role with your partner.

Laura was aware that when Joe retreated, and they remained emotionally disconnected, she felt panicky and afraid that he might not really want to be with her anymore. When Joe went out for a drive to cool off and get away from her pursuing, she would soon find herself in a downward spiral. First, she would tell herself that it was all his fault. But this strategy didn't work because it didn't last long, and the panic, hurt, and fear returned.

In therapy, Brent helped her take a step back and reflect. "Laura," he said, "I hear that you feel panic and hurt when you pursue Joe, and it still leads to disconnection between you. And I hear that this happens between the two of you repeatedly. I wonder though, what must it be like to be a wife in this relationship, finding yourself in this place of despair over and over? What's it like to be there?"

"It's awful," Laura said. "It's a terrible place to be. I raise my voice and criticize my husband until he can't stand me anymore and walks away."

She shared how she feels so bad about herself during these times and how lonely she is. She tries to get him back, tries to reconnect, but it hardly ever works. This leaves her in despair. "That's the worst place of all," she said. "When I'm no longer pursuing him, and he's far away emotionally, it hurts so much. What a terrible place."

"Do you think Joe is aware of all of this?" Brent asked Laura. "Do you think he realizes how you begin to start feeling a sense of panic as he withdraws? And that this leads to your feeling hurt because he's once again slipping through your fingers? Sure enough, the two of you disconnect, which leaves you, in your own words, in a terrible, awful place of hurt."

"He doesn't know," she said. "He thinks I'm just mad at him." But underneath the anger, Laura was being eaten alive with pain and hurt.

"Did you know she was going through this much hurt and pain?" Brent asked Joe.

"I had no idea," Joe said.

But how could he? While the arguments are happening, Joe sees Laura's reaction to her deeper panic and hurt — the critical anger. He doesn't see the panic, hurt, and ensuing loneliness. He had no idea that Laura feels terribly about herself after their arguments. "I see a woman who has it all together," Joe said. "One who's basically saying to me, 'Hey, get your crap together already!' I've never seen her pain and hurt."

Responding to your partner from secondary emotion — such as frustration, irritation, and anger — most often pushes him or her away. Instead, try risking by being genuine and showing your softer, more vulnerable emotions like sadness, fear, and hurt. This invites your partner to come toward you with understanding and care. It may not happen every time, and it may not happen the first time you try. But you'll find that when your partner senses honest vulner-ability from you, and begins to trust that, he or she will begin to come toward you, instead of pushing away. (For more on the different levels of emotion, see Chapter 4.)

When a negative cycle gets going, typically neither partner risks exposing primary, vulnerable emotion. Instead, both people play it safe and only show their armor — that is, their secondary, reactive emotion — which serves to protect them by pushing the other person away.

This was the case with Laura and Joe. When she sensed him withdrawing, even a little bit, she would press the gas and try to latch onto him before he got away. "Pressing the gas" meant talking more loudly, being more edgy, moving toward him. It wasn't effective, though. In fact, it had the opposite effect: It drove him away.

Both partners have good intentions and good reasons for their behaviors. But they too often find themselves emotionally disconnected and alone.

You and your partner may find yourselves in a situation similar to Laura and Joe's. You may be longing to defeat your negative cycle and connect with each other. If you're the more pursuing partner, however, you must get in touch with your fears before you can hope to break through and defeat the cycle. Fears often keep you locked down and stuck. Working through your fears, rather than cutting them off, allows you to better understand yourself and your needs, and to make healthier decisions. As your partner increas-ingly understands your fears, your true experience is much clearer to him or her as well, and your partner can help you with your fears. The idea is for both of you to begin to confide in and rely on each other.

Recognizing Your Fears

Fear is a powerful thing. Most people haven't thought much about their fears. In fact, when you begin to feel your fear, you usually act quickly to elude it altogether. That's what Laura did. As we uncovered her fears, she began to see that she was doing all kinds of destructive things to ward them off. This is problematic because she never really knew and dealt with her fears; she just reacted to the initial felt sense of them. She'd do anything to escape from that feeling of fear.

It makes sense that Laura would react to her fear like this, though. When she felt fear in her stomach, it was uncomfortable. She felt her face flushing, her heart rate increasing — her body was preparing for fight or flight. "I guess I'm not really aware of my fears," she said. "I just react pretty strongly when I start to feel those incoming fear signals in my body. I don't even think about it. I just react."

Fear tells us when we're in apparent danger. It makes sense that Laura was used to dealing with her fear by reacting to it — which in her relationship meant criticizing and pursuing Joe.

When you only react to fear, you cut off its message. As you learn to listen to your fear and not cut it off, you get more deeply in touch with your fears. You learn to *feel* that fear, and to be sad about it, rather than act to shortcut the pain. As you better understand your fear, you also became aware of the reasons behind it — reasons that may have their roots in your past. For example, if you're afraid that your partner will leave you, that may be rooted in the fact that your father died when you were a child.

In this section, we help you identify what the fear is about, and then find your needs emerging from those fears.

Seeing what the fear is about

In intimate relationships, fear falls into two categories:

- ✔ Fears about your partner
- ✔ Fears about yourself

These fears are intertwined. That's a testimony to how we're wired relationally. How others respond to you, from very early on, tells you something about how you're valued (or not valued). This process builds your idea of how you view others, too. The emotional climate between you and your parents teaches you everything from whether you're lovable to whether you can trust other people.

The emotional give and take between an infant and his or her parents unfolds long before the brain has developed words or thoughts. Words and thoughts come much later. The foundation for relationships is built on *affect,* that deep primary emotional state that we refer to as a kind of gut feeling. Affect is laid in place by repeated emotional exchanges with your parents.

EFT says that this same emotional process is the key to adult love relationships as well. Learn to plug into it and use it, and you're on your way to a long-lasting and significantly close relationship. Ignore it or push it away from awareness, and you may miss out on how real and genuine love can transform your life.

Fears about your partner

Sometimes pursuing in the face of emotional intensity has to do with fears about your partner. There may be fears around your partner

> ✔ Not loving you as deeply as you love him or her
>
> ✔ Wanting someone with a different personality
>
> ✔ Getting fed up and leaving
>
> ✔ Not having fun with you anymore
>
> ✔ Not wanting to spend time with you anymore
>
> ✔ Not finding you attractive

The theme running through all these fears is how negatively your partner may see you. The fear is that you're so deficient in these areas that the relationship will never be what your partner really wants. You may fear that your negatives will pile up so high that your partner will come to his or her senses and decide to move on without you. He or she will either live alone or find another partner to share life with.

Those who pursue are often surprised to hear that their partners don't know that they have these fears. Your partner may be very surprised, even alarmed, to hear about this kind of fear. It makes good sense if you think about it: What your partner mainly sees is that during times of emotional intensity, you tend to get loud and point out your partner's shortcomings. You likely come across as someone who wants your partner to shape up or ship out. But this is exactly the opposite of what's really happening underneath.

A note for partners of pursuers: When your partner pursues, there is a lot going on inside emotionally that's often unseen. The more you realize that there are fears stirring inside your partner when she pursues, the easier it'll be for you to step out of your negative cycle and typical behaviors. You can more easily empathize and seek to understand what fears your partner is battling.

As Laura experienced feeling alone and hurt while disconnected from Joe, it became clear that fear was a big factor for her. When she was alone and emotionally disconnected, fear seeped in that maybe, just maybe, Joe was getting tired of this relationship. Maybe he would eventually realize that he had had enough. Laura had this fear that perhaps his withdrawing was only a prelude to the final scene — in which he would withdraw from the relationship for good. What could she do to stop it from happening? When she tried to get him *not* to withdraw from her, it seemed to only hasten his withdrawal!

She rarely let herself experience this fear. But as she did go into it and increasingly felt her fear, an amazing thing occurred: She began to understand exactly what her fears were, what primary emotions they were connected with, and how she wanted to move out of being repeatedly stuck in her fear and pain.

EFT asks you to integrate your primary emotions into your daily life because they're there to give you clarity and guidance. You listen by allowing yourself to experience them and not shut them off. In turn, they give you clarity and motivation to act. Primary emotions begin organizing you to move out of being stuck and in pain, and toward a healthy resolution.

For Laura this meant the following:

1. When we're emotionally disconnecting I'm full of anxiety and panic. *(These are secondary emotions.)*

2. After we've emotionally disconnected, I get afraid that Joe's withdrawing may be a sign that, sooner or later, he'll want to end the relationship. This is very scary. *(These are fears about her partner.)*

3. I realize that I love him dearly. I have fears of losing him and of him no longer loving me. *(These are fears about herself.)*

4. As I experience this longer, I feel terribly sad. It leaves me very lonely. It hurts so much. *(These are primary emotions.)*

5. I'm sick and tired of this stupid cycle. And I've had enough of these awful, painful feelings. There has to be a better way of living. *(Experiencing her primary emotional state motivates Laura to act by moving toward a healthy resolution.)*

By fully experiencing her primary emotional state, Laura is moving toward fully recognizing and acting to meet her relationship needs. Needs become clear as a result of listening to your fears and primary emotional states. But before we address needs, you also need to understand how to handle possible deep-seated fears about yourself.

Fears about yourself

Some pursuers are afraid that there's something inherently deficient about them. They may rarely speak about it, but inside there is a longstanding, nagging fear that the real cause of problems always comes back to them. A part of them believes that they're the reason that their relationship is a struggle. When Laura experienced her fear, it wasn't long before this surfaced in her. "If I were a better person," Laura said, "Joe wouldn't withdraw." She blamed herself.

In psychology, this kind of fear is referred to as a *negative view of self* (see Chapter 2). This means that in times of relationship distress and emotional disconnection, people blame themselves, regardless of the evidence. They often have a sense of being unlovable or unworthy of their partners. Common fears associated with a negative view of self include fears of being

🗸 Unlovable

🗸 Usually to blame

🗸 Deficient

🗸 Unworthy of love

- ✔ A failure
- ✔ Unacceptable
- ✔ Disgusting
- ✔ Stupid
- ✔ Ugly
- ✔ Dumb
- ✔ Inferior

These partners may not often let others know about these deep-seated fears. But the fears are powerful nonetheless. Ironically, the fear of these things keeps you from opening up to your partner concerning these fears. When you share these fears with an empathetic partner, the burden can be shared and, thus, lightened.

As Joe learned about Laura's fears around a negative view of herself, he was moved to comfort her and dispel the fears. "You can talk to me about this," he said to Laura. "When you feel these fears, let me know. Let me help you with them."

Confiding her fears to Joe proved to be immensely helpful for Laura. She didn't have to be alone in her fears anymore. She learned to go to Joe and let him in by sharing her fears with him when she felt down. "Just having him hear me, reassure me that it isn't true, and hold me is enormously helpful," Laura said.

Finding your needs emerging from your fears

In relationships, allowing your fears to simmer and season without quickly reacting to them can pay huge dividends. Intertwined with fears are your primary emotions. But if you don't hang in there with your fears, you run the risk of pushing them away or quickly reacting to only the initial sense of fear. Doing this blocks your other primary emotions and the crucial meaning or messages they're carrying.

As you practice integrating your emotional experience more fully into your life, it becomes easier to do. And the more you glean the clarity of meanings, needs, and motivation to act that comes as a result, the more you'll want to continue. As one client said, "It's like a whole new world has opened up to me. A new emotional world that was always there, but I didn't have a clue that it was. It's kind of amazing."

A neat thing happens when you allow your fears and other primary emotions to simmer in your awareness: Your core relational needs become clear. Your needs are part of the message carried by your primary emotions. As usual, you have to slow down and listen to them. And when fear is involved, doing that can be scary or difficult, until you get used to integrating your whole experience into your awareness. This process is something that you can practice and get better at. If you've been doing the activities in this book, you're well on your way already.

As Laura sat with her fear and primary emotions longer, her core relational needs became obvious to her. It wasn't something she had to really think about. And that's the point. By sitting with your emotions, previously untapped meaning, clarity, and motivation follow. Building on the five-point list we started earlier, in the "Fears about your partner" section, Laura became clear on her relational needs and said, "I need to know that Joe loves me and won't leave me. I need his reassurance. I need to feel it, to know it," she said, putting her hand over her heart. Her relational needs have become clear.

Pursuing partners typically need one or more of the following:

- ✔ Reassurance that their partners love them

- ✔ Reminders of what their partners love about them

- ✔ Reassurance that they're not crazy

- ✔ Reassurance that their partners won't give up on them and the relationship

- ✔ Confirmation from their partners' actions (not just words) that they love them

- ✔ Time to be together, with no distractions

- ✔ Reassurance that their partners want them for more than sex

This activity is for the pursuing partner. Re-enter a recent or typical disagreement in which you and your partner ended up emotionally disconnected. Use the following steps and prompts to write down what comes up for you. We've listed Laura's words at each step in the process to help guide you in understanding what's being asked. Take your time and allow it to become as emotionally "alive" as possible. The more real it is, the clearer you'll be.

- ✔ When we're emotionally disconnecting, I feel _____. (List the secondary emotions you feel — for example, "When we're emotionally disconnecting I feel anxiety and panic.")

- ✔ After we've emotionally disconnected, I get afraid that my partner's withdrawing may be an indication that _____. (List your fears about your partner — for example, "After we've emotionally disconnected, I get afraid that my partner's withdrawing may be an indication that sooner or later he'll want to end the relationship.")

✔ I'm afraid that _____. (List your fears about yourself — for example, "I'm afraid of losing her and of her no longer loving me.")

✔ As I experience this longer, I feel _____. (List your primary emotions — for example, "As I experience this longer, I feel terribly sad. It leaves me very lonely too. It hurts so much.")

✔ I need _____. (List your relational needs — for example, "I need to know that he loves me and won't leave me. I need his reassurance. I need to feel it, to know it.")

Chapter 10

Facing Fears and Finding Each Other

Michael rarely acknowledged his own primary emotions (see Chapter 4), much less his fear and need for intimacy with Diane. Somehow over the years, they'd grown apart emotionally. Work and kids demanded that they keep things going, take care of business. But, like many couples, they'd come to a point in which one partner (in this case, Diane) started to step out of the daily grind and take a relationship inventory of sorts. Diane had been doing this for about two years when they came in for therapy. "I'm 30 now," she said. "I'm a mom and a professional. I love my husband with all my heart. I don't want another man — I want him. But something needs to change because we just aren't close enough. Something's missing."

As she shared more, one of your authors, Brent, felt a kind of sadness well up inside. As therapists, we listen to our inner feelings for guidance in listening to and understanding others — in much the same way you and your partner are learning to do in your relationship.

"You seem tired as you say that," Brent said to Diane.

"I am very tired," Diane said, slowing down her speaking pace.

Brent felt a sense of isolation. "I can't help but wonder if you feel lonely," he said.

"I am very lonely," Diane said, her eyes watering. We spent a little time mining her sadness for clarity. Then Brent turned to Michael.

"Michael," Brent said. "What's it like to hear about your wife's loneliness right now?"

"It's hard," Michael said. "I don't want her to feel alone. It makes me sad. I feel alone, too."

Many couples come to a place in which they feel lonely, much like Diane and Michael. They don't want to go anywhere; they just realize that something is missing. Do you ever feel this in your relationship? Maybe you long to be closer to your partner. Rather than just accept the status quo, many couples, like Michael and Diane, come to therapy because they want more. You probably have this in common with them — otherwise, you wouldn't be reading this book!

In this chapter, you discover how to face your fears, crystallize your intimate relationship needs, and find each other as allies, not enemies. We help those who withdraw and those who pursue to not only stop the old cycle, but also begin a new and positive cycle. This process takes a measure of courage and risk, but the reward is great.

Primary emotions are there to help guide you in your intimate relationship, but also in your parenting and in your work. Your emotions can help you in all human interactions. You're built to feel your emotions and those of others — this helps you understand and connect. It also advises you when you don't want to connect with someone else, or when you don't feel you can trust someone else. The more you become aware of your primary emotions and practice listening to them, the more you'll integrate this built-in navigation system.

The withdrawer's journey

When Brent started seeing Michael and Diane in therapy, Michael was almost totally unaware of his own emotions. He rarely, if ever, talked about or shared his primary emotions with Diane. "I just don't talk about my emotions," Michael said early on. "I don't know why exactly."

But two things happened in their second session that began, even at that early stage, to change both Michael and Diane. First, as we talked about how it felt to him after he and Diane argued, disagreed, said mean things, and then retreated to separate corners for days, Michael said that he felt "useless," "like a failure," and "sad."

Brent asked him to stay with those feelings in the session, to let himself feel them right then. He smiled and said, "I don't really know how to do that." Brent assured him that many men don't, but that he could help him learn.

"Imagine yourself alone after one of your fights," Brent said to him. "Let yourself go there right now. You're alone. You're working on your car, or you're lying in bed in the dark before going asleep. Don't push it away like you usually do. Instead, just let your feelings of 'uselessness,' 'sadness,' and 'failure' happen. Let them come. Don't try to escape them."

For maybe the first time in his life, Michael did this. After about ten seconds, his head dropped. He looked at the floor. His eyes watered. "Just let it happen," Brent said. "Where in your body do you feel it?"

"I don't know," Michael said.

"Are you feeling some of these emotions right now?" Brent asked him.

"Yes," he responded.

"Pay attention to them," Brent said. Some people feel them in their stomachs. Others feel it in their shoulders."

"I feel it in my heart," Michael said. "I used to get panic attacks after we fought. I actually thought I was having a heart attack, and we went to the hospital."

"Wow," Brent said. "These arguments and ensuing emotions are so strong that you actually thought you were having a heart attack. She means so much to you. It affects you so strongly, huh?"

"Yes, it does," Michael said.

"Do you feel it some in your heart right now?" Brent asked.

"Yes, I can," Michael responded.

"I wonder if you get really afraid that she might end up leaving you?" Brent asked.

"Yes," Michael said. "That's my greatest fear. That's the core of everything. I'm afraid that she'll leave me and take our daughter, too." Michael's voice was very low and soft as he said this. He was clearly "in" his primary emotion. Brent knew right then that Michael had this in the bag. He didn't know it yet, but he was doing exactly what he thought that he couldn't do. He was already well on his way.

Another thing happened in that second session that made a big difference: Diane finally saw Michael's core state — his primary emotions — and it greatly moved her. While Michael talked, Diane couldn't take her eyes off him. It was as if she was both powerfully drawn to him but also stunned at the same time. We see this repeatedly in emotionally focused therapy (EFT). When partners get into their emotional core state, it just steals the show. Both partners zero in on each other.

"What's it like to see him share that he gets scared that you might leave him?" Brent asked Diane. "That underneath it all, he feels sad and useless. Those are powerful words."

"They sure are," Diane responded. "I didn't know this. I never see this. All I see is anger, and I can't understand or connect to his anger. I can understand this — his sadness. I can connect to that." Diane then began to talk about how she felt sad for Michael, and sad herself. She shared how she feels so alone after they fight. She also touched her own fears.

It was then that Michael learned for the first time how much his wife needed to know about his fears and primary emotions. That was powerful for him to understand. Paying attention to and sharing his primary emotions was almost totally foreign to him. But as he saw how much it moved his wife and made her understand him more, he started to understand how he had to learn to share like this with her in order for their marriage to make it.

We worked hard at it throughout therapy, but when Michael experienced firsthand how greatly impacted both he and his wife were by powerful emotion, he never again questioned the necessity of feeling and sharing emotion with her.

"When I share from that place," Michael said, "that place that gets afraid, that place that I used to run from, feels close to me. And honestly, when she shares with me from her place of vulnerability, I feel close to her. We have to keep doing this. We have to."

Your journey may mirror Michael's in some ways. A whole new world began opening up to Michael in that second therapy session. The veil of the primary emotional world was lifted. This book may challenge you in similar ways. For Michael, seeing the powerful effect that feeling and sharing his core emotions had on Diane changed him.

In time, Michael grew to a point where, more times than not, he refused to withdraw. He was fed up with it and largely left that part of their

(continued)

(continued)

old negative cycle behind. But not withdrawing is only half the solution. Michael hadn't yet gotten to where he could share his fears, vulnerable emotions, and relationship needs directly with Diane.

Remember: Change in EFT comes from harnessing the power of emotion by listening *inside* and then sharing directly *between* partners. It's not enough to tune in to your own emotions. Each of you must then sincerely share your vulnerable emotions with each other. You each have to show tenderness and speak from the heart.

Refusing to Withdraw: Daring to Reach for Your Partner

At some point in the process of recognizing how you withdraw, and then unearthing the secondary and previously blocked primary emotions driving this behavior, you begin to get tired of the whole withdrawing idea. This may describe you now, or maybe you reached this point a while ago.

The more Michael, for example, began to regularly feel his fears around failing as a husband and partner, the more he hated being in such a position. "I get that sick feeling in my stomach," Michael said. "I'm afraid I'm failing. I hate that feeling. I'm tired of this crap."

This is a common situation for people in emotionally focused therapy (EFT), referred to as the *engaging withdrawer*. Michael is "engaging" back in to the relationship and is tired of the old, negative cycle.

"Look, I'm only as good as I am," Michael said. "But I'm trying here. And I can't stand feeling like a failure as a husband. I can't continue like this. It's got to stop."

Brent knew they were making solid progress when Michael said this from a place of really feeling and meaning it. The fact was, Michael had stopped withdrawing about a month ago. He stood his ground now when he and Diane fell into their negative cycle. He refused to withdraw. This, in turn, allowed Diane to feel his presence even when he said things that might have been hard for her to hear. It was great. They had made a lot of progress.

Michael had also recognized and felt his own fears and needs in the relationship. Now it was finally time for him to more fully organize these feelings and bring them directly to Diane. Reaching for your partner is daring. It takes courage.

It's not enough to recognize your own intimate relationship fears and needs. You must take the plunge and share them directly with your partner. You must risk asking your partner to meet you in your fears and to heed your needs. For this to have the greatest chance of working, you must reach while being in touch with, or experiencing, your fears.

Michael had to share with Diane his relationship fears and needs from a place of vulnerability within himself. That's the key. That's where the rubber hits the road. You're going to have to do the same thing. This is often referred to as speaking from the heart, not the head.

You need your partner to help you with your intimacy fears and needs. People are relational beings. Your own fears are intrinsically tied to your partner — they're relational in their very nature. It's your partner who can listen, heed, accept, and reassure you that your fears are not true. Your partner can do this by meeting you *in* your scary places, with the balm of accepting love and reassurance. And you can do the same for your partner around her own unique intimacy fears and needs.

Facing your fear as a withdrawer

Note: In Chapter 8, you begin facing your fears and recognizing your needs. You may need to revisit those lists for the work in this chapter, whether you wrote them down or just committed them to memory. If your fears and needs are not clear, take a little time and review Chapter 8 before moving forward. You'll need those for the next activity in this chapter.

Fear often arises very quickly, even at the onset of an argument. "When I hear that tone in her voice," Michael said, "that tone that comes out when she's upset or disappointed in something or, more likely, in me, my stomach sinks and my fear is alive." Fear hit Michael that fast.

A problem with fear is that it can shut you down. It can block you from your primary emotions. And it can block you from moving toward reconciliation with your partner. For some people who have gotten into a longstanding habit of actually being afraid of feeling their own fear, it can be crippling.

"I guess for my entire life, I've been afraid of my own fear," Michael realized. "When fear starts to happen inside me, I just do whatever it takes to not feel it. It's kind of amazing because I never realized I was doing this."

As therapists, we see this a lot in the process of EFT. Many people, both those who withdraw and those who pursue, are simply not aware of the degree to which they're automatically "running" from their own fear.

Fear may be *the* most important element in creating lasting change in both psychotherapy and your own relationship work with each other. We focus a lot in this book on helping each of you recognize and work with your fears. You each must find it and face it. You have to embrace your fear to have lasting change. It's that important.

Facing your own fears takes courage. You must learn to withstand fear's initial impact in you instead of bolting at the first hint of it. Your fear is preparing you by signaling that something very important is happening and that it could cause pain.

Fear *prepares* you. It isn't there to be ignored by pushing it away or shutting down. Fear sets the table for you to seriously engage with what is truly bothering you. It signals to you that you need to face the core of the issue at hand. In effect, fear says, "Okay, this is important to you. Stop whatever else you're doing and pay attention to your primary emotion and associated meaning wrapped in that emotion."

Again, we aren't talking about fear that arises when you're out in the woods and you hear a growl. We're talking about internal, recurring fears around relating with your partner. But if you stand with your fear and don't run from it, you'll find the gold behind it. This is when you're running on all cylinders.

Michael had grown in his ability to integrate his primary emotion into his current awareness. When his secondary emotions surfaced, for example, now he was able to tell himself that these were indeed reactive emotions, and then "see through" them and into his primary fear and genuine emotions. This was huge for Michael, and it will be huge for you, too.

Now that you're learning to listen to your emotions, you're getting much more in tune with how quickly they arise within you. That's a good thing. The more aware you are of your emotions in the here and now, the more you can receive their information, which is provided super-fast. Keep feeling. Keep listening. Practice can't "make perfect" in this case, but it can be pretty helpful. It's not about thinking in your head. It's about feeling in the moment.

Some people seem calm and "above the fray" because they ignore and cut themselves off from emotion. They appear unflappable, but research shows that inside they're boiling with emotion. This isn't healthy. Learning to see through your secondary emotions and into your fears and primary emotions is a process of healthy integration. It's holistic. And inside you won't be cutting off your emotions. Quite the opposite, you'll be using them to help guide you in the moment.

Being able to see through your own secondary emotions and into your fears and primary emotions is a trait that society ascribes to "wise" people. These people just seem more "centered" than most. They aren't tossed to and fro by the waves of life as much. When you talk to them, you get a sense that they're really listening to you. And when they talk, you realize that you want to listen to what they have to say. And when they laugh, they mean it!

Sharing your fears and needs

Opening up and sharing your fears and needs with your partner is a crucial step toward creating a new, positive cycle between the two of you. Although there is no rule, the withdrawing partner often arrives at the place of being ready for this step first. Maybe the pursuing partner needs more evidence that the other partner won't continue withdrawing when faced with strong emotion. This makes sense because, in some couples, the pursuing partner has been pursuing for quite some time and has become certain that the other partner will simply withdraw if he or she opens up.

When the withdrawing partner begins to share and open up, it can go a long way toward convincing the pursuing partner that it's safe to risk opening up from his or her own vulnerability as well. Pursuing partners often need to see and viscerally feel that the other is seriously here to stay now — no more withdrawing. Even when the now engaged partner says things that are difficult to hear, he or she is present, and that makes disagreements more tolerable. This creates an atmosphere that fosters the mutual sharing of fears and needs.

Receiving your partner's reach

Keep in mind how difficult it may be for your partner to show this kind of vulnerability and open up to you. At first, it may come across as awkward, but with time and experience, it should flow more easily. Your response, however, usually has a strong impact on your partner. If he or she feels unheard or blamed, the chances of your partner continuing to open up decrease dramatically.

Diane was very relieved when Michael began opening up with her directly. "I felt like I knew him better. I felt closer to him when he started sharing with me." Although Diane may not have liked everything Michael said or agreed with it, she learned the importance of their being able to share from deep places with each other. "Sometimes he says things that I disagree with and don't like," Diane said. "But I try to save that for later. When he's being vulnerable, it's not my time to be 'right' or 'wrong.' I need to hear and try to be caring with him."

When it came time for Michael to reach to Diane and share his fears and needs, it went like this:

> "When I feel distant from you, I start feeling afraid that maybe we won't make it," Michael said to Diane. "It scares the crap out of me. My biggest

fear is that you'll leave." *(This is a fear around his partner.)* "I know I haven't been the best husband. I'm sorry for that," Michael said. "I feel like I've let you down, let myself down." *(This is a fear around himself.)* "I don't want to feel like this anymore," Michael said. "I need to know that you won't leave." *(This is a relationship need.)*

"I won't leave," Diane said. "I want this to work."

"I need you to back off some and not be so critical," Michael said. "It's hard on me to face your anger. I need you to control your anger some. That would help me to stay present." *(This is a relationship need.)*

"It's great to see this vulnerable part of you," Diane said. "I feel closer to you. I understand more now. I don't want to be so critical of you."

Diane was spot on with her comments. She was great at creating an environment that welcomed Michael's explorations of his fears, primary emotions, and relationship needs. The pursuing partner in your relationship will be just as vital in creating that safe environment for sharing.

A note for the pursuing partner: Your partner is prone to withdraw when he or she feels your disapproval or criticalness. Hang in there with him or her. If you feel compassion, show that. If you feel your partner's sadness, tell him or her. Try to respond to your partner from your heart after he or she has finished opening up to you. If it's really difficult, take a deep breath, focus on your breathing, and breathe your way through it.

This activity is for the withdrawing partner. Drawing from the work you do recognizing your fears and needs in Chapter 8, it's time to start sharing with your partner. Take a minute to look over your list of fears and needs. If it's incomplete, go back and spend more time looking over the lists of typical withdrawer fears and needs in Chapter 8. Make sure to write down the ones that speak particularly to you.

Next, see if you can get in touch with your own fears and needs. It's important that this not be a simple "cognitive" exercise. It needs to come from your heart.

When you're in touch with your needs and fears, on a separate piece of paper, write out answers for the statements below. Fill in the spaces in your own words.

- ✔ Sometimes when we're emotionally disconnected, I begin to get scared that I _____.
- ✔ When this happens, I sometimes get afraid that _____.
- ✔ As I understand these fears more, I have come to realize that I need _____.

When you're done, share this list with your partner, reading it carefully and from your heart.

A note for the pursuing partner: At this point your job is to mainly listen. Don't respond, question, disagree, or try to explain. Simply listen. Try to recognize that this can be scary information for your partner to share. Remember that this sharing time is primarily focused on your partner. Later in this chapter, we walk through how you, the pursuing partner, also share fears and needs.

After the withdrawing partner shares the list, the pursuing partner should briefly share what it was like to hear him or her open up and share. Then the withdrawing partner should confide what it was like to share. Talk about whether there is something your partner can do to help you open up and share like this more often.

Resisting Pursuing: Sharing Your Fears with Your Partner

By now you're probably sick and tired of pursuing and chasing, all to no avail. In the end, it leaves you alone and emotionally disconnected from your partner. Your negative cycle has improved by this point, and you've just completed the beginning of your partner sharing fears and needs with you. The time has come for you to face your own fears and move toward sharing those fears with your partner.

Diane was mainly afraid that if Michael saw her for the "weak" person she was, he would be disappointed, feel misled, and want to leave her. Deep down inside, she was convinced that she wasn't someone whom others found very lovable. On bad days, she wondered if she was at all lovable or even worthy of another person's love. Of course, she kept this buried deep inside herself and never showed these fears to anyone, let alone Michael.

What Michael saw was a strong woman who seemed to have everything together. "You're almost perfect," Michael said. "You follow through with everything, have everything together. You're like Wonder Woman or something."

Although this sounds complimentary, unbeknownst to Michael, Diane found it awful. If Michael really saw that she wasn't "Wonder Woman," he would be disappointed. In fact, she was afraid that she wouldn't be able to please him or be the woman he really needed. When they argued and emotionally disconnected, powerful fear crept in and shook her to her core.

Michael had no idea about these fears. He was used to seeing a nearly perfect, strong woman who had it all together. He saw Diane as being fed up with him because of his weaknesses. He saw her anger and criticalness, which are totally different from vulnerable emotions. When she saw him coming to terms with his fears and reaching out to her for support, Diane knew it was time for her to do the same.

Facing your fears and being seen

As the pursuing partner, facing your fears and sharing those with your partner involves showing parts of yourself that you may not have shown before. For both of you, facing fear and opening up to the other person requires courage. But it also requires a desire to be emotionally close. To open up and share like this demonstrates a love that is to be commended.

Facing and listening to your own fears takes courage. You can learn to understand and tolerate fear's initial impact instead of distracting yourself at the first hint of it. Fear prepares you by signaling that something very important is happening, and that it could cause pain. Action is needed.

Fear *prepares* you. Fear is not built into human beings to be ignored. It's not healthy to push it out of your awareness or to shut down in the face of it. Your fear automatically sets the table so that you can seriously engage with what's important and what troubles you. Fear signals that you need to deal with the core of the issue. You do this by listening through your fear to your primary emotions. It's like fear is saying, "Okay, this is important! Feel me in your heart? Feel me in your knees? Feel me in your chest? Now I have your attention. Good. I'm not here to hurt you. I'm here to help you. I'm here *for* you. Stop what you're doing and focus your attention on your primary emotions here beside me. They'll guide and move you to action."

For pursuing partners, reaching out like this often involves a great sense of being seen, maybe in some ways for the first time. For Diane, this was a risk. Although she didn't like being put in the role of "Wonder Woman," she had a real fear that at the end of the day, if this facade was removed, what was really there?

Diane had some fears about herself. Her "view of self" at times was shaky at best. Deep down, she was afraid that Michael didn't know the "real" her. And if he saw that part of her, he might not like it. "It was very difficult for me to open up to him about some things," Diane said. "When it came to my fears around myself, that was tough."

This may be tough for you as well, but the rewards far outweigh the risks. We've seen this time and time again with couples. Hang in there!

You and your partner have the opportunity to uniquely listen to and reassure each other about fears. Couples who learn to do this are able to connect in their fears. They realize and seize this opportunity to find each other in deeper ways. Together, they agree, "Let's be afraid of this giant risk we're taking together instead of letting it push us away, leaving us to manage it all alone." Successful couples in EFT *connect in their fear.*

Many withdrawing partners are surprised to learn that their partners actually *don't* have it all together. When they hear that their partners have fears, too, they often feel relieved because they aren't the only ones who are "messed up." In a strange way, when the pursuer softens and presents her vulnerabilities, the other person often experiences relief and renewed hope in the future of the relationship.

Sharing your fears and needs

As the pursuing partner, take a look back at the work you did in Chapter 9. Take time and resonate with the fears and needs that you identified. Begin thinking about how you'll share some of these fears and needs directly with your partner. It's important to lead with your fears — fears aren't typically blaming in nature. And your partner can comfort and reassure you when you lead with fears. Plus, your fears lead to your primary emotions and relationship needs.

When Diane shared her fears and needs with Michael it went like this:

> "This is really hard for me to do," Diane said. "I keep this part of me pretty hidden. I'm afraid that if you really see me, you won't like what you see," she said, crying. *(This is a fear around self.)* "Maybe I'm not the wife for you after all," Diane continued. "I've always been told I could never please a man. And here it is, happening between us. If I were a better person, we wouldn't be having these troubles," she cried. *(This is a fear around self.)* "I need to know that I'm the woman you still want," Diane said. "I need your comfort and reassurance. I need to know you're there for me, and that you'll help me with my fears." *(This is a relationship need.)*

> "You're the only one for me," Michael said. "I'm here for you now. I didn't know all this. I feel closer to you when you let me in like this," he said, moving over and holding her hand, offering reassurance and comfort. "I'm not the most emotional person, but I want to learn to comfort you when you feel afraid."

Michael was able to put his own anxieties aside and put his entire focus on Diane and her needs during this exchange. That's exactly what the other partner needs to do during this activity.

Only one partner should share his or her own vulnerable emotion at a time. The other partner needs to put his or her own issues down and primarily be there for the partner who's doing the sharing. Let the disclosing, risking partner and his or her fears and needs have the total attention of both of you. Going one at a time helps slow it down and promote the care and attention needed for creating a safe, accepting environment, which is vital.

Responding to your partner's reach

A note for the withdrawing partner: Keep your own questions and pointers to yourself while your partner opens up to you in vulnerability. If you make it about you in the middle of your partner's sharing, it simply blows up. It's crucial that you keep your attention focused on your partner when he or she is sharing primary emotion with you.

Keep in mind that opening up can be very scary for your partner to do. So, handle it with care. If you feel your own questions coming up about your role in her pain, now is not the time to bring it up. This has nothing to do with "right" and "wrong," or who did what. Just keep yourself in the listening, comforting, and accepting role. Here are some tips on how to do that:

- ✔ Be sure to breathe regularly, and stay aware of your breathing.
- ✔ Maintain eye contact.
- ✔ Turn down your thinking — stay out of your head.
- ✔ Pay attention to your partner's emotions as he or she is sharing.
- ✔ Don't get defensive.
- ✔ Remind yourself to stay focused on your partner.

Sometimes the partner who's listening can fall into a trap of blaming himself or herself while the other person is opening up. For example, when Diane was sharing how she doesn't have it all together and fears that Michael may not be happy with her, Michael had a tendency to break in and begin to blame himself for this. "That's my fault," Michael would say. "If I were a better husband and told you how I feel more often, you wouldn't feel like this." Michael interjecting while Diane is sharing isn't helpful. It takes the focus off Diane, and leaves her feeling alone again in her fear.

In a way, Michael actually "withdrew" from Diane when he went into his own reactions like this. He had to learn that he could disclose these emotions when he was the sharing partner, but not when Diane was in the middle of opening up to him.

Many people find it incredibly fulfilling to learn that their partners "need" them. They often fear that just the opposite is true. When they experience their partners opening up and see how much they're needed, it often lights a fire in them. It's exciting to be needed by your partner. Through the years of conflict and distance, many people fear that they aren't needed at all. To feel their partners reaching to them because they still need and love them can be life changing.

These kinds of heartfelt exchanges entailing mutual openness and acceptance have the power to change your relationship for the long haul. Your partner is your adult love — risk, dive in, and go for it!

This activity is for the pursuing partner. Drawing from the work you do recognizing your fears and needs in Chapter 9, it's time to start sharing with your partner. Take a minute to look over your list of fears and needs. If it's incomplete, go back and spend more time looking over the lists of typical pursuer fears and needs in Chapter 9. Make sure to write down the ones that speak to you.

Next, see if you can get in touch with your own fears and needs. It's important that this not be a simple "cognitive" exercise. It needs to come from your heart.

When you're in touch with your needs and fears, on a separate piece of paper complete the following sentences. Fill in the spaces in your own words.

- ✔ Sometimes when we're emotionally disconnected, I begin to fear that I _____.

- ✔ When this happens, I sometimes get afraid that _____.

- ✔ As I understand these fears more, I have come to realize that I need _____.

When you're done, share this list with your partner, reading it carefully and from your heart.

*A **note for the withdrawing partner:*** At this point, your job is mainly to listen. Don't respond, question, disagree, or try to explain. Simply listen. Try to recognize that this can be scary information for your partner to share. Remember that this sharing time is primarily focused on your partner.

After the pursuing partner shares the list, the withdrawing partner should briefly share what it was like to hear the other person open up and share. Then the pursuing partner should confide what it was like to share this list. Consider whether your partner could do anything to help you open up and share like this more often.

Now what?

In a sense, the entire book up to this point sets the stage for the two activities in this chapter. You'll need to return to these two activities again and again in your relationship. We can't stress this enough. If you start feeling emotionally distant, sit down and use the map of these activities to find each other again. If you find yourselves emotionally disconnected, sit down and go through the steps in these activities.

The more you share with each other by following the activities in this chapter, the easier it becomes. It may seem somewhat forced or awkward at first, but stay with it. We find that sometimes couples start awkwardly, but before long, they "trip" primary emotions, and the environment quickly drops down into sacred places.

This may be a chapter that you each read repeatedly over time. We recommend reading the chapter together. You may need to return to Chapters 8 and 9 repeatedly as well, because they prepare each of you for the crucial activities in this chapter.

As you slowly learn to reach out to each other from vulnerable places, share your fears and needs, and ask for your partner to comfort and reassure you, you're well on your way to breaking your old negative cycle. In fact, each time you open up to each other and share primary emotions, you're creating new positive, loving cycles. These interactions are the building blocks of lasting love. You'll need to make this kind of emotional connecting a regular part of your relationship.

Michael summed this part up well. "The more we sit down and walk through these steps with care, the more we stay emotionally connected," Michael said. "It's not easy. But we've each learned to feel and recognize when we feel emotionally distant. That's our warning signal. It's up to each of us to grab the other and sit down and connect."

Chapter 11

Overcoming Common Blocks

*I*n emotionally focused therapy (EFT), couples make progress by increasing the safety and security in their relationships, which allows them to listen and respond more to each other's needs. Sometimes these new steps of listening and responding get blocked by past experiences of pain and insecurity. These past patterns of coping with pain may affect your present conversations and experiences.

Shame is a particularly pernicious block that can isolate partners and prevent sharing vulnerable experiences. Other blocks to vulnerability result from relationship injuries (or *attachment injuries,* in EFT-talk). Attachment injuries happen when there's a breach of trust or abandonment, making it difficult to trust your partner.

You and your partner can get along and work out your differences, but you may still be holding on to "good reasons" for not risking or expressing vulnerability because of the past. The blocks remain because you haven't worked through them. These blocks become more evident as you're working to increase the closeness of your relationship.

In this chapter, we help you identify blocks that are preventing you from reaching deeper levels of emotional closeness with your partner. You may find that talking about these blocks with your partner is a first step toward removing these barriers in your relationship. You may also find these topics more difficult to discuss together without the help of an emotionally focused therapist who can help you overcome these obstacles.

Dismantling the Power of Shame

Shame is fundamentally an emotion about your value as a person. In its mildest forms, shame signals that your behavior is unacceptable and isn't fitting with what's expected in your family or in society. You likely know this feeling as one of embarrassment, but shame can also signal — in a deeper, more profound sense — that you're "unacceptable."

If this is the message you carry about yourself, it makes sense that you would hide and protect yourself from revealing these "unacceptable" thoughts, memories, and feelings. You're afraid that if people saw those things, you'd be rejected. Trying to protect yourself because of shame often leads to isolation and withdrawal.

The power of shame to disrupt a couple's intimacy resides in its ability to turn partners away from each other and inward, toward themselves. Psychologist Gershen Kauffman describes shame as a "wound made from the inside." It's an internal emotion that interrupts a person's and couple's ability to connect at a deeper emotional level. Eye contact is broken as a partner drops into feelings of self-consciousness and stays away from communicating with his partner.

Consider the example of Will and Claire. Years of infertility treatment left their mark on Will and Claire's relationship. The couple worked to overcome the distance that grew between them during repeated attempts to have a child. As a couple, they could be caring and close, but Will's low sexual desire proved to be an enduring challenge for the couple. He tended to dismiss his lack of desire by attributing it to work pressure, aging, and overall fatigue. Claire *wanted* to accept his explanation, but she felt a nagging sense that there was more going on for Will than he would admit to.

In therapy, the couple identified Claire's tendency to pursue and Will's corresponding withdrawal (see Chapter 6). The couple made good progress in recognizing their conflict pattern and ways it kept them apart when they wanted closeness. Will shared how he knew he provided well for Claire but at times doubted whether he was really the husband Claire had hoped for. When Claire brought up their sexual relationship, Will became evasive or defensive.

In a therapy session, one of your authors, Jim, asked Claire, "What's it like when you find Will moving away?"

"It's hard for me to put my finger on," Claire said. "He's just there one minute and gone the next," she answered, as Will looked away.

"And that's happening now?" Jim asked.

Turning to Will, Jim said, "Will, can I check in with you? What's going on as Claire is talking about these times?"

"Nothing, I guess. I'm just frustrated, that there still has to be an issue. I'm still not doing it right, somehow," Will responded, looking down to avoid making eye contact.

"Yes, this has to be tough," Jim said, understanding Will's struggle. "You've both worked through so much, and you've fought hard to get through this together. Still, you hear her concern and what happens for you?"

"I feel sick — sick to my stomach," Will responded, visibly uncomfortable. In a frustrated tone, he continued, "Like I failed her again. You know we can't have kids because of me, and we don't have sex because of me. I'm a disappointment."

Will expressed regret, but his tone was laced with sarcasm, anger, and contempt. It was unclear whether these words were directed at Claire or himself.

Jim saw Will's withdrawal as Will looked away from Claire with an expression of defeat. "Will, it's like you feel you've let Claire down when she brings up these concerns. It's not just about sex — there's something bigger here. It's more about feeling like you failed, or like you're a failure," Jim said.

Locating shame in your own life

The experience of shame can run in the background of a couple's relationship. Leslie Greenberg described shame as having a "covering" response that blocks awareness and access to more adaptive primary emotions. Shame complicates the relationship between a couple's pattern and the emotions that underlie their pursuing and withdrawing. Shame covers over their underlying losses, injustices, and needs. These needs are obscured by a partner's negative view of self that then reinforces the shame that he or she is experiencing.

People commonly hide things they fear are unacceptable, and they even hide the fact that they're hiding them! The eventual result of shame is isolation.

Think of the last time you saw someone who felt ashamed. What told you he or she was feeling ashamed? Was it the person's expression, something he or she said, or how he or she acted? Here are some common indicators of shame:

- Avoiding eye contact
- Looking away
- Tilting the head down
- Blushing
- Staring but not connecting
- Displaying looks of contempt or disgust
- Being self-conscious
- Being shy, socially withdrawn, or isolated

- ✔ Having a self-denigrating sense of humor
- ✔ Controlling
- ✔ Denying
- ✔ Being a perfectionist
- ✔ Feeling like an imposter
- ✔ Feeling deficient
- ✔ Feeling inferior or as though you don't fit in
- ✔ Being afraid of being seen as stupid or incompetent
- ✔ Feeling uncertain and insecure

The combination of these attitudes and actions can create an emotional state of self-doubt, rejection, alienation, and inferiority. How you see yourself can be organized around these themes of being unwanted, ineffective, or deficient.

Understanding shame

When people share an embarrassing moment, they often laugh and feel a sense of togetherness. That togetherness comes from the fact that everyone has done something embarrassing before. And the laughter they share is a form of validation — other people understand and accept the experience.

Often, though, in the moment, your immediate response to an embarrassing situation is to hide from others what has just happened. Societal pressures to fit in with your social group often reinforce these experiences. Efforts to "save face" are important in guiding social practices.

Jamie and George fondly remember their honeymoon, including one of Jamie's most embarrassing moments. After hours of playing in the surf, the couple decided to be more adventurous and try their hand at body surfing in larger waves. After several tumbles in the surf, Jamie called it quits and headed to the beach. Disoriented and exhausted from fighting through the waves, she didn't realize that the top of her bikini was riding around her waist as she walked from the water to her towel. She noticed several people staring at her, suddenly discovered her "wardrobe malfunction," and raced to her towel. George found her later, hiding in their car, where she demanded, "Get me out of here!" They laugh about it now, but in the moment, Jamie felt humiliated by the situation and there was little George could do to comfort his embarrassed wife.

Think of a time when you did something embarrassing. Put yourself back in that moment. What was the first sign that you felt embarrassed? What did you do? What were you feeling? What was happening inside your body in that moment? If you were to put words to that feeling what would they be?

More than embarrassment, secondary emotions of shame can have a strong theme of self-criticism and rejection. Feelings of shame may show up in embarrassing moments when a person not only feels awkward socially but also feels bad about himself or herself at the same time.

As a child, Salvador was self-conscious about his appearance. He often wore secondhand clothes that didn't fit well, and he was overweight as a teen. He never felt like he fit in with his group of friends. As an adult, he can easily recall the taunts and jeers he heard from those who bullied him as a kid. Salvador's career success and social standing are a striking contrast to his childhood, but he admits his success is only "skin deep." Deep down inside, Salvador may *act* the part of a successful attorney, but inside he's running scared and never feeling like he really belongs.

Think about a time when you didn't feel like you fit in. Maybe you felt rejected or disregarded. Ask yourself the following questions:

✔ How did you feel about yourself? What word would you use to describe that feeling?

✔ Can you recall other times when you felt a similar way?

✔ What happens inside your body when you reflect on this feeling? What word would you give to this feeling?

✔ How often does this feeling come up for you?

✔ When it does come up, what do you typically do?

At an emotional level, shame is similar to guilt. Guilt involves the breaking of a moral standard, rule, or expected behavior. When you violate your morals or values, you can feel guilty, and often these feelings can direct you to take some corrective action to address that wrongdoing. You can correct guilt, but sometimes people turn their guilt into shame through self-blame.

Clarissa apologized to Thomas for hiding her credit card debt. Thomas became aware of her lying after the couple failed a recent credit check. Clarissa apologized and took steps to work out a payment plan with Thomas to help restore the trust that was broken. Inside, Clarissa felt like she not only failed the relationship but also failed herself by being so manipulative and dishonest. Even though she made peace with Thomas, she continued to see herself with contempt. This contempt impacts her relationship with Thomas because she often fears that he'll never really trust her again.

Partners who experience shame may have anxious thoughts fueled by fears of rejection. Perfectionistic standards and performance can drive their attempts to manage their fears of rejection. For example, Clarissa manages her fear of Thomas's rejection by anxiously pursuing Thomas for reassurance on all financial matters, which he finds overly dependent.

Saying no and drawing boundaries may be difficult for these partners because they fear being ignored or left out. Seeking approval becomes a primary means to manage a negative view of self, and this approach to coping often reinforces this negative view when you can't sustain perfectionistic standards (because no one can). Feelings of disgust and contempt are commonly directed to the self. Shame can fuel harsh, self-critical responses. Anger can keep others (and yourself) away from the vulnerability that's at the core of the patterns of shame that may dominate your sense of self.

Brad believes that he never gets it right with Lauren. He focuses much of his attention around her needs and expectations. Brad takes Lauren's happiness as a sign of his efforts to be a "good husband." Their biggest fights occur when Brad feels criticized by Lauren. Lauren will try to correct Brad, and he reacts in bitter anger, resenting that she doesn't give him credit for how much he does for her. Then he turns on himself saying, "I failed again. I work so hard to make her happy. I'm no good." His self-contempt leaves Lauren in a double bind. She tries to tell him what she needs, which he's expecting, but too often her words set him off in rage, directed either toward her or toward himself. Ironically, Lauren often feels there is little room in the relationship for her to express what she wants or needs.

Shame can result from the harsh judgment of others or the harsh judgment of yourself. Understanding your relationship history (see Chapter 6) can provide a deeper understanding of the triggers of shame in your relationship. Negative experiences in childhood can result in enduring feelings of being unwanted or unacceptable. Parents can send "shaming messages" about a child being weak (mainly directed toward boys), aggressive (mainly directed toward girls), lazy, unlovable, selfish, or stupid. Over time, these rejecting messages of childhood become the rejecting messages about self in adulthood.

This was the case for Will and Claire. *Disappointment* was a loaded word for Will. Claire knew that he hated that word because his father used it to motivate Will in sports and school. Will found himself in the shadow of his older, more accomplished brother, who was often used as a standard for Will to live up to. As an adult, Will kept distance in his relationship to his father and brother. Still, the messages of comparison and falling short live within him. He prided himself on the thought that when he became a father, he would make sure his children felt valued and accepted.

Patterns of shame are associated with depression. The experience of self-rejection and criticism are more common among partners with a relationship history that includes a lack of parental interest or, more extreme, parental rejection. Will's low sexual desire is linked to his ongoing struggle with depression and his struggles with feeling unwanted and deficient. He initially resisted going to therapy because he thought it was a sign of weakness, a sign that he had failed in some way.

Other sources of shame result from relationship histories that involve past abuse and victimization. Memories of these events can be personally humiliating, especially when the actions involved are socially unaccept-able. Keeping these events hidden protects a partner from social shame and stigma for actions that they didn't choose. In situations of sexual abuse, part-ners may feel "dirty" or "spoiled" in some way.

Shame can provide a sense of control over the disruptive violation of abuse. Retaining a sense of responsibility may provide a semblance of control over events that shattered your assumptions about safety and security in the world. These patterns of shame and responsibility may be directly or indirectly implied by perpetrators, who often tell the victim that he or she was to blame.

Taming the voice of shame

Shame can block the experience of other, often painful emotions. In EFT, the process of working through shame involves allowing pain and brokenness, working through the brokenness, and then transforming the brokenness. Change occurs as you're able to acknowledge your brokenness and make allowance for the feelings that are more adaptive than shame. Facing your brokenness in this way often increases self-compassion and a better under-standing of your needs.

In EFT, the first step in working through shame is allowing for a person's pain and brokenness. Shame provides protection from unwanted vulnerability, including emotions that may threaten rejection or abandonment. Fear and anxiety are common when facing these powerful underlying experiences. The process of moving into this level of vulnerability requires care and concern for these fears.

Allowing your pain and letting go of shame

In the following sections, we walk you through the process of facing your pain and working through the shame that often blocks it.

Step 1: Facing fears in facing pain

The initial step of this process requires accepting feelings of hopelessness and helplessness as you release control and begin to trust your partner and yourself with these emotions that you've safely managed up to this point. Often, these experiences include more desperate emotions, which can seem overwhelming and can reinforce both the fear of allowing them and the ten-dency to control these emotions.

At first Will was reluctant to engage his disgust at the word *disappointment,* but Jim helped him explore the contempt he expressed about this word and the idea that he might be seen as a disappointment. Jim said, "Sounds like a hard place, this feeling of disappointment. You don't see yourself this way and it's tough when others express disappointment and it involves you? It's almost like they're saying that *you're* disappointing?"

"I guess it was hardest when it became clear that the infertility issues were more my issue than Claire's," Will said slowly. "I felt sick inside, like I had let her down. I had put off seeing a specialist for a long time, too long maybe. I know rationally that it's not something I can control, but still I felt horrible. Sick inside."

"Nauseous?" Jim followed Will's experience. "Do you feel something like that now?"

"Yeah, just like I did when I was a kid with my dad looking down at me, telling me how disappointed he was that I wasn't trying hard enough and wasn't living up to my potential. I could feel the same disappointment all over again," Will said. He looked down, and pain filled his face.

"Can you talk about that disappointment?" Jim asked. "This pain that cuts so deep?

"I don't know. I don't let myself go there. It's too overwhelming. I just keep it walled away," Will said.

As the session unfolded, Jim guided Will between his fear of the past and his wounds of disappointment. Jim accepted Will's fear as an expected response, given how little of his pain he allowed others or himself to see. Claire sat close and touched Will's arm in moments where Will's pain was most clear. Though she had seen firsthand her father-in-law's critical and condescending manner, this was the first time she saw its impact on Will.

Step 2: Recognizing blocks to pain

The process of allowing pain leads to working through other emotions and past efforts to manage these hurts. Opening up to these hurts may surface other emotions like sadness, anger, and shame. You may feel anger over a past violation and at the same time experience a fear that you aren't entitled to be angry. Shame can push down this emerging anger because you say to yourself: "You shouldn't be angry over that. How can I be angry about that when I'm also to blame?"

Will made clear that he had learned to "live above life's disappointment" by being positive and future oriented. He used his optimism to keep his pain away. This strategy was useful in defending himself against his father's critical eye. Will said, "I used to tell myself that I would prove my father wrong. He would see one day that I measured up. And I certainly told myself that I would raise my children differently. I would make sure they knew they were valued, just for who they were."

Will's response was colored with emotion. His voice rose in defiance as he spoke about his father and fell into softer tones of sadness when talking about his own children.

Jim picked up on Will's sadness and said, "That's what's so tough, right? So tough about the infertility and your future? It's really tough to 'live above that disappointment.'"

Both in therapy and in his story, Will expressed themes of failure, feelings of sadness, and holding on to hope. His optimism helped him stay on the surface as he used reason to keep his distance from the loss he felt both in childhood and in fatherhood. "What could I say to my father? He wouldn't care — he'd just make some comment about not having a grandchild. It would be just another reason for him to be disappointed." Will paused.

Jim added, "In you?"

Step 3: Letting go of barriers to pain

Seeing your pain more clearly helps you also see how you've coped and managed to block your hurt. When you're able to see the shame or distractions that block your pain, you're freer to let go of these distractions and controls. Letting go of the shame requires a new step of vulnerability. Without the shame that has controlled and covered your pain, you begin to see yourself and others in a new way.

Jim asked Will to revisit the doctor's appointment where he received news of his diagnosis. Will was matter of fact in describing the scene and how he responded. Claire explained that, although they had discussed treatment in detail, they hadn't yet had a conversation about Will's feelings. "I just knew not to go there," Claire acknowledged. "He would politely put me off or close off in anger."

Jim acknowledged and validated Will's tendency to block Claire out: "After all, you were coping with this painful situation in the best way you knew how. And it's not like you've had a lot of times in your family when someone came alongside you in your hurt."

"Right. It's what I know to do. I do it without thinking," Will said.

"And now that you've felt some of this pain, this disappointment that the future won't fix, when you go back to that moment in the doctor's office, what's that like?" Jim said, slowly heightening Will's awareness of loss.

"Difficult," Will said. Then he tearfully added, "Completely devastating."

Will felt awkward with a spotlight on his pain. Trying to recover he said, "It's hard, but you can't stay there. It's not like I'm *really* damaged goods."

"Right, and this is how you've coped. Reassuring yourself is how you've gotten through, but the pain remains," Jim said. "Can you go back there, back to that moment and the doctor's words?"

Will leaned forward, his eyes focused and welling with tears. Jim acknowledged the presence of his pain and the fears of feeling the sadness and grieving his disappointment. Will spoke from his grief about his struggle to make sense of his pain without feeling it. He felt he needed to keep it at a distance, because it wasn't to be trusted and it wasn't to be shared — that was weakness.

Will's shame covered the grief of his loss. He could see his grief because of his fear of being vulnerable and being deficient. Ironically, his way of coping with this loss kept the wound alive but inside, where no one could see, not even Will. The loss Will began to experience was the loss of being able to comfort himself through being a different kind of father, knowing he had no way to redeem his own pain.

If you can see yourself in pain, you can begin to see yourself as worthy of compassion and care that was previously dismissed along with your pain. When you see yourself in a new way, you may also be able to see others in a new way. As you experience your pain differently, leaving how you coped with this hurt in the past, you become a person who can deal with this pain, no longer needing to avoid it.

Expressing emotions and mourning losses

When you face your pain, you're better able to see the impact of setting this hurt aside. Expressing these emotions helps you to see more clearly how you see others and how you see yourself in relationship to the pain. Being able to be angry in response to a violation says something against those who have hurt you but also says something about your value and worth: "I'm worth defending, and I didn't deserve to be treated that way."

Will's risk to let go of his shameful feelings about his hurt and vulnerability enabled him to be more compassionate with himself and with Claire. As he recognized more clearly that his pain of disappointment wasn't a weakness but a wound, Will was able to express his sadness and anger toward his father.

"It mattered to me what my dad said. I tried hard to meet his expectations, but that didn't matter. It just never counted," Will said, his tone sounding cross. "His opinion mattered to me — he should have known that. He cared about himself, not about me."

"For so long, you've seen your father's actions as justified, not living up to his standards," Jim responded. "Your anger makes sense, especially because you see now, as an adult, that his standards weren't fair. He should've treated you differently It wasn't right what he did." Jim validated Will's struggle for his father's acceptance.

"Yes, exactly. Kids need support and to know they're important," Will asserted. "That's what I would've given to my kids."

Will's shame covered the anger that he didn't feel entitled to. He didn't want to become like his father. Under his father's critical eye, Will held back his anger, finding "good" reasons for his father's criticism and rejection. Over time, he held onto his shame of not being the son his father wanted him to be. He struggled to accept his own needs, including his need for care and support. Jim helped Will explore and expand his underlying emotions of grief and anger over his father's mistreatment of him as a child.

Shame is a covering emotion. It protects and blocks primary emotions when those emotions are associated with actions that are unacceptable or when the person herself fears that she's unacceptable. Allowing and engaging feelings enables you to access these underlying feelings, which provide important information about your experience that is more adaptive (see Chapter 3).

Facing yourself

The process of letting go of your shame and accessing your sadness and anger can provide you with a renewed awareness of your value and worth. As you work through your pain, letting go of shame in the process, you're better able to speak for your needs and take responsibility for your interests.

As Will set aside his fears and shame about his own vulnerability, he began to see himself differently. Facing the pain of his father's rejection and his anger over his father's ignorance of his own needs enabled Will to have greater compassion toward himself and toward Claire. In therapy, Jim asked Will what it would be like to show concern to himself as if he were a father caring for his son.

"I wouldn't be so hard on him, and I would want him to know that I believed in him. You know, like I really saw him as he is, not who I thought he should be," Will said.

"What would it be like to begin to offer *yourself* some of this care and concern now?" Jim asked.

"I never really saw that, but that *is* what I need. It's something I think Claire has been trying to give me, but I couldn't take it from her. I didn't accept it for myself," Will said.

Will's voice showed the peace he was beginning to feel as he recognized not only what he needed but also what he could give. Later, he turned to Claire and thanked her for being kind and caring. "I'm sorry that I couldn't take what you were trying to give to me. I can see now that you cared, and I just pushed it away." Ironically, Claire's efforts to show concern for Will triggered the couple's conflict pattern. Will was able to see this clearly when he was able to see how difficult it was for him to be compassionate to himself.

This experience gave him a new way to see Claire's own need for care. He had a similar need, one he struggled to take in. Will said to Claire, "I didn't know what to say to your needs. I know I tried, but I'm sure I came off as uncaring. I couldn't take it in. I just gave to you what I gave to myself: more expectations and little compassion."

Letting your partner in

Ultimately, shame turns us away from others and inward toward ourselves. Sharing the broken parts of yourself with your partner can open new ways to see your partner and yourself. In a safe and secure relationship, one in which your partner is responsive and accessible to your hurtful memories, there is no need for shame, and your partner's compassion can be a resource for your self-compassion.

Findings from studies of adult attachment show that partners in more secure relationships are more likely to have a more positive and better understanding of themselves and less likely to have struggles with anxiety and depression.

In EFT a therapist's goal in addressing shame is to help people face their fear of closeness and risk sharing and respond to new levels of vulnerability. The "hiding" function of shame makes these conversations more difficult for both partners in different ways. If you're battling negative feelings of self-acknowledgment, opening up to your partner means facing the internal tension of self-rejection head-on and finding the strength that comes from facing these internal struggles together. The affirming presence of your partner means you no longer have to walk alone in these painful places.

It's not uncommon for those who know about their partners' fear and vulnerability to steer conversations away from these painful places that can trigger anger and defensiveness if touched. You may feel hesitant to step into these places with your partner, for fear that these conversations will lead you back to your conflict pattern and reinforce the fragility of your relationship. It's best not to push these conversations but to respect the readiness of your partner to take on shame.

Responding to your partner's feelings of shame can be challenging. Your frustration is understandable, especially when your best efforts at care and concern are dismissed and disregarded.

Often, a person has good reasons for protecting past hurts and vulnerability with shame. So, it's important for you as a partner to also see the possibility of change by how you respond in these moments. Your care and concern are important even when they don't have the impact you desire.

Here are some ideas to keep in mind when your partner is trying to work through shame:

- ✔ **Shame is often colored by fear.** It's helpful to keep in mind that your partner is vulnerable and self-protective when his shame has kicked in.

- ✔ **Don't be surprised by feelings of fear and hopelessness.** Your partner is moving into new territory and facing emotions he or she has kept at a distance.

- ✔ **Keep in mind that a struggle with shame is an internal battle with oneself.** Your partner's defensiveness may feel personal, but when shame is the issue, the defensiveness is self-protection. *Remember:* It's not about you.

- ✔ **Show appreciation for the risks your partner is taking and the courage it takes to face shame.** If you can recognize that shame is something that's difficult to share or discuss, you're more likely to offer a place where your partner's vulnerability can be seen.

- ✔ **Your acceptance and acknowledgment of your partner's struggle are essential building blocks for safety and security.** Meeting your partner where he or she is in the process of letting go of shame gives him or her permission to take the next step.

- ✔ **You can communicate understanding through validating your partner's experience.** You don't need to have gone through your partner's pain to understand it. Just look for ways to understand how your partner has coped in the past and offer your support in the present.

When your partner has had a history of rejection and harsh treatment in his or her childhood, often without care and compassion, your partner may struggle to be compassionate to himself or herself, and to you. In turn, your partner may be more prone to being defensive around these experiences of the past. Keep in mind that your partner's emotional landscape may be very different from your own. Let your partner be your guide.

Will took a moment to gather his thoughts. Then he looked at Claire and said, "I know you tell me that I'm not a disappointment to you. It's hard for me to believe that because that is the message I heard most of my childhood. I held onto the hope that I could raise our kids differently, but the infertility has made that uncertain and made me feel like less of a man. I know that isn't the case, but I'm afraid that you might see me that way. I don't like to show you that part of me."

"Thank you for letting me know, Will." Claire responded. "I know the infertility has been tough on both of us, but in no way do I see you as a disappointment or defective. You're my husband, and I love you. None of these things will change that. I understand why you would feel this way, and I want to reassure you that I'm here for you."

Overcoming Broken Trust

In the development of EFT, Sue Johnson and her colleagues found that some couples would make significant progress in treatment but wouldn't fully recover. In a number of cases, these couples reported a specific incident that involved one partner's breach of trust or abandonment. In EFT, these events, where a partner's past actions were linked to an experience of relational betrayal, are considered *attachment injuries*.

Attachment injuries can appear as relational traumas that affect a couple's ongoing relationship. Attachment injuries can become the standard that is used to gauge whether a partner can be trusted and to what degree. Couples fail to develop deeper trust or risk vulnerability until these attachment injuries have been addressed. Attachment injuries create obstacles that block trust and must be worked through as a couple.

Attachment injuries focus on specific events where the degree of trust and dependence in a relationship changed. A partner's affair is an obvious breach of trust, but in other cases the significance of the injury isn't found in the action itself but in the *impact* the action has had on the injured partner or what the action represents (for example, abandonment or rejection).

Tyrone was laid off after his company restructured. He took his job loss personally, even though the company was disbanding his whole department. He looked to Justine for support, but she was preoccupied with the family's financial situation and responded with fear and contempt. "How could this happen to us!" Justine exclaimed. She fired off a series of questions upon hearing the news, each laced with anxiety and urgency. "Was it something you did? What are you doing to get a new job? What's your plan?"

Breaking the news to Justine was difficult for Tyrone because he felt ashamed, but her contemptuous tone and anxious reaction led him to hide his fears and vulnerability. In therapy, Tyrone acknowledged that, ever since then, he hasn't really opened up about his needs in the relationship: "Yeah, I just don't go there with Justine. I love her, but it's hard to believe she would care. She needs me to be strong."

Everyone has a natural tendency to seek care, contact, and comfort in the face of distress. This is a basic survival strategy for regulating emotional distress, especially in couples' relationships (see Chapter 2). Attachment injuries interrupt this natural tendency and tend to reinforce coping responses that increase the likelihood of isolation and alienation for couples.

Think of a time the trust in your relationship was challenged. How did you handle this? Use the following questions to assess the effect this event had on your relationship:

✔ Did you both talk about the event? What was the result?

✔ Does that event ever come up in your conversations? In your conflicts?

✔ Do you still have unresolved feelings as a result of that event? How do these feelings affect your relationship today?

✔ What steps did you take to strengthen the trust in your relationship after the event?

✔ What steps might you take in the future to strengthen the trust in your relationship?

Attachment injuries are inherently difficult to resolve because one partner has become both the source of and the solution for emotional pain. This results in making the relationship inherently insecure. Partners choose not to trust again as a way of managing this insecurity. Some injuries happen without the offender knowing it. These injuries can go unspoken in a relationship even though their impact affects a couple's level of closeness.

Couples develop secondary emotional responses around these injuries that make it difficult for them to move beyond the injuries, much less acknowledge them. The enduring impact of the injury can change the way couples make sense of their relationship.

Rick and Tracy sought therapy to communicate better and work out differences they had with the balance of work and leisure in their relationship. At the end of the fifth session, Rick responded in anger: "How can I really trust her? Not after the affair seven years ago. I want to trust her, but how can I let that go?"

Rick went on to share that even though it had been years since the affair, since starting therapy, he had been fighting nagging doubts about Tracy. "Sometimes I have images of Tracy having sex with that guy, and I wonder whether Tracy has told me the whole truth about him."

Although they've made progress addressing their concerns, according to Rick, "I want to trust Tracy, but I'm afraid to let down my guard. I'm not sure I'll ever be able to ever trust her again, at least in the way I used to."

Identifying common areas of broken trust

Attachment injuries can occur in a variety of situations. Some of these situations are more obvious than others. Here's a list of situations where attachment injuries are most common:

✔ Relationship betrayals, including infidelity and other intimate relationships

✔ Absence of a partner during a time of life transition (for example, the birth of a child, having a child move out of your home, retirement)

✔ Absence of a partner during a time of loss (for example, a miscarriage, the death of a child or family member)

✔ Absence of a partner during a time of uncertainty (for example, medical illness)

A partner's absence may be physical or relational. In a couple, partners who rely on each other count on each other to be there for them in the moment. They count on each other's physical and emotional presence. If your partner isn't providing the care and support you need, feelings of fear and abandonment become primary, and the whole relationship can be deemed unsafe.

An attachment injury can shatter assumptions that you have about your relationship, your partner, and often yourself. Janet remembered the exact moment when things changed with Matt — it was when he failed to respond to her grief following a miscarriage.

"He was distracted by work, and we had just returned from the doctor," Janet said. "I didn't know what I needed, and I dropped on the couch sobbing. He stood on the other side of the bedroom while I was weeping and said, 'It's probably the impact of all your hormones, you know, all this intensity.'"

Janet felt the absence of Matt's concern and the pain of his seeming disregard. She found herself turning away. Her questions revealed her shattered assumption: "I needed him, and he wasn't there. Can I count on him? Do I really matter to him?"

Matt could tell his response wasn't what Janet needed, but he felt overwhelmed, not knowing what to say or do in the moment. So, he tried to be hopeful and downplay the pain, increasing the distance between them.

An injured partner may have symptoms that are similar to having been exposed to a traumatic experience. These symptoms can include

✔ **Intrusive memories:** Attachment injury victims may experience unwanted memories of the injury event. These memories can include a mix of painful feelings, images, and memories from the past.

✔ **Avoidance and numbing:** Attachment injury victims may cope using self-protective responses such as emotional numbing, which creates an emotional distance in the relationship.

✔ **Hyperarousal:** Attachment injury victims may show signs of hyperarousal and vigilance around protecting themselves from potential threat in the future.

Carrie shuddered when she walked into the den and saw Jack switch the computer to a different screen. Her immediate bodily feeling was one of alarm and tension. Her immediate thoughts were: "Why did he do that? Did he break his promise? Is he back on those porn sites again? How can I trust him?" On the outside, she stayed calm, trying not to leave a hint that she suspected that Jack had been returning to the porn sites she had discovered months ago. She felt on edge as she studied his face for the slightest indication of guilt, desperately fearing he had returned to his old habit.

"Is everything okay?" Jack asked politely.

Carrie felt the tension of whether to admit her fear, seek Jack's reassurance, and face a possible eruption of their cycle, or simply respond as if she had no concern. She chose the latter and returned to her reading. In her mind, she replayed the memories of the first time she found the hundreds of pornography files on Jack's computer. She fought her feelings of disrespect and distrust as she left the room to distract herself with a favorite TV show. Then the storyline of a celebrity's affair flashed across the TV screen, and her fears rebounded with a vengeance.

The more you are without emotional or physical support, the more likely you will find it a challenge to regulate your emotional experience.

These responses make sense given the threatening experience an injured partner has faced, but over time these protective responses contribute to increased distress in the relationship. Patterns of self-protection create blocks in the relationship that prevent couples from healing past wounds and engaging new levels of intimacy.

Discovering the blocks that protect

Attachment injuries usually emerge after a couple has made progress in therapy. Couples who report less emotional distress and react to each other less may be getting along, but not touching deeper places in the relationship that they've walled off. As the emotionally focused therapist invites couples to take more emotional risks in trusting each other, these injuries come to life.

Sometimes the injury is openly discussed as an ongoing complaint made by the injured partner. The injury doesn't get resolved because the offending partner dismisses the significance of the injury. In other cases, the offending partner's rejection of the injury silences discussion of the injury, and the couple gets along without ever talking about the past hurt. In both cases, the attachment injury remains dormant until the couple is asked to begin to trust one another in new ways.

Attachment injuries can remain unresolved because of injured partners as well. An injured partner may not be receptive to the offending partner's efforts to address the injury. The injured partner may say, "I just can't trust that he has really changed. How do I know that he really means it? Those are just words." Likewise the injured partner may be afraid to risk being vulnerable again. He may say, "I can't let my guard down. I let it down once before. It's just too much of a risk." Repairing attachment injuries requires more than an apology — an injured partner must feel that his or her partner cares and is connected to the pain that the injury caused in order for the remorse and apology to heal.

When you or your partner deny, dismiss, or rationalize a relationship injury, this prevents the injury from being resolved. These past hurts may remain hidden for some time, but the impact on your level of trust in your partner remains.

EFT researchers have identified seven steps in the process of resolving an attachment injury. Typically, couples aren't able to resolve these injuries on their own. The following steps describe what the process of working through an attachment injury may look like if you're the injured partner. The first two steps involve uncovering the blocks of self-protection associated with the attachment injury:

1. **Identify the injury.** The essence of this first step includes naming the specific violation of trust. This includes reviewing a time you felt alone or abandoned by your partner. Reviewing these memories can bring up a mix of intense emotion associated with the injury. Your partner may dismiss or deny the importance of this event or your more intense feelings. The first step requires identifying the injury and connecting to the emotions around the injury.

2. **Feel the impact.** In time, your therapist helps you see more clearly the ways in which the injury impacts you and your relationship. The key to this step is being able to express your understanding and experience of this violation of trust at a deeper level. You're able to see how the injury damaged the closeness and trust in your relationship. Anger often softens to sadness as you begin to see and experience the loss and hurt from the abandonment or rejection of your partner.

Note: The remaining steps are in the following sections.

Kate and Ethan found peace after several sessions with their emotionally focused therapist. Kate felt less pressured by Ethan and experienced more space in the relationship. Their fighting lessened as each of them understood their conflict pattern and the vulnerabilities that they felt in trying to cope with the painful distance that had developed between them. This suddenly changed in therapy, when Ethan erupted with intense anger, recalling how he couldn't trust Kate. He had learned during the week that Kate had a detailed personal conversation with a former boyfriend on Facebook. He summarized his feelings saying, "How can I trust her? I thought we had dealt with this."

Jim helped Ethan identify a past injury when Kate had developed a close relationship with a work colleague. Ethan had been traveling extensively for business, and Kate befriended a younger man, Craig, at the office, whom she spent hours with outside of work. She also confided in Craig her disappointment and her growing concerns about her marriage. In one moment, Kate defended her actions by saying, "At least Craig understands me. He listens to me. He's there for me, and you're always gone."

At that moment, Ethan felt violated, as though Kate had chosen another man over him. Her words still haunt him today, but when he thinks about that conversation, he tries to put it out of his mind.

In the sessions that followed, Jim helped Ethan express the anger and hurt he felt in his relationship with Kate specific to this former relationship. The therapy helped Ethan get underneath the rage of abandonment that often ran just below the surface in many of their conflicts. Kate expressed fear at Ethan's anger. "I try to keep my distance. I want to heal our relationship, but I get overwhelmed by his anger, and I stay away." Jim helped the couple see their conflict pattern and the ways that Ethan's angry protest and Kate's protective distance made sense in light of this injury that remained unresolved.

This made room for Ethan to begin to explore this past injury that blocked the couple from regaining trust and security in their relationship. Ethan expressed feelings of panic, when he recalled the moment he learned about Kate's relationship with Craig. "I felt my whole world slipping away," Ethan said. "I had to be gone for business, and I knew she was lonely, but I had no idea she would turn to another man. It broke my heart."

Facing damage done

The emotionally focused therapist helps the injured partner explore how the injury has impacted the relationship and an injured partner's sense of worth. As this unfolds, the injured partner is better able to identify the needs he had at the time of the injury and the damage done to his trust in his partner. The therapist also helps the offending partner begin to accept and understand the injured partner's pain and need for a secure and trusting relationship. An offending partner responds with remorse and regret when impacted by these hurts and the hoped-for needs that weren't met. These needs of trust and support are often evidence of that partner's commitment to the couple's relationship.

Here are the next three steps in the seven-step process (see the preceding section for the first two steps):

3. **Hear the pain.** Your partner becomes less defensive as there is more focus on the pain of the injury. Shifting the focus onto the impact of the

injury on you and your relationship opens new ways for your partner to see you and the value of your relationship, not just the injury.

4. **Grieve the loss.** As you're able to express a deep sense of loss related to the attachment injury, your partner is confronted by the impact of his or her actions that led to the injury. This grief is shared from a place of vulnerability.

5. **Acknowledge responsibility.** In this step, your partner moves forward to take responsibility for his or her actions and their resulting impact. Although apologies may have been given in the past, this time the remorse is expressed with both empathy and responsibility for the injury. The expressions of remorse and regret are more believable because you can feel your partner's more vulnerable emotions.

Ethan shared more openly how he still struggled to trust Kate as much as he did in the past. "I don't really worry about her relationship with Craig anymore," Ethan admitted. "It's more the lingering questions of whether I'm enough for Kate. Will she one day just give up on us and leave me? That's what keeps me up at night."

Jim helped Ethan engage his fears about the future of the relationship and the losses he felt more personally.

"I feel like I lost confidence in how she sees me," Ethan said. "If she could turn to someone else this way, how do I know she really wants me? At the end of the day, I don't know if I matter to her."

Kate was used to seeing Ethan's anger and was unprepared for the depth of his grief. Tears fell from her face as she heard how much her actions had shaken Ethan's confidence in her love. She, too, felt the losses in their relationship. The carefree moments were fewer, and Ethan seemed more guarded, especially when he was out of town. Kate said, "I hate that my words don't comfort him the way they used to. I do my best to convince him, but I feel his distrust, and I just shut down. It kills me to see that what we once had is no longer there. I had no idea that what I did caused so much damage."

Kate's experience of Ethan's pain and loss helped her better see the losses in the relationship and prompted a deeper level of remorse and responsibility. Kate was able to meet Ethan in the grief she felt and express this with heartfelt regret. Weeping, she said, "I'm so sorry, Ethan, for turning away from you like that. I hate what this did to us. I hate what this has done to you. I know it's hard for you to really believe what I say, but I'm really so sorry."

Beginning to trust again

In the final stages of healing an attachment injury, the offending partner provides a caring and protective response to the needs of her partner. When trust is repaired in the relationship, the couple can move to positive emotional patterns. Couples who have successfully resolved an injury in treatment reported greater levels of forgiveness toward their partners.

Here are the final two steps in the seven-step process (see the preceding sections for the first five steps):

6. **Reach out.** Finally, you're able to reach out to your partner with your needs for comfort and caring. As a couple, you've fully faced the injury, but this step is an additional step of vulnerability because you're asking for the care and comfort that you haven't received. You're requesting the reassurance and support you needed but didn't get.

7. **Respond back.** The response of your partner provides an antidote to the injury. As you work through your injuries together, you can tell a new story about your relationship. A story that includes an understanding of how the injury happened, including the offending partner's response and how, through this process, you both have found a way to heal this past hurt.

Ethan found hope in Kate's apology and her own grief for their relationship. He had let go of his anger, but at times he was still gripped by fear. Jim helped Ethan express his fears of rejection and worries that Kate would give up on him. In the midst of experiencing these fears, Ethan was better able to see his needs.

"Right now, what do you need from Kate?" Jim asked

"I need to know that she's there. That she's not going away," Ethan said. "I need to know that she chooses us, that she chooses me."

"Would you like to ask her for that right now?" Jim said. "Can you look her in the eye and say in your own words, 'I really need to know you'll be there for me. I really need this when my fears take over. I really need your reassurance that I'm who you want to be with.'"

Looking at Kate, Ethan said, "I do. I need to know where I stand with you, Kate. You mean so much to me. I know I don't show it much, but I need that, too. I need to know that I matter to you."

In that moment, Kate responded to Ethan's need for reassurance. This opened the way for the couple to share more openly about their needs in the relationship. Jim helped Kate be more explicit about her needs in the relationship, particularly those times when she felt alone in the relationship. Both of them were able to move toward greater strength and security in the relationship as Kate engaged her needs (see Chapter 8) and Ethan softened his tendency to control and pursue Kate (see Chapter 9). Resolving their attachment injury, both Ethan and Kate were able to face their fears and needs together, instead of focusing on the injury from the past.

Forgiveness is a critical step in the process of recovery for partners who have attachment injuries. Acts of forgiveness include accepting the offending partner's taking responsibility and expressing remorse, apologizing, and working to rebuild trust again in the relationship. Injured partners are less likely to punish offending partners because they've let go of their self-protective responses.

Couples who take these steps of forgiveness are more likely to form more positive assumptions about their marriage, their partners, and themselves. Typically, there is greater commitment to the relationship among couples who are able to move through the processes of healing an attachment injury.

The process of healing an attachment injury strengthens the security couples find in their relationship. Making mistakes and recovering from them strengthens a couple's bond. When you avoid these injuries, you weaken your relationship, but in facing them and finding healing, security is built in your relationship.

Chapter 12

Dealing with Infidelity

*I*nfidelity often spells the end of a relationship. Many couples fail to make it back from the broken trust and shattered memories following an affair. Divorce is two times more likely as a result of an affair, and infidelity is often listed as the principal cause for divorce. For those who decide to stay married after an affair, significant challenges and obstacles must be overcome in order to regain trust.

Healing may take time, and some wounds appear long lasting. As one injured partner described it, "As time goes by, things are getting incrementally better for me. I feel like an animal in the wild that broke its leg. It goes on, lives on, and has happy days. It survives — maybe even thrives — but it has a permanent limp now. I feel this way about my marriage, too."

Infidelity causes couples to face a storm of negative emotions. Betrayal, deception, abandonment, and rejection intensify many of the common patterns couples have for coping with negative emotion. Couples who aren't able to work through this intense negativity often fail to develop the resilience in their relationship necessary for healing and growth after the affair.

Recovery means facing the emotional realities in a relationship. Another injured partner described healing as a process: "We sometimes struggle with the decisions my husband made in the past. However, I acknowledge the work he has done today to grow from the experience. And he acknowledges the pain, sadness, and anger I struggle with. We've found that recovery isn't about remembering how to be in love or romantic with each other. It's about discovering yourself (good and bad), sharing these parts with each other, working to heal the wounds of the past together, and making decisions every day that you can be proud of. That's what has worked for us."

In this chapter, we give an emotionally focused therapy (EFT) understanding of affairs and how to heal from them. We want you to be clear on the challenges and opportunities facing couples who seek to rebuild the broken trust in their relationship. Throughout this chapter, you find practical suggestions for dealing with the emotional challenges of recovery.

Gaining an Emotionally Focused Understanding of Infidelity

Affairs create attachment injuries. These traumatic relational experiences interrupt your ability to turn to each other for what you need most in times of distress. Your instinct may be to seek comfort or care from your partner, but after an affair, your partner is both a source of comfort and a source of pain. Simply put, you may feel abandoned, rejected, and betrayed. This mix of emotion can erode the strongest emotional ties and diminish the most positive emotional memories.

Initially, couples cope with the effects of infidelity individually. Partners use the coping resources they've practiced for years in their relationship, but often they use these resources in new ways.

Helen had complained about the lack of closeness in her relationship with Pierce for years. Now she bitterly complains about his unfaithfulness. The effect on Pierce is largely the same — her scorn and contempt keep him at a distance. "I try to help Helen see that I'm different and that I want this relationship," Pierce said. "But after a while, I just give up and try to keep the peace." The couple's pattern is much the same as it's been for years, but now it's organized around the affair.

Relationship patterns may contribute to the dynamics that make affairs more likely, but they don't *cause* affairs. Partners cause affairs. Dealing with the offense *and* the pattern is necessary for healing a relationship.

The process of forgiving an emotional injury like an affair requires partners to connect their secondary emotions of contempt, anger, and disgust to underlying primary emotions and vulnerability. Partners who are able to access their feelings of loss and sadness are better able to find compassion and care for themselves and their partners. The process of healing requires finding new levels of empathy and care. Forgiveness is found in being able to empathically step into the shoes of your partner at an emotional level that takes seriously the impact of the affair on your relationship and your partner. Forgiveness begins with whole-hearted remorse from the partner who had the affair and may include regret from the injured partner whose actions to cope with this injury caused harm.

An emotionally focused therapist helps both partners to face the painful emotions that define the aftermath of an affair. Focusing on the negative patterns that perpetuate escalating emotions, the therapist engages partners in transforming these patterns with new, more responsive ways of connecting through compassion and love. The emotionally focused therapist facilitates change through experiences that offer each partner a safe and secure relationship where deep understanding of hurts and fears promotes new understandings and opportunities for couples to re-engage a relationship that has become damaged and distressed.

Researchers have found that EFT is successful in helping couples recover from infidelity. In one study, Sue Johnson and colleagues found that two out of every three couples treated for attachment injuries recovered from these injuries through EFT. These couples sustained these changes when evaluated three years following treatment.

In this section, we explore how affairs impact both partners in different ways. An affair is an action that one person takes that damages the trust in the relationship and injures the other partner who was not involved. This injury can be traumatic. The process of healing must address this injury. In many relationships, the affair is a symptom of an enduring problem in the relationship. Not all affairs happen for the same reasons.

Seeing infidelity from both sides

In a distressed relationship, partners find themselves playing more fixed roles. Over time, and through more relationship distress, these roles become patterns that define the couple. In relationships where there has been an affair, these patterns may influence a partner's decision to go outside the relationship. However, these patterns by themselves don't cause an affair.

Travis worked long hours chasing a partner position in his accounting firm. This often meant he was traveling most weeks of the month. He told Tina that he would have to travel at least until he secured his place in the firm, and she accepted this as a temporary sacrifice for a better future. As the years went by and the demands of raising children fell increasingly on her, Tina grew more and more frustrated with Travis's work. Similarly, Travis was tired of having to defend his efforts at work and countered by pointing to the lifestyle that they both enjoyed. Eventually, he withdrew emotionally from Tina and her constant disappointment. They shared a classic pursue-and-withdraw pattern.

"I didn't realize what was happening," Travis shared in session. "I shut off my feelings at home, at least as far as Tina was concerned. There was no pleasing her, and it felt like she was always unhappy with me."

"So, you kept your distance emotionally?" one of your authors, Jim, asked.

"Yeah, but not intentionally," Travis said. "I just hated how I felt at home. So, when I was away, I tried not to think about it. Then Claire, my associate, gave me all this attention, and we were working well as a team. That opened the door."

"*You* opened that door! *You* left this relationship, not me," Tina's anger flashed in response. She was tired of hearing Travis rationalize his absence and the affair based on work demands and her negativity.

Jim responded, matching her intensity: "This is where you feel Travis doesn't get it, right? You hear his explanation as an excuse. He really does have a part in this and it does matter how he responds to you. Like not going away, not shutting you out. The affair is much more than avoiding problems and that's what you hear him saying. Right?" Jim made sense of Tina's anger over the affair, making clear that the affair is separate from other issues in their relationship.

"Exactly. Things weren't good between us. I know that," Tina acknowledged. "But his way of dealing with it was to run away. And he did that with her."

Tina's anger and frustration were fueled by the affair as well as Travis's tendency to avoid his emotions and withdraw in silence. His withdrawal from Tina made him more vulnerable to an affair and their inability to connect at a deeper emotional level increased the pain and loneliness for both partners.

The impact of discovering that your partner has been unfaithful can be emotionally devastating. Injured partners may find their sleep or concentration interrupted by vivid images and disturbing memories. Similarly, those injured because of a partner's affair find it difficult not to obsess on details of the disclosure and the infidelity itself. Over time, an injured partner may emotionally detach from the relationship and through numbing out, avoid emotions related to their partner's violation.

In the following sections, we point out common emotions felt by both partners in a relationship following an affair.

Common emotions felt by injured partners

The emotional impact of infidelity on the injured partner often results in a number of powerful emotional responses, including the following:

- ✔ **Anger:** Confronting a betrayal leads to primary emotions of anger at the injustice of an offending partner's unfaithfulness. Rage over the abandonment and protest over the violation mean that this anger is powerfully intense.

- ✔ **Avoidance:** Feeling the traumatic impact of an affair may send injured partners into emotional avoidance as a primary coping strategy. Avoidance can provide a short-term emotional equilibrium in a time of crisis.

- ✔ **Depression:** Facing the shattered assumptions about your relationship, your partner, and yourself can lead to a deep sense of personal uncertainty and loss of hope. These negative feelings can linger, and periods of depression are common.

- ✔ **Vigilance:** Losing trust in your partner because of another relationship can fuel feelings of fear and uncertainty. Jealousy may also erupt in the face of fears about a partner's commitment (or lack thereof). Efforts to cope with these fears can result in active efforts to assess and monitor the actions of an offending partner.

- ✔ **Powerlessness:** Finding yourself on the injured side of betrayal is disempowering. Discovering your partner's independent actions may undermine your own confidence in your ability to influence and impact your partner.

- ✔ **Fear of abandonment:** Dealing personally with feelings of rejection and negative feelings about your worth can fuel self-doubt and fear of abandonment.

- ✔ **Loss of personal and sexual confidence:** Making sense of your partner's infidelity can trigger questions of your own confidence and value. Measuring yourself against what you know or imagine about the other man or other woman can undermine your confidence in your sexual and physical desirability.

Common emotions felt by the partner who had the affair

Partners who are seeking to rebuild a relationship after having had an affair face their own mix of emotions, including the following:

- ✔ **Guilt:** Walking through the pain of healing can trigger deep feelings of regret and remorse for the offending partner.

- ✔ **Shame:** Dealing with one's own decisions and their impact on others can increase feelings of self-reproach and a questioning of one's worth and value.

- ✔ **Defensiveness:** Coping with an injured partner's raw anger and intense rejection often results in defensive responses, particularly as efforts at repair are dismissed or ignored.

- ✔ **Loss:** Assessing the costs of infidelity on others and one's own life means facing changes and losses. Offending partners must grieve losses in the face of their own decisions. This may complicate efforts to grieve as the offending partner may get lost in feelings of shame.

- ✔ **Uncertainty:** Facing the emotional upheaval of a partner's response to an affair may leave the offending partner confused and uncertain regarding what to do in the future and in the present.

- ✔ **Relief:** Admitting to an affair brings relief from lies and deception. An offending partner often has to manage significant anxiety in covering up his or her other life and the fear of being found out. Relief may also be felt in facing old issues in the relationship through confronting the affair.

Shattered images

An affair can shatter your assumptions about your relationship, your partner, and yourself. Discovering your partner's infidelity can be traumatic, shaking the essential beliefs you have about your relational world. You can see this impact of these shattered assumptions in three areas:

- ✔ **Your beliefs about your relationship:** "I believed if you stayed committed, did the right things, made your relationship a priority, you were safe. That's naïve. There are no guarantees."

- ✔ **Your beliefs about your partner:** "I thought I knew him. I thought I could trust him. How could he do this to us, to me? I'm confused about anything that's related to 'us.' Everything has been turned upside down. I can't really count on him in the same way, especially when I really need him."

- ✔ **Your beliefs about yourself:** "I used to feel really confident. Now I'm not sure. She said I mattered to her and that she was happy, but that was when she was with the other guy. I can't be sure if I'm enough for her."

Loss is a common feeling when your core beliefs are shaken. Injured partners often need both time and space to grieve. A betrayal of trust can leave partners vulnerable to depression because these losses can impact their own sense of value and well-being. Anger and avoidance can be powerful ways to manage despair and a loss of hope. They can also prove challenging obstacles to couples and partners seeking to move beyond these losses.

Recognizing that not all affairs are the same

Not all affairs are the same. They have different emotional impacts, often depending on the level of involvement of the offending partner. There are three types of affairs an offending partner could be involved in:

- ✔ **Emotional affairs:** These relationships include emotional attraction but no physical involvement. Here, a partner may turn to someone outside the relationship to meet unmet emotional needs. Business relationships, friendships, or online chatting can form the basis for more intimate relationships. These relationships are more common among women than men. People who have emotional affairs are more likely to say they fell in love with the other person. Emotional affairs are more typical of couples with low levels of relationship satisfaction. Although women are more prone to emotional affairs, women also find it more difficult to forgive a partner's emotional affair than other types of affairs.

- ✔ **Sexual affairs:** These relationships are based more on sexual involvement. Men are more likely to have sexual affairs than women are. In these affairs, greater emphasis is placed on the sexual experience, and less attention is given to the relationship with the other person. Although men are more prone to these types of affairs, they find it more difficult to forgive their partners for sexual affairs than other types of affairs.

> ✔ **Sexual and emotional affairs:** These affairs pose the most difficulty for couples who seek to rebuild a relationship after infidelity. Partners in these relationships tend to be among the most dissatisfied in their relationship.

The type of affair can change over time as relationships evolve. The complexity of the affair is one of the factors that may make recovery difficult, but other factors can influence a couple's progress in recovery, including the following:

> ✔ The injured partner has a history of low self-esteem or has difficulty trusting others.
>
> ✔ The affair is one in a series of broken promises and betrayals.
>
> ✔ The offending partner is unwilling to discuss the affair or acknowledge wrongdoing.
>
> ✔ The offending partner is unwilling to break contact with the affair partner.
>
> ✔ There are other problems in the relationship unrelated to the affair.

Understanding attachment strategies and why they matter

The ways partners respond to and then cope with the aftermath of an affair make sense in light of each partner's unique relationship histories (see Chapter 6). Relationship histories have also been tied to why partners get into affairs in the first place.

For withdrawing partners — that is, those who tend to shut down or avoid their emotions — an affair can offer an emotional form of escape. For pursuing partners — that is, those who tend to anxiously need contact from their partners — an affair can compensate for what they aren't getting in their relationship. (See Chapter 6 for more on withdrawing and pursuing.)

Rich felt life closing in on him. Downsizing at work triggered longer hours, and the demands of raising two young children left him without much of a life. He believes his affair was an escape from all the pressure he felt. He didn't want to deal with the constant demands, and his sexual liaisons helped him feel more like himself even though he knew they meant little to him personally. "I don't expect Marie to believe me, but that affair was more like a distraction, not a relationship. I never looked at it like what we have," Rich said.

Partners who tend to withdraw in times of relational distress are more likely to avoid unwanted emotion. Researchers have found that partners who rely on these attachment coping responses are more likely to have an affair that has less emotional involvement. For Rich, the affair was a way to avoid pain in his life. It gave him an outlet and a sense of freedom.

In contrast, partners who tend to pursue others in times of relational distress are more likely to seek out an affair as compensation for a distant partner. These partners may have an affair as a way to cope with feelings of loneliness and their partners' neglect. An affair can be about finding someone who will care about "me."

Marcia admits that she was playing with fire. She had been flirting with a neighbor for months, sometimes in front of her husband, Greg. Greg never seemed to catch on, and Marcia's need for affection and attention soon gave way to the affair. "I knew it was wrong, but part of me just felt like Greg had lost interest, and I was alone all the time. I felt special again," she said, "like I was wanted. The romance was intoxicating. It's been a long time since I felt that way with Greg."

Attachment strategies can also impact how partners respond to an affair. If a partner uses a more withdrawing attachment strategy, she may have a more difficult time forgiving her partner and letting go of the affair. Research has shown that the more you cope through dismissing and avoiding your emotional response, the likelier you are to retain stronger feelings of resentment. This coping response may also block your ability to find empathy for your partner who hurt you.

Greg knows he must forgive Marcia for the affair. He doesn't like to talk about it because he finds himself getting upset for days. He would rather just put the affair behind them and move on. He admits that even though he can put these things aside, he still has a hard time trusting Marcia and resents that her actions have made this so difficult. He expected more of her and finds it hard to grasp why she would make such a stupid mistake.

Partners with a more anxious or pursuing response to relationship distress respond to a partner's affair by seeking their partners' reassurance. You may feel intense negative feelings about yourself and your value, so it seems only logical to seek reassurance from your partner — even though your partner's actions are a source of your insecurity. The result of these strong needs for reassurance lead more pursuing partners to suppress their negative and angry feelings.

This strategy works temporarily because when they receive some acknowledgment and support from the offending partner, these negative feelings return — only stronger. If this is your coping response, you're more likely to show intense anger and hostility. These negative emotions often color how you see your partner and the security you feel in the relationship. Your partner's reassurance is fleeting in the face of an overwhelming flood of angry feelings. You may get stuck on these feelings, and a sense of sadness and failure may result.

Marie would do whatever it took to save her relationship with Rich, even after finding out about his affair. She told him that she was fully committed to working through the issues that caused the affair, if only for the sake of their marriage and children. She described herself as weak and unpredictable because out of nowhere she found herself in intense anger and rage. She hated the impact this has on Rich, but she felt helpless to contain her pain — especially in moments when Rich was more open and caring. She saw this as her flaw, a reason Rich may not want her.

Overcoming Affairs and Healing Injuries

Affairs damage relationships, but they also damage people. Infidelity may be a sign of a failing relationship, but its impact on the person having the affair is different from the impact on the person who has remained faithful. It's helpful to remember that most disclosures or discoveries of an affair come as a shock. They're emotionally traumatic.

Sharon remembers what it was like to learn of her husband's affair: "I heard it first from one of his friends. I can remember that like it was yesterday, like everything froze in place. All my worst fears and suspicions were being confirmed, and it felt right and horrible, all at the same time."

As Sharon described this moment, her face grew tense and her eyes focused. "I was in shock at first," she said. "Then when I saw him, I felt rage. All these feelings of betrayal, all the hours of talking myself out of my fears, came out in raw anger. He tried to explain, but I heard nothing he said. My heart was cold, and my anger was fierce. My world changed in that moment, and there was no going back."

Coping and relationship first aid

Partners healing from affairs are dealing with emotional injuries. These injuries can be traumatic and require special care for both those who were injured and those who offended. There are several ways in which partners can bring first aid to the wounds of their relationship. These include facing flashbacks, building boundaries, and creating confidence by talking about an affair.

Facing flashbacks

Flashbacks involve re-experiencing images, experiences, and negative emotional experiences from the past. Flashbacks aren't unusual and can be emotionally disruptive. It's helpful if you talk about ways to handle these unwanted memories as a couple. Sometimes, you'll need to cope with these experiences on your own; other times, your partner may be helpful in walking through one of these disruptive experiences.

Flashbacks may be triggered by certain events, locations, and even smells. You can be triggered by simple actions that your partner does, actions that trigger a painful memory or spark a fear.

For example, Carl forgot to call home one evening as he stayed late to work on a project. When he walked in the door two hours late, Sylvia nervously asked why he was late. "I had to work late and forgot to call," Carl said, in an anxious way. Sylvia was triggered when Carl looked away and seemed to avoid eye contact, and memories of Carl's disclosure of the affair came rushing back.

If your injured partner has a flashback, do your best to respond in an understanding way, and avoid responding defensively. Offer your partner reassurance and comfort, which can help your partner in these difficult moments. Later, take time to identify the trigger together. In some cases, you can take steps ahead of time to avoid triggers. Or, if the triggers are unavoidable, you can better respond to the situation and your partner.

Keep in mind that sometimes a partner may need to walk through his or her flashback alone. If you need to cope with your flashback on your own, it may mean that you don't feel safe enough to risk trusting your partner when you're re-experiencing a traumatic memory.

Offending partners also may have intrusive and unwanted memories of the affair. Sharing these experiences with an injured partner won't be helpful, so you need to find another resource of support to address these experiences. This way, you can take seriously the effect of the affair *and* protect your relationship and partner from intrusive memories.

Infidelity experts Douglas K. Snyder, Donald H. Baucom, and Kristina Coop Gordon, in their book *Getting Past the Affair* (Guilford Press), provide helpful guidelines for managing a flashback following the discovery of an affair. Review the following steps you can take, either as an injured or offending partner.

Ways to manage your own flashback

If your partner had an affair and you're dealing with flashbacks yourself, try the following methods for managing those flashbacks:

- Reflect before you respond to your partner.
- Identify your feelings and what triggered them.
- If your partner asks what's happening, help him or her understand your feeling in the moment.
- Share the trigger and plan a response (if the trigger was something your partner did).
- Share the trigger and your emotional response (if the trigger was a memory about the affair).

✔ Help your partner know what you need in the face of these strong emotions.

✔ Work together on steps to remove triggers, to identify supportive responses, and to develop ways to care and comfort yourself following a trigger. This may include taking time for personal meditation, journaling, or physical activity.

What to do with your partner's flashback when you're the one who had the affair

When your partner is having flashbacks after you've had an affair, you need to respond with understanding. Here are some suggestions:

✔ Give space for your partner's fear. These thoughts are often involuntary.

✔ Invite your partner to share what he or she is feeling (if you're aware the flashback is happening).

✔ Make space for your partner to share or not share. This shows you're focused on your partner's needs.

✔ If invited, help your partner find what triggered his or her memory.

✔ Stay focused on the present. Respond with support to your partner's present distress.

✔ Stay connected. Provide reassurance by being understanding and available to your partner's strong emotions.

✔ Take steps to reduce triggers, if possible.

Building boundaries

Making clear boundaries is necessary to protect your relationship from a former affair partner. These boundaries will be more effective when they're clearly stated and imposing to outside parties. Managing the possible encounter with the other person involved in the affair requires a level of planning and awareness. Boundaries work well when they can be kept; try not to set unrealistic and inconsistent boundaries.

Disclosing to an injured partner any boundary crossings is important to protecting efforts to rebuild trust. Be sure to tell your partner about any contact you've had with a former affair partner and the situation under which you saw this person. These contacts may be incidental, but disclosure is important in restoring the safety and security in your home.

Creating confidence by talking about an affair

One way to begin to rebuild trust and confidence in your relationship involves having open conversations about the affair. When talking about the affair, you and your partner need to have a clear idea of the conversation's purpose and focus. Keep in mind that you're working with your future in mind. Healing an affair and working through painful emotions takes time. The pain may result from the damage caused by the affair and its aftermath as offending partners struggle to acknowledge a painful past in the relationship prior to the affair.

Couples who share their experience have more to offer each other in gaining an understanding of their relationship than those focused on isolating the past and not recognizing its impact on the present.

Setting limits on your conversation helps to create a structure that provides protection for the power of negative emotional patterns to take over and organize around defensiveness and avoidance. You may want to put limits on when you do talk about the affair and when you don't, or how long conversations about the affair are tolerable. Finally, limiting details of discussions about the affair can protect the injured partner and the relationship from vivid details of experiences. For example, talking about detailed sexual activity may create more obstacles and painful memories to overcome. Injured partners should know the extent of their partners' physical involvement, but without all the details.

Healing as a process of forgiveness

The process of healing from an affair takes place in three phases. Research has shown that as couples work toward healing, they're more likely to find that their relationship has increases in trust and that feelings of security return. It makes sense that as you work through the relationship hurts and loss of trust, you would build greater trust and security through taking risks and needing security to take those risks.

In the following sections, we cover the three phases of healing from an affair.

Apples and oranges: Avoiding comparisons

Typically, affairs focus exclusively on meeting two people's desires. Couples who are married, raise children, and share financial commitments have, by nature, more complicated relationships. Affairs are free from the demands of couple relationships. It's not fair to compare a marriage to an affair. The relationships are different: more exclusive, less complicated, and illicit. It's not possible to make a fair comparison between your partner and someone with whom you were involved in an affair.

Affairs are often associated with excitement, fun, and few demands. Infidelity can be one partner's attempt to change his or her negative experience of a spouse or marriage. The power of an affair can also be driven by its secrecy, where an unfaithful partner's efforts to keep a secret relationship going increases the intensity of the emotions shared. The nature of an affair will make it virtually impossible to make a fair comparison.

Phase 1: Weathering emotional storms

This phase is marked by a range of responses, including anger, ambivalence, introspection, and greater self-awareness. This is a time when intense emotions are expressed and then avoided. Couples find it difficult to manage conflicting feelings. Confrontations can be intense exchanges between two people who are finding it difficult to express their pain and at the same time hang on to some sense that they need each other.

Phase 2: Understanding the affair

The second phase of healing from an affair focuses on understanding the affair. At this stage, the immediate impact of the affair wanes, and more attention is given to making sense of the affair and why it happened. This process still has emotional intensity, as partners try to construct an understanding of what happened and how they'll make sense of the affair in their future as a couple.

A common challenge faced by couples in this phase is finding a way to talk about the affair without further damage. Injured partners may focus on their need for details about the affair as a way to unmask past deception and to gain understanding about the affair. Other couples focus only on "business-type" conversations, handling day-to-day matters but avoiding the pain and uncertainty of the affair.

Emotional and practical supports help partners navigate the stormy emotional patterns that persist. Although the emotional volatility of the crisis has passed, strong eruptions of emotions can be common. Friends and family can be key supporters in healing at a personal and couple level, particularly as support from a partner is either uncertain or unavailable.

Couples who gain an understanding of the affair itself and its role in relating to a relationship are able to move more quickly through the process of healing.

Phase 3: Building trust

Healing is a process of regaining trust. The final phase of recovery marks a couple's efforts to re-engage and explore investing in new levels of commitment together. The offending partner's efforts to take responsibility for the affair and other actions that previously undermined trust in the relationship open the door for trust to be renewed. New risks are taken to trust again and reach for care and comfort. Overcoming the betrayal is found in efforts to reconnect at intimate levels. Couples find new ways to reassure each other and to take risks in sharing their needs. The focus now is on the relationship, not the affair.

Offending partners seeking to repair their relationship often feel like their apologies have little effect until this final phase of healing. The injury of affair and the survival responses of an injured partner make it difficult for the injured partner to trust the offending partner's words enough to risk accepting remorse. Offending partners often apologize for their actions, but it takes getting to this phase for an offending partner to really grasp the damage done to the relationship and to his or her partner. Regret and remorse at this level open the way for restoring trust.

Healing the Injury of Infidelity in Emotionally Focused Therapy

Healing attachment injuries in EFT follows a series of steps, moving partners toward risking and reaching from their softer side of emotion. These steps are the same ones followed in healing attachment injuries (see Chapter 11). In this section, we focus on the specific issues important to working through an affair.

Walking through emotional storms

The first stage of recovering from an affair requires facing the emotional storms of relationship betrayal. Emotions are raw as partners realize the emotional costs of the affair. This is a difficult period for couples because the injured partners may shift unpredictably between intense anger and periods of detachment. These times of avoidance and withdrawal become means for protecting themselves from their partners and the emotional intensity the affairs have wrought.

This emotional roller coaster creates periods of emotional confusion for both partners. An injured partner may respond vindictively, seeking revenge on a partner or the partner's lover. An injured partner may feel paralyzed by the pain over what they lost. The unpredictability of emotional responses creates an emotional storm, fueled by the shock and despair of a partner's unfaithfulness.

In EFT, we approach affairs as attachment injuries that block partners' efforts to seek care and comfort from one another. These blocks to care and comfort make sense for an injured partner because the defenses they use provide not only a sense of protection but also a way to manage the emotional chaos they often feel.

There are two primary steps in beginning to work through an affair using EFT:

1. The therapist helps the injured partner begin to open up about the emotional impact of the injury. The therapist helps this partner begin to engage and share these overwhelming emotions, helping the injured person express the impact of the betrayal.

2. The therapist anticipates the offending partner's defensive responses that often result in response to Step 1. These reactions are a failed attempt to respond to the pain and hostility of the injured partner and often organize around attempts to dismiss or disregard the pain being expressed by the partner they injured.

Tina found a suspicious note in one of his suits and confronted Travis about the situation. Travis admitted that he had a brief affair with a work colleague that ended a year ago. He reassured Tina that it was over and that he no longer had contact with the woman after he changed departments at his company. Tina and Travis sought therapy to save their relationship. Tina was ambivalent about whether they would make it, but she felt little hope after months of painful arguments and avoidance around Travis's affair.

In therapy, Tina relived the night she confronted Travis. She described the moment of his confession in vivid detail: "It was like watching a priceless vase falling to the ground and breaking into a thousand pieces." Tina's emotions were intense as she moved from furious accusations to times of silent disgust. "You made our marriage a joke," Tina said, with fury in her eyes. "Do you know how humiliating it is for me to know you invited her to our home and played me the fool? How could you?"

Travis sat frozen. His apologies and attempts at reassurance had little effect. When he did try to explain, he felt Tina's withdrawal and was powerless to repair the damage. His explanations felt like excuses to Tina, and she doubted he really understood what he had done to her and their marriage.

"I'm not sure what else to say," Travis said. "I've apologized every way I know how, and I've tried to make this right. I want to find a way to help us move on."

Tina glared in silence. Her disapproval seemed to disqualify Travis's attempt to show commitment to their future.

In these early stages, Jim created a safe space for both Tina and Travis to feel the impact of this injury. Sometimes Tina's angry protests gave way to feelings of isolation and abandonment. These moments were brief, as her pain often touched off her anger. Travis felt less pressure to respond to Tina directly after she pushed away several attempts. He, too, felt pain and shame over what he had done. Jim seemed to get this, even though Tina had little patience for Travis's regrets.

Making sense and recovering hope

As a couple confronts the emotional impact of an affair, they create opportunities to better understand the affair and their relationship. The shattered assumptions about their relationship require new understandings and experience. As they move beyond the initial stages of sharing the emotional impact of the affair, they're better able to understand the influences that led to the affair. They also begin to have more realistic assumptions for what they can expect from each other at a time that their relationship bond remains largely broken.

Emotions are more than feelings — they carry meaning as well. So, when an injured partner is able to grieve the loss of what he believed he could trust in a relationship, he's also expressing the value of that relationship. Your hurt is an expression of something that matters.

In the next phase of attachment injury work, the emotionally focused therapist helps couples to deepen an understanding not only of the affair but also of their relationship by helping them move through the varied emotional responses they have to the affair and each other. Working through the pain and loss from the affair helps couples see and understand how they responded to the affair and how they respond to each other. This opens the door for couples to begin to see each other again.

There are three steps in EFT to help couples move to a deeper understanding of the affair and their relationship:

1. **Move toward pain.**

   Moving beyond the protective avoidance of the injured partner, the emotionally focused therapist invites the injured partner to experience the losses, disappointment, and hurt that resulted from the affair.

2. **Promote compassion.**

   Shifting toward more vulnerable emotions opens new opportunities to understand the impact of the affair on the injured partner. The experience of an injured partner's primary emotions often primes feelings of compassion from the offending partner. The emotionally focused therapist gets partners to express and engage these softer, more vulnerable emotions more effectively.

3. **Open up.**

   The injured partner shares more directly about the injury and grief and fears about the loss of the relationship.

The more Tina talked about the affair and its impact on her, the more she was able to talk about its personal impact. "I took things for granted. Things like counting on the fact that Travis would be faithful to me," Tina said, choking back her sadness. "That's what's gone, the confidence that he's there for me. I used to trust it, but now I can't even remember what it felt like to feel safe with him." Jim helped Tina stay with her hurt and sadness around her loss. Through this, she was able to express a deeper, more vulnerable level of grief, one Travis hadn't noticed before.

Travis felt the impact of Tina's grief in a new way. Most conversations they had turned quickly from pain to blame. In these moments, Travis responded by explaining and often minimizing the meaning of the affair or promising to do better. His efforts failed to comfort Tina, and as a result, Travis endured Tina's rage but kept his distance. As Tina poured out her hurt, Travis felt caught between wanting to pull away, feeling ashamed about what he had done, and wanting to comfort Tina in her pain.

"I've done a lot of damage here," Travis said, searching for what to say. "I broke her heart. I can see that," he said softly, with regret. Tina was used to hearing Travis's regrets, but this time she heard something different, his sorrow.

The emotionally focused therapist walks alongside couples as they uncover new layers of the brokenness between them. Exploring these losses helps both partners experience and understand what's important about their relationship. The pain and fear can result from an ongoing struggle to reconnect or get their partners' attention. Jim helped Travis make room for Tina's distrust and acknowledge her loss from his own depth of grief.

Sometimes Tina wonders whether they can actually recover from the affair. "Some days I tell myself I'll just have to accept this and move on, but other times I look at what this has done to our marriage, and I wonder if the wounds will really ever heal." She feels better that they're actively discussing the affair because she struggles with uncertainty and her own doubts: "Did he tell me the whole truth? Do I really know what's going on? Can I really count on the changes he says he has made?"

Tina's fears and hurt take on new meaning. Working through her fears and identifying her needs with Jim in therapy have helped Tina and Travis reach toward the next step of recovery.

 Couples who develop a more realistic understanding of the affair and their relationship are more likely to move toward forgiveness. In EFT, this understanding comes as the therapist helps partners access and make sense of moments of emotional distance and emotional vulnerability. Partners are better able to see how they respond to fears, hurt, rejection, and abandonment and what choices they want to make moving forward.

Offering forgiveness and risking trust

The final phase of healing an attachment injury following an affair involves rebuilding trust, exploring loss, and risking sharing one's needs. Forgiving may not mean forgetting, but it does mean letting go of feelings of distress and unmet needs from the injury. Letting go of feelings of anger, grief, sadness, and hurt may be necessary for resolving past injuries and significant disappointments.

At this point, the injured partner's negative feelings are less intense and more predictable. Each partner has a better understanding of his or her negative emotions and the effects those emotions have on the relationship. Partners tend to have a less distorted view of each other and their relationship. The injured partner is better able to see the offending partner's weaknesses and strengths and is better able to manage negative emotions and take the risk of trusting that he or she can truly begin to emotionally rely on his or her partner.

Some partners don't reach a point of reconciliation from an affair. The obstacles to safety and security may be too significant for some relationships to overcome. In this chapter, we focus on couples who *do* make it to the other side of an affair. Couples who are able to make it through find ways to take new steps together in trusting and investing in a relationship that matters to both partners.

Working toward reconciliation requires both acts of forgiveness and new responses of trust. Sue Johnson, in her book *Hold Me Tight* (Little, Brown), suggests that an emotionally effective apology involves the following:

- A clear appreciation for the pain caused to your partner
- Acceptance and acknowledgment of your partner's emotional response to the injury
- Acknowledging responsibility for what you did that caused the injury
- Expressing regret and remorse
- Offering reassurance to support and help with healing

In the final stages of attachment injury work, the emotionally focused therapist helps partners take steps toward forgiveness and reconciliation. These steps include the following:

- **Taking ownership:** The offending partner takes ownership for the affair and resulting injury. The offending partner shows responsiveness to the injured partner's pain through expressing empathy, regret, and remorse.
- **Reaching for caring:** The injured partner faces fears of rejection and abandonment and asks for caring and comfort that weren't available in the relationship at the time of the affair.
- **Responding with comfort:** The offending partner responds in a supportive way, restoring trust and building a new basis for caring and comfort in the relationship.

In EFT, the therapist helps couples move to primary emotions (see Chapter 4) because they prompt more adaptive responses of caring and concern from each partner. Fear blocks partners' efforts to connect, and as a result, partners are less effective in communicating their needs and desires. Engaging partners' fears and working through what blocks sharing them is a crucial step in the EFT approach (see Chapter 10).

Infidelity heightens partners' fears associated with their need to know that they're important and cared for in a relationship of primary significance. This is particularly true for these final steps, where injured partners are asked to accept an offer of forgiveness by the offending partners but also risk trusting them again in a most vulnerable way.

Travis felt Tina's pain. It was the affair, their relationship, and the doubts she carried about herself. Tina lost confidence in herself and struggled in a profound way with whether she could really believe Travis when he said he "loved her" or that she was "special to him." Jim helped Tina express the fear she now held and the pain of what she had lost.

When Tina was in pain, she spoke from her pain and Travis felt an ache inside to comfort her. "I want to know if I can hold her hand," Travis looked at Jim, unsure whether Tina would want his comfort now. As Jim checked with Tina, she nodded yes. "I am so sorry," Travis said. "I know what I did was wrong and I hate myself for it. But worse, I see what this has done to you and to us. I'm sorry for the pain I've caused you and these doubts you now feel. It's my fault, and I am so sorry."

Through Tina's pain, Travis understands what his actions and the affair have done. He's able to stay more connected to Tina as she expresses her emotion in a primary way. Instead of pulling away in defensive explanations, he tries to comfort Tina by acknowledging her pain and his part in it. He acknowledges her losses and offers his care.

Tina's biggest fear was that Travis was somehow just settling for their life together. She knew that the affair was out of character for Travis and that he was committed to the family. She just didn't really know if he wanted her, at least the way he used to. "It's good to know that he cares, but it's hard to really believe it," Tina said to Jim. "I know he's sincere when he apologizes like this. That feels good, hopeful even. It's just that, deep down, I have these lingering doubts. Does he really love me? Can I really count on him?"

Jim asked Tina to talk about these doubts and fears. She had trouble finding words because she struggled with a deep sense of uncertainty. "He tells me all the time that he's different, that we're different. I can see that. But . . ." Tina paused. In tears, she continued, "I'm afraid to really let him in."

"Do you know what you need from him in these moments of terrible fear?" Jim asked.

"I guess I just need him to tell me and to show me, over and over again," Tina said.

Vulnerability is a game changer. For months, Tina and Travis talked about the affair and the changes they had to make if their relationship was going to survive. Travis couldn't count the number of times he apologized or promised things would be different. Likewise, Tina didn't hold back from letting Travis know how she thought the affair had damaged their family and their relationship. In all these conversations, someone was defensive, and although their intentions were good, the result tended to be the same: Travis felt like there was nothing he could do to address the fear Tina felt when the affair took center stage.

This moment was different. Jim asked Tina to share her fear and let Travis know what she needed. As she struggled to find words, Travis held her close and said, "I get it, honey. It's going to take time. I'll be here for you, I want you to count on that, and I know this is going to take time. I'll be here." Unlike before, Travis remained focused on Tina's need and was able to respond effectively to her fear. His presence in her moment of need brought a real sense of safety and care.

Forgiveness doesn't mean that you condone an affair or minimize its destructive impact on your relationship. It *does* mean that you're able to gain a more balanced understanding of your partner and his or her unfaithfulness, developing more empathy, and letting go of the strong negative feelings toward your partner.

For Tina, the most important thing is not what happened with Travis and the affair but what both she and Travis have learned in working through it. "It's something that happened in our relationship, but it no longer defines our relationship," Tina said, reflecting on where she is now. "Of course, I wish this had never happened, but I'm grateful for what we have now, having walked through this together. One of the most important things for me is that Travis is more open now. He talks about what he's thinking and feeling. I feel like I know where he is. For the longest time, I had to make myself believe he cared about me and about us. I'm starting to believe it again. It's hard, but we've been through a lot to get to this point."

Protecting Your Relationship from Affairs

Infidelity by itself does not end a relationship. It's what a couple does with the broken trust and emotional consequences that makes or breaks a relationship. Couples who know this also know that prevention begins with taking care of each other and your relationship. Your commitment to each other is evident both in what you say and in what you do. So, being open about your needs, fears, and concerns is important in staying close and building a secure relationship.

Recognize that feelings of sexual attraction are normal and expected, even with others who aren't your partner. Knowing how you deal with these feelings is important in setting boundaries and honoring your partner and your relationship. Being clear about your expectations and how to support each other furthers the felt sense of safety in your relationship.

Researchers studying infidelity would say that having a strong relationship and strong commitments to be faithful may not be enough to keep your relationship from an affair. Here are some steps you can take to protect your relationship:

- ✔ Discuss expectations and standards you have as a couple for the kind of relationships you'll have with others outside your relationship.

- ✔ Pay attention to danger signals and fears that may result. Responding to these moments protects your relationship from the insecurity that can easily result in rejection and abandonment.

- ✔ Invest in activities that increase your relationship satisfaction.

- ✔ Develop friendships with others who will encourage commitment and provide support for your relationship.

- ✔ Know yourself and where and when you may be vulnerable.

- ✔ Invest in friendships where you can be open about developing interests or personal risks that could lead to an affair.

- ✔ Take your relationship to therapy. Avoid ignoring relationship issues and get help for problems before they become longstanding.

Couples rebuilding their relationships after affairs often point to positive changes that resulted from learning from their mistakes, taking new steps of commitment, and experiencing greater closeness. Old relationship patterns are challenged, and changes are made because many of these patterns from the past created obstacles to resolving the threat and damage infidelity wrought. The infidelity creates a crisis that partners must respond to in new ways. Being more assertive, staying engaged in conflict, and risking vulnerability provide new resources for couples who have worked through the broken trust of infidelity and built a more resilient bond as a result.

Part IV
Moving Forward Together

The 5th Wave   By Rich Tennant

©RICHTENNANT

"When I asked you to put on some mood music, 'On Wisconsin' wasn't the mood I was going for."

In this part . . .

*I*n this part, we take a look at how couples work out the everyday issues of life from the security of an emotionally effective relationship. You find ways to increase your awareness and responsive to your partner and strengthen positive emotion to promote a thriving relationship.

This part also offers practical steps that guide you in strengthening the intimacy you share. You see the importance of sharing stories and attachment rituals as ways to enhance the meaning and value in being a couple. You also find our insider advice for finding a good emotionally focused therapist and getting the most out of therapy as a couple.

Chapter 13

Finding New Solutions to Old Problems

*W*hen couples are able to face their fears in a responsive and supportive way, the everyday struggles of life together are much easier to address. Past issues that triggered escalating fights no longer have the same power to drive partners apart. Still, most couples will confront common issues that can trigger a return to previous patterns.

If you're like most couples, you won't jump as often to your reactive position when you have a more emotionally secure place to stand. Gaining awareness of your experience and your partner's experience builds confidence as well as awareness. When you can see your conflict cycle, you're better able to find the exits and, at this stage, take more constructive steps to address differences and difficulties.

When you work together at a more secure emotional level, you can navigate differences, and you're less likely to get caught in intense cycles of negative emotions. Stepping out of these patterns also enables you to invest more positive emotions and develop confidence in your ability to work together.

Couples at this stage in emotionally focused therapy (EFT) see issues in their relationships as less of a threat. Instead of having issues divide them, leaving partners to face off against each other, couples are better able to join around their differences and strengthen their relationship as a result.

In this chapter, we focus on steps you and your partner can take to deal with practical issues in your relationship. These pragmatic issues may have been triggers for escalating your negative patterns. This chapter helps you find and practice ways for understanding specific issues in your relationship and taking practical steps to respond when these issues arise.

Getting Back on Track after the Cycle Returns

Conflict patterns are common. You can work hard to avoid them, but it's more realistic to expect that they'll show up from time to time. These patterns are built on the coping responses two partners bring to a relationship and are common when facing distress. The sooner you identify a pattern, the quicker you can take steps to work out of one of these cycles. Increasing your awareness of your pattern is crucial to being able to recognize it in motion. See Chapters 4 and 5 to deepen your understanding of your conflict pattern.

Too often, couples are neck deep in their conflict pattern before they realize that it has taken over and they're caught in a vortex of emotional reactions. However, if you know your tendencies and those of your partner, you stand a chance of exiting a reactive process before it has a negative impact. In the final stage of EFT, therapists help couples anticipate the triggers for these patterns, as well as identify steps that can be taken to avoid greater emotional insecurity.

Refusing to panic

Slipping back into a conflict pattern can be alarming. Couples who fought hard to work beyond their patterns can start to panic when past patterns of defensiveness return. In these moments, it's important to recognize that fear is often at work. Name it for what it is. Your fear is a warning sign, as well as information about what you need in the moment. Naming your fear helps you see what's really going on in the moment. Speaking your fear helps both you and your partner see what's happening in the moment (see Chapter 10).

Slow down. Keep in mind that your emotional process is also a physical process. When defensiveness and tension rise in response to an argument, your body will respond. Noticing bodily responses increases your emotional awareness and helps you identify what's happening in the moment. If you can recognize your triggers and responses, you can begin to slow the process, stopping a cycle before it takes over.

Julie knew their argument had crossed a line. She had pushed Bryan too far. He told her he couldn't handle the arguing any longer and then left the room. She waited, knowing that if she followed, things would only get worse. Ten minutes later, she found him reading a book upstairs. Julie tried to engage Bryan again, and he ignored her, eventually leaving to run some errands.

"This is just like it used to be," Julie said to herself. Her heart raced as she thought back to the nights she spent waiting for Bryan to return. "He swore to me that he was over going to the bar, but how do I know he's not back there again?" She could feel the tension mounting as she began to play out what she would say to him if he'd been out drinking.

Then she stopped and remembered her therapist's words: "You'll likely find yourself in this cycle again. Now you know a way out. You have to learn to trust that."

Julie tried to slow down and replay this advice. She remembered how Bryan said that he would close down when he felt he needed to escape. Julie played back his words when, in tears, he said, "I go away when I'm overwhelmed. I can't meet your needs and I know it. I feel like a failure."

Julie took a deep breath and held onto this moment, remembering that Bryan did care about her and did want to make their relationship work. She decided to give Bryan his space and let him know when he returned that she wanted to start over on the conversation, when he was ready, rather than press in on him the minute he walked through the door.

Regaining your balance after an escalating argument may take time. You may need to step away from a difficult conversation. Taking a break can be helpful to stop an escalation, particularly when you're able to see your cycle and what has triggered you. Taking a timeout to slow yourself down creates space to tune into your underlying emotions and to listen to your unspoken thoughts and feelings. Seeing your responses in terms of your conflict pattern gives you a new resource in facing difficult topics. In these moments, regulate your own emotional responses by taking a moment to calm yourself, reflect on your experience, and use your breathing to put the brakes on an escalating situation.

Talk with your partner about a recent time when you got caught in your conflict pattern. Try to avoid talking about the issue and instead focus on what it was like in that moment when you were pushing in or pulling away from your partner. What was going on inside of you when you felt the need to go after your partner or to pull away from him or her? Answer the following questions about that moment:

- ✔ What was the first sign that you noticed you were reacting to this situation rather than simply responding to the issue being discussed?

- ✔ What did you do to let your partner know you were headed into trouble?

- ✔ What could you do differently to let your partner know that you were getting triggered?

Check in with your partner. Review your answers and respond to the following questions:

✔ What did your partner need from you in that moment?

✔ What did you need from your partner in that moment?

✔ How could you let your partner know what you need in the future?

Seeing the big picture

Julie was able to step back and see a different side of their pattern by recognizing her reactive responses in their argument and remembering what it was like for Bryan in the past in similar moments. Their work in therapy made clear to her that Bryan wasn't rejecting Julie — he was just overwhelmed by their conflict. Similarly, Julie didn't mean to pressure Bryan, but she often felt panic when he withdrew from her. This time, Julie held onto the idea that past patterns can repeat themselves, but you can find a way out of them.

When you've done the hard work of making sense of your patterns, you have a bigger picture of what they're all about. EFT helps couples find their way in the midst of disorganizing emotions by being able to access emotions that offer meaning and needed information. When you know your pattern, and you're more aware of your primary emotions (see Chapter 4), you have a clearer understanding of the needs you both share in your relationship. Seeing the big picture means you can step back from the intensity of a heated moment of conflict and reflect on your experience as well as what's happening in your relationship.

Ask yourself the following questions:

✔ What am I responding to?

✔ What's behind my reactive response?

✔ What's going on inside of me?

✔ What do I know about my partner?

✔ How does my partner respond when I react?

✔ How do I let my partner know what I need?

You will inevitably get caught in your pattern, particularly in stressful situations that trigger longstanding differences or concerns. Deepening the security in your relationship gives you new options for responding to situations that trigger your pattern. Being able to recall your pattern is a first step in your escape from escalation.

When Julie pressed Bryan about the credit card statements, Bryan reacted by shutting down. Inside, he heard a familiar refrain: "You're a screw-up. You're not doing it right. Nothing will get done if it's up to you."

Later, Bryan said, "I didn't handle that well. I knew I was late on a payment and felt bad about that, but I shouldn't have shut down. I want to do this differently."

Bryan knew that Julie felt like she wasn't important to Bryan when he didn't seem to pay attention to details that mattered to her, and especially when he withdrew. She experienced this as rejection. They knew their dance from the inside out, and it got the best of them this time.

Tackling Common Sticking Points

Building a solid bond in your relationship means facing differences and challenges that come up between you increasingly relying on each other for love, care, and support.

In this section, we cover some common areas that challenge couples. You and your partner will be better able to face these challenges when you've established a more emotional, secure relationship.

In-laws and extended families

Family relationships can be both a resource and a challenge for couples. Extended-family relationships may provide social, emotional, and practical support, especially in the early years of a marriage. At the same time, these relationships can create obstacles between partners that can endure for years. In-law relationships are, by nature, third-party arrangements, and these third parties often expect or hope to influence the choices couples make.

Rick and Diondra have the biggest fights after family gatherings with Diondra's family. She values her close-knit family and expects Rick to join her at most family occasions. After ten years of family gatherings, Rick still sees himself as an outsider. Diondra wishes Rick made more of an effort to get along with her parents, but he remains passive, after being blamed for Diondra's decision to continue pursuing her career rather than start a family. Rick and Diondra often fight on the way home from family events because neither of them feels the other supports what's best for their relationship.

Research studies show that couples who lack supportive relationships with their extended families are more likely to report lower marital satisfaction over time. The effect of these relationship issues can be felt by couples well into two decades of marriage. If couples have challenges in these relationships, they're more likely between the mother-in-law and daughter-in-law and father-in-law and son-in-law.

Relationship dynamics get more complicated when parents or partners try to use their influence indirectly. This can happen when a wife tries to influence her husband by complaining about his behavior and at the same time indirectly comparing him to her father. In the same way, a husband might ask his wife to tell his mother that they won't be making it home for the holidays, because the husband usually gives in to his mother's disappointment.

In-laws and extended family members often require couples to navigate a three-way relationship. You may find this challenging, particularly when there are emotional issues at stake. One of the key signs of trouble occurs when one person tries to influence another person through a third person. In these situations, the emotional needs of the relationship aren't being directly addressed. These patterns can show up in different ways:

- ✔ **Escape:** One or both partners flee negative family experiences and expect their relationship to meet emotional needs that their families did not. Although the couple's relationship can be healing in many ways, the expectations of unmet needs from the past can trigger a couple's pattern.

- ✔ **Competing attachments:** Couples can get split by extended family relationships when partners get caught between the obligations they feel to a parent or family member and their emotional commitments to their partner. These loyalty conflicts can cause couples to re-engage their reactive patterns when insecurity is fostered from competing allegiances.

- ✔ **Go-between:** Here partners put their partner in the middle between themselves and their parents. For example, in a marriage, one spouse assumes the responsibility for managing the family relationships of both families. When you're caught in the middle, you can feel like it's impossible to meet everyone's expectations, and you find that *your* needs aren't important or are taken for granted.

- ✔ **Taking sides:** This is a two-against-one pattern that is similar to the escape pattern, but in this case one of the partners is the outsider. If you're on the outside, you feel pressure from your partner to conform to in-law expectations. This pattern can escalate when you're compared to one of your partner's parents, who is seen as an ideal father, mother, or spouse.

Your approach to coping with relationship distress rooted in family relationships is also shaped by your family history. How you cope in the present can impact your partner in direct and indirect ways, especially when your family is involved. Being able to talk about these moments can help couples use the security in their own relationship to explore new ways of responding to old family patterns.

Trying to change your partner's behavior in a relationship you aren't a part of seldom pays off. As much as you might hope your wife can help her mother accept you, your best shot at making this relationship different is through relating to your mother-in-law directly. Putting your wife in the middle is putting all three of you in a no-win situation. Similarly, you may wish that your husband had a better relationship with his family, but no amount of advice you give him will make a difference unless he engages in that relationship differently. The expectations and pressure from these situations are more likely to increase conflict rather than improve these relationships.

You and your partner chose each other, but you didn't choose your partner's family. If you're like many couples, you and your partner have to work at navigating the expectations of family members. These expectations and family values can come between couples in a number of areas:

- ✔ **Gender roles:** In-laws may express opinions about the roles women and men should take in a family.

  Sara's family expected that her husband, Carl, would be the "breadwinner." They express their concern for Sara, who is juggling a career and parenting, while Carl pursues his passion as a freelance journalist.

- ✔ **Child rearing:** Grandparents may express their opinions about the parenting practices and decisions of new parents.

  Lauren's parents offered to pay for her daughter's parochial education. Paul feels like her parents are intruding and trying to influence the values of their daughter.

- ✔ **Values and money:** A couple's decisions about receiving or giving financial support from other family members can lead to division.

  Grace resents Peter's refusal to support her desire to reduce her work schedule to part-time. Peter argued that the couple needs the income to support his aging parents, because in his family that's expected. Grace believes Peter is choosing his parents over her.

- ✔ **Affection and love:** Families have particular ways of sharing affection. Family rituals including holidays and celebrations can symbolize commitment and love.

  Terry fights the pressure he feels from Sara to attend most of her family's holiday gatherings. He often feels he's an outsider at these events and resents that Sara insists on not missing events because her parents would feel that they were no longer important to her.

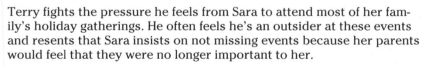

Couples can get caught between differing family expectations when fears about the priority of the couple's relationship are challenged by allegiances to a partner's extended family. These issues can create competing attachment relationships where one partner questions the commitment of the other or questions his or her own worth and importance. When these issues are critical to a partner's felt security in the relationship, attachment injuries can result. (See Chapter 11 for steps to address these injuries.)

Theresa felt abandoned by Warren after Warren's mother criticized Theresa's decision to return to work following the birth of the couple's first child and Warren sat in silence. Theresa was furious with Warren for siding with his mother and not standing up for a decision that they both made together.

Take a moment to think about the family expectations that impact your relationship. Answer the following questions:

- ✔ What is one expectation that your family or parents have that impact your partner? What does your partner do in response?
- ✔ How do you respond to your partner if he or she raises a concern about your extended family's expectations? What does your partner need in these moments?

Now take time to discuss your answers as a couple.

- ✔ Do these issues trigger your conflict pattern?
- ✔ How have you found ways to avoid getting into your cycle over these issues? Make sure your partner knows what you need in these moments.

Finances

If you're like most couples, you spend a significant amount of time talking about money and related issues. Couples can get caught in an escalating cycle when financial issues trigger fears about worth, influence, and responsibility. Dealing with money decisions requires you to define priorities and expectations, even if these decisions mean that you and your partner will handle your money issues separately.

In many cases, it isn't a financial issue that activates a couple's conflict pattern but how a partner handles a monetary issue that has symbolic importance. The key concern is whether the issue the couple is facing creates a threat to their felt security. Financial stress can threaten a couple's sense of stability, just as arguments about handling money can threaten issues of trust. In both situations a partner may ask, "Can I count on you to be there for me when I need you?"

Some financial decisions made unilaterally by one partner can impact the couple to such a degree that this decision creates an attachment injury. When one partner's excessive debt, gambling losses, or investment speculation has a significant impact on a couple's financial well-being, attachment injuries often result. (See Chapter 11 for steps to resolve these injuries.)

Jordan bid on a weekend resort package at his company's silent auction. The bidding went higher than he expected, but he was pleased to surprise Felicia with an extravagant weekend getaway. Felicia's initial appreciation withered as she soon realized that Jordan had just committed to a trip that they couldn't afford.

Jordan responded, "This is a once-in-a-lifetime trip. Let's not worry about the money."

Felicia interrupted, "You need to check with me before you commit us to an expense like this. Besides, this really feels like something you want for yourself more than for me."

Jordan withdrew in anger after hearing her accusation, and their cycle began.

Other times, couples have trouble discussing money issues because they approach the issues of saving and spending with inherently different values. One partner's solution can become another partner's problem when they hold different beliefs about the role of money in their relationship. Here are some different ways partners may look at money:

- **Security:** Money is like a security blanket.

    Jill's father was often unemployed when she was a child. She has vivid memories of nights when the family didn't have enough food. She takes comfort in the savings that she and Lisa have acquired and hates to spend a dime that they don't have to spend. Lisa understands Jill's history but hates that they can't enjoy spending some of the money they've worked hard to earn.

- **Pleasure:** Money is a source for the good life.

    Reggie sees himself as a generous man and appreciates that others see him that way as well. He enjoys giving to others for the joy that it brings and thinks nothing of spending lavishly on others or himself. Money may not buy love, but in Reggie's world, it can buy some happiness. Carol isn't so sure when she pays the credit card bill and sees their unpaid balance rise.

- **Control:** Money represents options and choices for self-determination.

    Megan takes pride in her ability to live independently. She's hard working and values the choices that her earnings bring. The more financial resources she has, the freer she feels. Jeff appreciates Megan's work ethic but finds her concern with control a bit obsessive, especially because she refused to accept his parents' support for a down payment on their first home.

- **Status:** Money signals success.

    Doug doesn't mind the long hours. He makes good money and has plenty to show for it. He expects to stretch their resources now and then for the right purchase. Violet is afraid that they spend too much on luxury items and that they should save more, but Doug dismisses her concern, saying, "What's the point of my hard work if we don't have something to show for it?"

When couples encounter differences in these values, they can easily become divided. Often, fear is at the root of these concerns. These fears can be about any of the following:

✔ **Circumstances:** Economic pressure puts strain on a couple's relationship. If your partner doesn't share your values, you can feel more vulnerable. Spending can impact your sense of well-being and security. If one of you is more risk tolerant and the other is more risk averse, the same financial decision can be experienced by one person as an opportunity and by the other as a threat.

✔ **The relationship:** A couple's struggle in financial decision making can foster distrust. If you find comfort in control and security and your partner values pleasure, his purchases may seem foolish and unwise. If you're the partner who values status or pleasure and your partner questions your decisions, you may feel judged and as though you need to defend not only your decision but also your sense of worth. A couple's lack of trust breeds fear, and you can easily get drawn into a cycle without knowing it.

✔ **Personal value:** When couples share financial resources and responsibilities, financial decisions can impact how they rely on each other. If you make independent decisions and you fail to consult your partner, your partner may fear that you don't trust him or that his opinion doesn't matter. Other times, differences in opinion about a "wise financial decision" can communicate distrust in the perceived competence of a partner. In both of these cases, the one-down partner often feels fear about his or her own worth in the relationship.

Dealing with debt can have a significant impact on a couple's well-being. Research findings suggest that the more a couple's debt increases, the more likely they are to argue and the less likely they are to spend time together. Arguments about money tend to last longer, include more negativity, and are rarely fully resolved. It isn't a surprise to see that finances are a common reason couples cite as a reason for divorce.

Take a moment to think about the conversations you and your partner have about money. Answer the following questions:

✔ Which of the four values — security, pleasure, control, or status — best describes how you think about money? Which of the values best describes your partner's view of money?

✔ When you're discussing money together as a couple, are you more likely to push to a conclusion on an issue or postpone and avoid getting to a specific decision? What is your partner's response to your actions?

✔ Often, fears get in the way of couples being able to make progress in resolving money issues. Which fear do you identify with? In moments when this fear takes hold, what do you need most from your partner?

Now talk with each other about your answers. Do money issues trigger your conflict pattern? How have you found ways to avoid getting into your cycle over these issues? Make sure your partner knows what you need in discussions about money and planning your future.

Sex

Couples feeling heightened levels of distress limit or cut off physical intimacy because emotional safety erodes from the relationship. Others go through the motions, but their sex becomes increasingly one dimensional. In contrast, couples who have worked through their conflict patterns and faced their fears together find renewed passion in their sexual relationship. The security they reclaimed brings with it a greater freedom to explore and play at an intimate level.

Other couples continue to find sexual intimacy a relationship minefield. Even though a majority of couples face adjustments and difficulties at some point in their relationships, couples who struggle sexually can find that attempts to improve this area of their relationship trigger their conflict cycles.

Some couples face significant obstacles in making their relationship more secure sexually. Infidelity and other attachment injuries can block a couple's efforts to connect in a more open and vulnerable way. (See Chapters 11 and 12 for steps to resolve these injuries.) Other partners have histories of childhood sexual abuse or rape that can disrupt feelings of safety and security in sex. Couples need an appropriate level of support for dealing with these sensitive issues. A competent therapist with experience helping others through past traumatic experiences is needed as a first step in helping couples walk through the real fears and hurts associated with past abuse.

Insecurity and anxiety dampen sexual desire and increase the likelihood that couples will experience negative feelings being associated with sex. Specific sexual problems including low sexual desire, premature ejaculation, and erectile dysfunction can become the focus of a couple's sexual life or a reason to avoid sex altogether. At times, efforts to address these issues can heighten anxiety and performance pressure that exacerbate these problems.

Partners' relationship histories often inform their response to feelings of insecurity in their sexual relationship. Partner responses may mirror similar ways they cope with other threatening experiences including conflict:

- **Anxious partners:** Anxious partners tend to approach sex seeking reassurance and as a way to reestablish an emotional connection. Physical affection is important — maybe even more important than sex — because one partner's ultimate goal is reassurance.

 Carly struggled in her marriage to feel close to Tim. She often accommodated his sexual advances because, for the moment, she felt desired. But Carly also made it clear that sex was not enough for her and would often criticize Tim's lack of affection.

- **Avoiding partners:** Avoiding partners tend to approach sex with more focus on the physical rather than relational experience because, at an emotional level, they're keeping their distance. Sex can become more about a physical connection than a relational one.

Jessie used to feel alone with Blake in bed. "We were physically close, but it felt distant. He cared about whether I had an orgasm, but it was more about how he did in bed than my needs."

Negative cycles in a couple's sexual relationship lead to less desire and lower arousal. If you're in one of these cycles, you're likely to feel more insecure and avoid being physically intimate. If sex has been a place of criticism and complaint, it may take time and effort to face your fears from the past.

Sexual issues — including loss of sexual desire or premature ejaculation — can heighten performance pressure and anxiety in your relationship, especially if you're making progress at strengthening your relationship. Struggles with arousal or erectile dysfunction can trigger underlying feelings of inadequacy and shame. It's important to keep in mind that the pressure to get your sexual relationship back on track can have an adverse effect of undermining desire.

Anxiety and pressure are the enemies of sexual arousal. Keep in mind that reassurance and moving at your partner's pace are critical for calming fears that can take sexual desire off course. Safety comes before vulnerability, and couples who feel safe with one another are free to explore and play.

As you take steps to face these fears and rebuild the security in your relationship, you may continue to face sexual issues related to low desire, premature ejaculation, and erectile dysfunction. Couples who are able to reassure each other emotionally are better able to address performance issues in their sexual relationship.

Take a moment to think about your sexual relationship and think of two or three times when you and your partner had great sex. Answer the following questions:

- ✔ What made these moments special for you?
- ✔ What percentage of your needs were met physically, emotionally, and relationally in these moments (for example, physical = 80 percent, emotional = 60 percent, and relational = 90 percent)?

Think of two or three times when you and your partner had what you would say was disappointing sex. Answer the following questions:

- ✔ What made these times difficult for you?
- ✔ What percentage of the disappointment was related to a physical, emotional, or relational need not getting met (for example, physical = 70 percent, emotional = 70 percent, and relational = 80 percent)?

Think about one thing you could do and one thing your partner could do that would move your sexual relationship one step further toward meeting your needs at these three levels: physical, emotional, and relational. Make sure you come up with an answer for all three.

Now talk with your partner about your answers. Compare thoughts with your partner. Remember that sharing needs can often create expectations, and expectations can heighten pressure on couples to perform. Use this activity to help your partner increase awareness of your needs and desires.

Check yourself: Are you communicating an expectation to your partner or an invitation? Understanding the needs you and your partner share are critical to keeping sex safe and creating more room for play rather than pressure in this key area of your relationship.

For more practical tips on strengthening your sexual relationship, see *Sex For Dummies,* 3rd Edition, by Dr. Ruth K. Westheimer, with Pierre A. Lehu (Wiley).

Working Through Old Issues with New Resources

Marriage therapist Dan Wile makes the case that when you chose a partner, you also chose a set of problems. These problems may be differences in personality, differences in ethnic background and culture, or differences in gender assumptions. What Wile and couple researcher John Gottman both recognize is that these problems are inevitable and most likely perpetual.

Couples in EFT work hard to rebuild the security of their relationships. Through the steps they take to recognize their patterns, understand the needs they have as couples, and face their fears, they're more resilient, more skilled, but not problem free.

Relationship conflict is inevitable. Conflict can even be a sign that a relationship is growing.

You can find yourself in trouble when the conflict styles of the past reemerge in the presence of a current problem. On the one hand, this should be expected, given that each of us has a well-honed set of responses to negative emotions. These responses can be almost involuntary. You need to remember that, in these moments, you have new opportunities to work out problems together instead of having the problem work against you.

Emotions are a resource. They provide information you need in relationships. They help you stay in touch with your partner. They also help you see your pattern.

Seeing the pattern

Staying aware of your pattern and the role you typically take in a conflict gives you resources for working out conflicts before they get out of hand. Here are three things to watch for in identifying your pattern (see Chapters 4 and 5 for resources for understanding your pattern):

✔ **Knowing how you respond:** Starting with your response helps you see more clearly what's happening with you in an escalating conflict. This exercise helps you step back and see your side of the pattern. Ask yourself the following questions to track your response when a conflict starts to heat up.

Check your actions:

- Do you turn toward your partner and become more active in the argument?

- Do you turn away and try to calm things down?

- Do you shut down and check out from what's going on?

Check your thoughts:

- What do you say to yourself in these moments?

- What thoughts about your partner run through your mind in these moments?

- What do you say to yourself when things seem to be getting worse?

Check your feelings:

- What does your body feel like in these moments?

- Where do you feel the intensity of the conflict?

- What emotion words would you use to describe what you feel inside in these moments?

- What are the nonverbal signals you send your partner? What is the message they're trying to send?

✔ **Owning your emotional response:** Take a moment to look deeper at your response. Ask yourself what's going on in these moments. Look at your thoughts, feelings, and actions and ask yourself the following questions:

- What's the emotion behind my reactions?

- What is my primary emotion (see Chapter 4) when I turn away or turn toward my partner? What is your experience on the inside when you experience vulnerability in these key moments?

- What is it that I need in this moment from my partner?

- Do I have a fear that blocks me from sharing my need? If so, what is the fear about?

✔ **Recognizing your impact:** Now look back over your answers and think about how your partner responds in these moments. If your tendency is to withdraw and pull away, what does your partner do next? Try to keep your eyes on the big picture of what happens in a conflict rather than the specifics of the issue you may be fighting about.

Use the following questions to focus in on your partner's response. Think about what happens when an argument is starting to escalate between you:

- What does your partner usually do in these moments?

- What is different when you increase your intensity, trying to get your point across?

- What is different when you try to calm things down to keep things from getting worse?

- What does your partner usually say in these moments? What do you guess your partner says to himself or herself in these moments?

- What nonverbal responses do you see? What signals do you look for that give you a clue of what your partner is feeling but maybe not saying?

The conflict patterns that play out in a relationship follow a sequence of *react–respond–react–respond.* The reactions are often to a partner's negative emotional response. These responses are how partners instinctively cope in situations of threat or concern. It doesn't really matter how the pattern started — when it gets going, the pattern takes on a life of its own. Your goal is to see the pattern by recognizing your *react–respond* tendencies and those of your partner. Even recognizing one of these tendencies can help you see your cycle taking off and then exit an escalating pattern.

Take out a piece of paper and draw out your pattern. Think about a recent argument you had that got heated. Perhaps it was about one of the issues we discuss earlier (in-laws, finances, sex). Try to slow it down in your mind. Play back the start of the argument, and use the following questions to help you focus on breaking down your pattern:

1. **Start with something your partner said or did that you had an emotional response to, and write that down in the center of the page.**

2. **Think about what you did in response, and draw a quarter-circle with an arrow to your partner's side of the page.**

3. **Write down on your partner's side how he or she reacts to your response, and draw an arrow to you, indicating your partner's response. This should start a second circle.**

Note the impact you think your response has. Think of this as your partner's reaction.

4. **Try to complete the cycle for at least three turns.**

Note the actions first, and then go back and add the emotions for each of the responses. Use arrows to illustrate the emotions. Guess at what might be underlying your partner's response. Think about the primary emotion underlying these secondary responses.

This exercise should give you a clear picture of how you experience your conflict pattern. Once you've drawn this out, you can compare your diagram with your partner's diagram, or you can do this exercise together. Either way, be sure to do this exercise when you both have some distance from the reactive issue you plan to discuss. See Figure 13-1 for an example of what Julie and Bryan's cycle might look like.

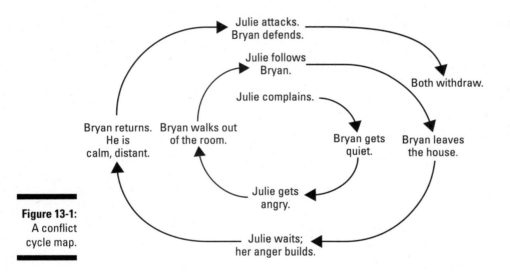

Figure 13-1:
A conflict cycle map.

Julie attacks.
Bryan defends.

Julie follows Bryan.

Both withdraw.

Julie complains.

Bryan returns. He is calm, distant.

Bryan walks out of the room.

Bryan gets quiet.

Bryan leaves the house.

Julie gets angry.

Julie waits; her anger builds.

Stopping the cycle

Taking time to write out your pattern and discuss it together gives you an advantage in stopping the cycle before it gets the best of you. You're most likely to recognize the immediate responses rather than the secondary reactions you or your partner make, because the responses are often instantaneous.

Your reactions to a situation are what you to do when you have a response. Your *response* may be fear, but how you *react* is defensiveness. Both are important, but your partner almost always sees your reaction (for example, defensiveness) and rarely sees your response (the fear that informs that defensive reaction).

When you can see that you're responding in an increasingly defensive way, you can draw attention to what's happening between you and take one of the following steps to slow the escalation and stop the cycle:

- **Make it known.** When you see your pattern in action, call it out: "You know, I think things are heating up between us. I think we're caught in our cycle." Your goal is to bring conscious awareness to the escalating pattern. Keep in mind that the actions you take in your cycle are often predictable.

- **Share your feelings.** In your pattern, you're more likely to enact your feelings rather than share them. One of you will show frustration through tone of voice or an angry look. If you can label your feelings and share your experience, you give each other a better chance of focusing on your relationship rather than getting lost in an issue. For example, you might say, "Okay, I'm getting frustrated now. I can feel the tension, and I don't think you're hearing me."

- **Affirm your intent.** You're more likely to contain an escalating argument if you can share your intent. Often, couples increase the intensity of their emotions when they aren't feeling understood. This then makes it more likely that your partner hears your intensity, not your intent of getting his or her attention. Saying what you want or what you intend can help your partner know where you're coming from. Frustration looks very different when it's directed at an argument that is happening rather than at the person you're arguing with.

Putting this together, you can stop a cycle by drawing attention to it, sharing what's happening for you in the moment, and letting your intent be known.

For example, Bryan might say to Julie, "Can we hold on here? I feel like things are starting to get out of hand. I mean, I can feel myself wanting to shut down right now, and I don't want to do that. I do care about what you're saying, but it just feels like we're getting back into our old pattern."

Most couples have many fights but only one pattern. You may argue and get stuck on different issues, but the way this happens between you and your partner is often the same. Seeing the pattern and the emotions that shape that pattern gives you a resource you can use for any number of differences and disappoints you'll face.

Moving to vulnerability

Stopping a cycle opens the way to make clear what's at stake. Typically, the emotional alarms that set off a cycle are fears that something needed is missing. This may be the need for recognition, reassurance, or simply understanding. The underlying questions partners feel touch on basic questions of adequacy and worth: "Am I what he or she wants? Am I lovable?" Taking time to acknowledge these underlying needs can short-circuit your cycle and help you more effectively respond to a critical concern in your relationship.

Acknowledging your needs means moving to vulnerability. Safety in a relationship makes this possible. Keep in mind that your ability to focus on your partner is just as important as the issue you're facing. Your willingness to listen and respond to your partner's need increases the emotional security in your relationship.

Julie came to Bryan and said, "Sometimes when you don't respond to me, I think you see me as stupid or think I don't have anything to offer. I felt that way a lot growing up, and I do get very angry in those moments. What I need most in those times is to know that you do hear me and care what I have to say."

You can also ask your partner about his or her needs. Showing that you're available and responsive can open the door to your partner's vulnerability. Stopping an escalating cycle can give you an opportunity to better understand your partner's needs by learning more about his or her side of the pattern. Think of this as an invitation you're offering rather than an expectation you're giving, a new experience of your relationship

"I know you were starting to shut down earlier," Julie said to Bryan. "I'd like to know what happened then, because I didn't mean to push you away, but that's what happened. Can you help me understand?" This opens the door for Bryan to share more about his experience. Julie giving him space to talk about his need to withdraw makes room for Bryan also to talk about what he needs from Julie instead.

Practicing Emotional Engagement

Couples who are able to express and respond to primary emotions are more resilient. By taking time to understand your cycle and the reactive patterns that organize your relationship under distress, you've given yourselves deeper insight into how your relationship works. These cycles also can work based on positive emotion. The more you engage and respond to the joys and surprises of your partner, as well as your partner's hurts and fears, the more confidence you'll both have in your relationship.

This confidence is a form of emotional security. The more practice you have responding to one another (especially in moments that matter), the more you invest in this security. Sharing and caring for the emotional needs of your partner increases the likelihood that in times of trouble your partner will give you the benefit of the doubt, even when you don't respond exactly as he or she might need.

You can be sure that you'll miss your partner's needs at some important moments in your relationship. What you do in response is more important than not making a mistake in the first place. If you're able to show care and concern in response to your partner's fears and concern, you'll maintain the emotional connection you need even when times are tough. Your resilience as a couple is based upon your ongoing ability to respond and engage in the joys and sorrows life brings your way.

Tuning in to what matters

When you can stay emotionally attuned to your partner, you don't have to work as hard at managing your relationship. The emotional security you share makes it safer to be more open about expectations and needs. Reading and responding to the emotional cues of your partner will strengthen this security.

Checking emotional cues

Growing in your emotional awareness helps you stay in tune with your partner. Paying attention to nonverbal responses when talking with you partner can help you be more aware of the impact you're having in the moment. Most couples read these cues carefully in the early stages of a relationship when each partner is trying to read the interest and intent of the other. Over time, you can take the relationship for granted and miss important signs that help you stay in tune with your partner.

Here are some ways to stay in tune:

- ✔ Maintain eye contact. Show your interest.
- ✔ Notice changes in your partner's body posture. Is he or she opening up or closing off?
- ✔ Watch for changes in your partner's facial expression. Has something changed?
- ✔ Listen to your partner's tone of voice. Does it match what he or she is saying?
- ✔ Use your partner's words and key phrases. Show you're listening.
- ✔ Check in with your partner's feelings. Show you care.

Tom heard tension in Lori's voice when she was recounting her workday. Tom responded, "It sure sounds like you had a tough day. Do you want to talk about it?" He invited Lori to share more about her day but also picked up on her distress. Tom showed Lori that he was aware and tuned into her world. This made her feel comforted and connected.

In the past, Tom would've heard her distressed tone and assumed it was about him. He would have become guarded and quiet. In turn, Lori would've provoked him with frustration over his lack of response. Today, Tom has more confidence that he and Lori are on solid ground as a couple. As a result, he's more open to Lori. He can hear her frustration without reacting, and this helps Lori to recover and respond more quickly to his care.

Check your ability to read your partner's emotional experience. Complete the following sentences, thinking about your partner's response:

- ✔ When my partner feels frustrated, I'm most likely to see it when he or she _____.

- ✔ When my partner feels angry, I'm most likely to see it when he or she _____.

- ✔ When my partner is hurt, I'm most likely to see it when he or she _____.

- ✔ When my partner is sad, I'm most likely to see it when he or she _____.

- ✔ When my partner is afraid, I'm most likely to see it when he or she _____.

- ✔ When my partner is scared, I'm most likely to see it when he or she _____.

Review your answers with your partner. Take time to help your partner tune in to your emotional responses, and allow your partner to help you tune in to his or her emotional responses, too. Responses may vary from situation to situation, but do your best to identify the common emotional signals you see in your relationship.

Catching attachment themes

The most important emotional responses in a couple's relationship tend to organize around two central themes. These themes are expressed in the question "Can I count on you to be there for me when I need you most?" Your answer to this question expresses (1) your confidence that you can trust your partner, and (2) your belief that you matter to your partner. The more emotionally secure your relationship is, the more confidence you'll have that you matter and that you can trust your partner.

Reactive patterns typically organize around a fear that you don't matter or can't trust your partner in a time of need. Of course, it would be simplest if you and your partner could just check out these fears and get reassurance on these core issues, but that's difficult to do in the face of these fears. When insecurity takes over a relationship, couples increasingly rely on more indirect ways of responding to these questions or avoid them altogether. Yet with confidence in the security of their relationship, couples are better able to make their needs known.

Lori told Tom about the horrible day she had at work. She explained how a business deal had fallen apart and her boss took her team to task for the loss. "I know it wasn't my fault, but still I couldn't help feeling like I lost their confidence," Lori shared, with tears running down her face. Tom reached over to touch her shoulder, and Lori leaned into his chest, finding comfort as he embraced her. His embrace was the reassurance she needed.

In the past, Tom would have problem-solved Lori's situation and inadvertently dismissed her fears. This is how Tom tended to handle his own fears, so he thought he was helping Lori when he would try to help her "think through" her response to the situation. Lori would reject Tom's advice and, rebuffed, Tom would react defensively by criticizing and then shutting her out. This time, Tom heard Lori's worries as her fear, and having faced their fears together (see Chapter 11) he knew she needed his reassurance more than his reasoning.

Catching attachment themes becomes easier when you know your partner's relationship history and have more awareness of the primary emotions that are part of the cycle. Tom understood that Lori grew up with a critical father who was difficult to please. She was sensitive to criticism and could get triggered by others' disapproval. Tom also learned that his support and reassurance helped her the most. Initially, this was difficult for Tom because he had his own triggers about being "good enough" and struggled to give Lori what she needed because of his own fears. Knowing about their cycle and understanding more about the way fear played in their relationship gave Tom what he needed to respond in a way that mattered to Lori.

Taking steps to invest in your relationship can strengthen the confidence you share in the strength and security of your relationship. Taking time to actively invest and prioritize time together can proactively strengthen your relationship by demonstrating commitment and value to your partner. (See Chapter 17 for ways to strengthen your relationship.)

Engaging vulnerability

If fear is one of the main factors keeping your pattern in place, facing fear gives you a way to respond that's more likely to draw you together rather than push you apart. Fear can be tricky because it's often expressed defensively, as an accusation or a form of blame. Someone might say, "You're scaring me. Of course, I'm afraid — anyone would be, given the way you treat me." This is a secondary reaction to fear, not an expression of vulnerability.

Opening up about your fears often means opening up about the core themes of trust and value in a relationship. Escalating patterns of negative emotions can propel fears of abandonment and rejection. These core themes can be difficult to shake in moments of uncertainty, especially for couples who have endured a crisis in their relationship or a period of extended distance or conflict.

Facing the uncertainty and the fears associated with these moments can open new opportunities for couples to re-engage and reassure each other. When you share your fears, you're letting down your guard and letting your partner experience your vulnerability. This is a risk that couples in the later stages of EFT are ready to take (and must take) together to continue to avoid their previous conflict patterns.

In recognizing and sharing your fears, you're also better able to communicate your needs. These needs most often relate to the attachment themes of being valued by your partner and having confidence that you can trust him or her. Couples often talk about needs for influence in their relationship: "I need you to help more around the house" or "I need you to be more understanding about my schedule." These are legitimate needs, but they don't address the more crucial needs of knowing that you matter, or knowing that you can count on your partner.

Couples who are able to risk sharing these needs are more effective in responding at the emotional level that's needed. Engaging vulnerability requires sharing more openly and vulnerably about how you depend on each other. In sharing your fears and needs, you create the opportunity for your partner to respond to the ultimate relationship question: Can I count on you to be there when I need you most?

Responding to one another

If your partner takes a step of vulnerability, your response is crucial. The starting point for an effective response is your emotional presence. Often in these vulnerable moments, you can feel pressure to respond. Take a moment. Stay focused on your partner. If you've been tracking your partner's emotional responses, you're in a better position to respond. Keep in mind that one of your partner's questions may simply be: "Can I count on him?" or "Does she really care?" Showing that you're listening and that you're present helps your partner know that you're available.

Showing empathy with understanding helps your partner know that you're with him or her. Responding to the content of what your partner is saying may be less important than responding to what he or she needs at an emotional level. Remember that relationships are organized by emotion, and in moments of vulnerability, you need to respond to the emotional signals first.

In many cases, your partner's risk to share his or her fears and needs may be more important than the content of your response. Responding to fear with comfort and reassurance and clarifying what a partner needs in the moment matter more than having a specific answer to a big question. You want to show that you're available and that you care about your partner's concerns.

Taking time in these moments to make sure you're meeting your partner's needs can help you more effectively respond. Tracking and responding to your partner's emotional cues and listening for attachment-related themes help you better address your partner's reach for care and comfort.

Finally, after taking these risks together, make sure you appreciate what you've done together. Using new solutions to face old problems begins by facing these tough issues together. When you can do this by exiting your pattern or staying out of it altogether, you make it more likely that you'll stay out of these patterns in the future. Affirming your partner and your relationship is another way of investing in the emotional security of your relationship.

Chapter 14

Securing Your Future

*E*motions play a vital role in resilient relationships. Couples face numerous changes in their relationships, particularly when children are involved — researchers may debate the degree to which children negatively impact a couple's relationship satisfaction, but there is little question that children offer additional joys *and* challenges to a couple's relationship. Career changes and health crises also may create relationship strain. Yet couples who are able to work at an emotional level are more effective in fighting together against these common and sometimes unpredictable challenges of life.

In emotionally focused therapy (EFT), couples develop new ways of enhancing their relationships by staying emotionally connected. Facing your fears and sharing deeply with your partner increases your confidence and ability to maintain a strong relationship, even in times of adversity. The investments you make at an emotional level and the positive emotions you experience will reap significant benefits over the life of your relationship.

In this chapter, we fill you in on steps you can take to strengthen your emotional bonds and invest more deeply in your future. Typically, couples who work through the process of EFT find greater resilience in their relationships because they're better able to share the joys and challenges of life as they walk through them together. At the heart of it all is a simple and enduring commitment to making your relationship and your partner a primary source of joy, comfort, and purpose.

Telling Your New Story

If you listen to a couple tell stories about their relationship, you can learn something about their past and future. When researchers examined the stories couples told about their pasts, they were able to predict over 80 percent of the time whether the couples would eventually break up. The strength of a couple's emotional bond was found to be key. This study showed how a couple's view of their past is an expression of their present and, to a greater extent, a glimpse toward what they may expect in the future. The stronger your bond, the more likely you are to have a bright future.

Couples who have strong emotional bonds are more likely to share a more secure attachment. When you have a secure bond in your relationship, you're more likely to describe the story of your relationship in specific ways. For example:

- ✔ You're able to recognize and appreciate difficulties you faced together.

- ✔ You recognize and appreciate the differences between you and their impact.

- ✔ You focus on the importance of your relationship.

- ✔ Your partner is seen as a personal priority and someone who really matters in your life.

- ✔ You recognize how your life together has grown and changed.

- ✔ You recall specific memories of positive moments in your history together.

- ✔ You can see how this relationship makes a difference to others.

When your relationship is a secure base, you can look at the past and honor the difficulties you worked through in positive ways. Researchers have found that couples who are able to talk about their relationship in these shared ways are often more satisfied not only with their relationship but also with their individual lives. A couple's shared story is a sign of growth and often healing in their relationship.

Typically, the stories couples tell focus on the loving and satisfying aspects of the relationship. Couples who've faced more difficult circumstances may focus on the more dissatisfying aspects of their life as a couple. EFT helps couples work through these negative experiences and find ways to balance their emotional responses, even to the most difficult circumstances.

It isn't the absence of differences and difficulties that makes a relationship secure; it's how partners face these issues together.

Robyn received the news of her breast cancer as a terrible shock. Derrick initially overwhelmed Robyn with his attempts to understand her cancer and its various forms of treatment. Soon Robyn felt invisible to Derrick; she felt like her cancer was not only consuming her body but also her relationship. The more anxious Derrick became, the more withdrawn and distressed Robyn felt. Through EFT, the couple faced Derrick's fears of losing Robyn and Robyn's own fears of losing part of herself and even her life to cancer. Looking back, the couple now expresses the strength they found in facing these fears and finding in each other a source of love and comfort that they needed to weather this difficult journey.

Identifying the characteristics of a secure relationship

Couples who make the investment in a more secure relationship often work together to keep their relationship on solid ground, emotionally speaking. Here are some common practices secure couples follow to keep their relationship strong:

- ✔ **Keeping on track:** Partners work to keep a more emotionally balanced relationship. They work together to find ways to get back on track when facing difficulties. Secure couples find ways to repair emotional damage following a conflict and seek new resources of comfort and support.

- ✔ **Seeing the positive:** Couples who have satisfied relationships tend to organize around the positive experiences in their relationship. They're more likely to acknowledge and encourage a partner's actions that bring more positive emotions to the relationship.

- ✔ **Working as a team:** Partners check in on each other if they sense there is some sense of distress. They take initiative to monitor and support each other.

Secure couples can count on each other to be available in times of need. More often than not, couples with a strong sense of security turn to each other when they feel a sense of desperation or uncertainty. Sometimes these are direct requests; other times, the bid for help may be more tentative and less obvious. The key question is whether the partner will respond.

Think about ways you signal your partner when you feel uncertain or need his or her support. If you wanted to let your partner know you needed support, how would you do so? Look through the following options, and circle those that you use to signal your need:

✔ I ask for help.

✔ I get quiet or respond with few words.

✔ I withdraw and act as if I'm unavailable.

✔ I show my uncertainty and appear as if I need help.

✔ I express my need indirectly — I tell stories about others.

✔ I complain and try to motivate my partner to action.

✔ I look afraid or scared, hoping my partner will respond.

✔ I become passive, hoping my partner will act.

Add any other ways you signal your partner with your concerns. Which of these signals is most effective for you? Which of these is least effective? Ask your partner about his or her experience. What bids for support does he or she recognize?

When you and your partner are effective in responding to these bids for support, you'll grow in the security and safety you experience as a couple. If you can confidently reach to your partner for comfort and support, your ability to handle increasingly distressed emotions will increase. As a couple, you'll become more resilient.

As a couple, think of a time recently when you experienced a distressing situation and found a way through it. Use the following questions to walk through this adversity together. Think of a time when you specifically looked to your partner for help. Use the following questions to highlight the steps you took together to stay secure.

✔ When did you first notice your distress?

✔ What did you do or say to reach out to your partner for help?

✔ How did your partner let you know that he or she was willing to help? To be there for you?

✔ What did your partner do in the moment that made the biggest difference for you?

✔ What was it like to receive your partner's help? How did your partner's help impact you at an emotional level?

✔ How did having walked through this difficult time impact how you see your relationship? How do you see your partner?

Now think of a time when your partner was facing a difficult situation and reached for you. Use the following questions to walk through a time when your presence made a difference for your partner.

- ✔ When did you first notice your partner's distress?

- ✔ What did your partner do or say to reach out for help? How did this impact you?

- ✔ How did you know to respond? What did you do to show your support?

- ✔ What did you do that made the biggest difference for your partner?

- ✔ What was it like for you to make a difference for your partner, especially in his or her time of need? How did this impact you at an emotional level?

- ✔ How did having walked through this difficult time impact how you see your relationship? How do you see your partner?

You can choose a common situation and take turns walking through these steps or take different situations and share first what is was like to be in the receiving position and what it was like to be in the giving position. The strength of a secure relationship is being able to move back and forth between give and take, especially in a time of need.

You can use these questions to think of other times and situations where "being there" for each other made a big difference in your relationship. Consider these situations when reaching and responding as a couple made a difference for you:

- ✔ A time of celebration (for example, promotions, awards, graduations)

- ✔ A time of illness (for example, hospitalization, prolonged illness, loss of functioning, fear of death)

- ✔ A time of financial hardship or struggle (for example, unemployment, overwhelming debt)

- ✔ A time of transition (for example, moving to a new area, a new job, retirement)

- ✔ A time of family change (for example, birth of a child, death of a parent, empty nest)

Take a moment and write out one of these stories of adversity or triumph. Focus your story on those moments where being a couple really mattered to celebrating a success or overcoming difficulty. Pay attention to what you both did to stay strong together and what a difference that makes today in how you see yourselves as a couple.

Strengthening a secure base

When you have a secure relationship, you know with confidence that your partner will be available and responsive to you when you need him or her. In her book *Hold Me Tight: Seven Conversations for a Lifetime of Love* (Little, Brown), Sue Johnson describes three characteristics of couples that relate to each other in a secure way: being accessible, being responsive, and being engaged.

✔ **Accessibility:** Couples who are accessible to each other stay connected through thick and thin. Accessibility focuses on each partner's ability to be available to the needs of the other. Couples who are strong in accessibility are able to say

- We pay attention to each other.

- We connect on an emotional level.

- We make each other a priority in our lives.

- We don't feel left out or alone in our relationship.

- We share intimate thoughts and feelings together.

✔ **Responsiveness:** When couples are responsive to one another, they're tuned into each other at an emotional level. Partners who are responsive are aware of the emotional cues that couples use to signal their needs for closeness and space. Couples who are strong in responsiveness are able to say

- We can turn to each other for care and comfort.

- We know the signals we use to tell each other what we need.

- In times of confusion and uncertainty, we can support each other.

- We respect each other even in the face of our differences and conflicts.

- We find ways to reassure and support each other.

✔ **Engagement:** Secure couples are able to be emotionally present with each other. They are able to show their tender sides and accept vulnerability. Emotional engagement shows how much partners care about each other, and a genuine willingness to make this a bedrock of their relationship. Couples who show their love through active emotional engagement with each other are able to say

- We enjoy and find comfort in being close.

- We can feel close even when we're apart.

- We're concerned for each other's feelings.

- We take risks to be vulnerable in our relationship.

Review each of these three qualities of attachment security and think about your relationship. Then ask yourself:

- ✔ Which of these areas is a strength I bring to this relationship?
- ✔ Which of these areas could I do better in?

Now look at these two areas and discuss the following with your partner:

- ✔ Identify one of the statements listed in your area of strength that really fits for your relationship.
- ✔ Identify one of the statements listed in your area of improvement that most stand out to you as an area that you could improve.

Take some time as a couple to share other strengths you considered. Be sure to affirm one thing that your partner does that contributes to this strength in your relationship. Take some time to talk about the areas where you would like to grow. Remember to focus on your own growth and what you may need from your partner to support your efforts to improve.

Reflecting on your progress

Couples who face the challenges of negative patterns and the underlying emotions that organize these cycles find healing in being able to openly share their emotions and the needs that accompany these experiences. Couples who are able to look back on what they've done are able to appreciate the ways in which *not* addressing these vulnerabilities left them stuck in destructive cycles. They can also see the growth and healing they've found in relating at a deeper level.

Emotionally focused therapists Lynne Angus and Leslie Greenberg, in their book *Working with Narrative in Emotion-Focused Therapy* (American Psychological Association), identify the importance of being able to describe moments of healing as a story. Telling a story of change and recovery helps each partner strengthen his or her experience of the relationship as a source of love, hope, and peace.

The positive experiences that result from working through emotional blocks in the relationship provide ways for couples to break the negative cycles and emotions that once dominated their relationship. Couples caught in negative patterns tend to focus on what was lost in their relationship, whereas couples who've taken risks to face new ways of being with each other can focus on the resilience and vitality of a relationship of safety and security.

Turn your focus to the progress you've been making as a couple. Think about a recent time when you experienced any of the following:

- ✔ Your partner responding to you in a way that you experienced love
- ✔ Your partner acting to make himself or herself available to your needs
- ✔ Your partner showing care for a fear or concern you had

Write a story about your relationship where the focus of the story is on a positive moment of change. As you write about the problem or negative events that you experienced, describe what you did differently. In your story focus on the following themes:

- ✔ **Accessibility:** We found ways to be more available to each other.
- ✔ **Responsiveness:** We found ways to be more aware of our needs.
- ✔ **Engagement:** We found ways to stay connected.

Now talk as a couple and answer the following questions:

- ✔ What title would you give to this story? How does this title honor what you've done?
- ✔ What does this story say about you as a couple? How do these positive changes give you hope for your future relationship?

Honoring how far you've come

EFT offers couples a new experience of their relationship by transforming reactive patterns of negative emotion. By accessing and engaging with each other at new levels of vulnerability, you show each other how much you care. Honoring the progress that you and your partner have made plays an important role in making sure these changes last.

EFT helps couples not only resolve distress in their relationship but also find new resources that strengthen their relationship. Looking back on times of distress can give couples new appreciation for how much growth has occurred both within you and as a couple.

The process of working through fears and embracing the most fundamental needs in a romantic relationship provides partners with new perspectives that make a difference in dealing with old issues. You can move more freely in the relationship and move away from actions that were driven by fear and self-protective responses.

Consider how Sandy and Craig found new resources by facing Craig's fear of failure together: As a couple, they often struggled with Craig's long work hours. In Sandy's mind, Craig was a workaholic who would sacrifice his personal health and their relationship just to get ahead. Craig endured Sandy's protests and harsh criticism until the tension and distance left them both seeking help.

Through their EFT sessions, Craig shared his fear of rejection that drove his tendency to withdraw from Sandy and overcompensate by trying to prove himself as a worthy provider. His fears also followed him to work, where his tendency toward perfectionism and overwork helped him cope with his feelings of inadequacy. His shame blocked the loneliness and sadness he often felt with Sandy.

"It's hard to believe that I thought I could solve this on my own," Craig admitted. "I made excuses for the long hours and ignored what I really wanted. I tried to convince Sandy that this is just what I had to do, but in reality, I was just running from my fears."

"I always knew something was wrong, and I just thought it was me," Sandy acknowledged. "I figured that he found his work more important and more rewarding, and I was just his companion rather than someone he wanted to share his life with." Sandy went on to explain how these emotions of fear and hurt went unacknowledged and how their efforts to cope drove them apart.

Things are different now that Sandy and Craig have laid down their barriers of self-protection and are able to talk more openly about their fears and needs. "Looking back, I wanted to trust Sandy with this side of me, and now I do," said Craig. "I got the message growing up that men don't show fear, and certainly my office was not a place to let on about my weaknesses, but the funny thing now is that I can talk to Sandy about these things and I feel less intimidated about work and even better about myself. I feel like we're in this together, and there is just less to fear as a result."

Investing in Your Future

Researchers Scott Stanley and Howard Markman recognize two types of commitments that shape a couple's relationship:

- **Constraint commitment:** This type of commitment is focused on external forces that keep a couple together, including having children, financial commitments, values, and religion.

- **Dedication commitment:** This type of commitment involves investing emotionally in the relationship. Sometimes you have to sacrifice your own interests for those of your partner or your relationship.

Couples who are strong in dedication commitment invest in improving their relationships. These couples take active steps to work on their relationships — for example, having a date night, going on a weekend retreat, taking cooking classes together, or sharing a common hobby or sport. These activities are investments in the relationship.

Sharon and Levi meet most nights of the week for a glass of wine and the sunset at their beachfront home. For over 30 years, they've made a ritual of watching the sun set over the Pacific. "Sometimes we talk, and other evenings we sit in the quiet of the moment," Sharon said. "I can't imagine our life without these moments. One day one of us will be gone and it won't be the same. These moments are about us." Their ritual is an expression of their dedication and a symbol of what their relationship means to both of them.

Looking at common relationship rituals

Couples develop routines for how they spend time together. If you're like most couples, you have typical ways of beginning or ending the day together. You may have certain things you do on weekends. These patterned activities fit the rhythm of how you live life together. These routines have more to say about what you *do* as a couple than who you *are* as a couple.

Rituals are different from routines because they're symbolic acts of importance. Rituals bring purpose to shared activities because both partners share in what they value. Rituals provide meaning-filled practices that help couples in several ways:

✔ **They create a sense of belonging.** Stacey and Steve follow their favorite football team religiously. They buy season tickets, and each home game is organized around a series of tailgating parties that they often host. Sharing a common love for their team and reliving celebrations and losses helps keep this couple strong.

✔ **They foster closeness and intimacy.** Christine and Will have a favorite escape. They plan an annual retreat to a mountain cabin for a weekend alone. After the couple had children, these getaway weekends became an important time to prioritize their relationship and renew their intimacy free of other demands.

✔ **They create opportunities for communication.** Ben and Pam plan a regular weekend getaway around a road trip. The long car drives provide a space for them to have uninterrupted conversations. The freedom of being out of their daily routines creates a unique setting to talk about the life they share.

- **They symbolize commitment and consistency.** Celebrating birthdays and anniversaries are a priority to Danny and Jennifer. Each occasion is an opportunity to emphasize the importance they have in each other's lives. They communicate this in writing, focusing on what they find special in one another.

- **They promote identity.** Sofia and Diego make tamales and share them with their neighbors on Christmas Eve. They're often away from their extended families at Christmastime, and this is a way for them to re-create a tradition they value and celebrate their common Mexican heritage.

- **They increase security:** Pete and Liz are like many couples who use a kiss as a ritual for saying hello and goodbye. Liz appreciates how Pete turns back after leaving if he has forgotten to give her a kiss. It reminds her of how important she is in his life.

- **They communicate values.** Samantha and Pierce end their day by saying a prayer as a couple. Their faith is important to them personally and gives significance to the bond they share.

Couples who participate in meaningful rituals are more satisfied with their marriages. Couples and families who have regular rituals have more positive and emotionally close relationships.

Making rituals of your own

Creating a ritual can be as simple as taking a routine and giving it purpose. You can set aside time to talk, take a walk, or go on a date where you and your partner devote time to focusing on your relationship. Rituals involve times of anticipation followed by a shared experience. Although rituals need to have a clear ending point, their effect over time can be enduring.

Fran and Michael decided to organize a ritual around planting their garden each spring. They both enjoyed gardening, and the process of planning their garden gave them an opportunity to express their creativity. Gardening was a hobby for Fran, and she could get lost in a seed catalogue or garden magazine, whereas Michael loved being outdoors and working in the garden. During the summer, the couple savored quiet moments on their deck overlooking the garden, where they would discuss what they had created together. One evening, some friends marveled at how beautiful their garden was and how much they must love gardening. Fran and Michael smiled in appreciation for the compliment, but also in the realization that the garden was an expression of the love they shared.

Couples can engage intimacy rituals that follow a similar pattern, or they can plan ordinary or special activities that express value in their relationship.

You can use the examples in Chapter 17 as a starting point. Then follow these steps:

1. **Identify an activity that you both enjoy and would like to share more often.**

2. **Discuss what you enjoy about the activity and identify what matters to you specifically.**

3. **Explore how this activity can provide an opportunity to focus on your relationship.**

4. **Make sure the activity is mutually rewarding.**

   You may get different benefits from the same activity, but it's important to find activities that you both find meaningful.

5. **Choose how often you'll schedule this activity.**

   Some activities require more resources (money, time, effort), so err on the side of being conservative. It's more important that your ritual is consistent and achievable than at a frequency you aren't able to sustain.

6. **Discuss how you'll share responsibility for making this planned ritual a reality.**

7. **Take time after the ritual to discuss the impact of the activity.**

   Did it meet your individual needs and your needs as a couple? Was the investment of time and energy worth the benefit?

   Some couple rituals involve partners sacrificing their individual needs for the good of the relationship. This must be balanced with opportunities for both partners to express their individual needs.

Take time as a couple to review a ritual you share. Follow the preceding steps and discuss whether the ritual is working as it should. Use the following questions to help you determine whether you may need to revise a ritual:

- ✔ Does this ritual express our shared interests?

- ✔ Do we count on this ritual?

- ✔ Is this ritual something we plan or organize around?

- ✔ Do we share in the planning and performance of the ritual?

- ✔ Is this ritual something we want to do or something we have to do?

- ✔ Does this ritual continue to express a value we share?

If you answer "no" to one of these questions, discuss this ritual as a couple. Consider the following:

- ✔ Has anything changed in how you practice the ritual?
- ✔ Is something missing from making this ritual meaningful?
- ✔ Does something keep you from consistently practicing the ritual?
- ✔ Has this ritual simply become a routine?

If you answer "no" to more than one of these questions, discuss as a couple the possibility of revising the ritual or finding a new ritual to replace one that has lost its meaning.

Most couples have to fine-tune their rituals. Be sure to stay in touch about your expectations and needs to ensure that a ritual is fulfilling its intended purpose. Stay flexible to the changing needs of your relationship. What works in one season of life may lose its value in another. Flexibility and adaptability are important in continuing to renew and invest in your relationship.

Beware of some of the warning signs that rituals have lost their meaning. Here are some signs that a ritual may be ineffective:

- ✔ **Rigidity:** Your ritual has become an inflexible rule and involves rigid expectations.
- ✔ **Triviality:** Your ritual has become a hollow activity that you do just because it's something you've always done.
- ✔ **Exclusivity:** Your ritual is valued by one partner but not valued by the other. One partner initiates the ritual while the other person passively engages in the activity. The ritual may express only one partner's values, but the other partner's values are excluded.
- ✔ **Inconsistency:** A ritual will lose its effectiveness when it can no longer be counted on. Partners may express an intent to maintain a ritual, but lack of consistency reduces its impact and meaning.

Practicing these rituals give couples an opportunity to anticipate and come to count on these events, which serve to strengthen their dedication commitment. You can use rituals to invest in your present, as well as your future.

Levi and Sharon's ritual (see earlier in this chapter) began one sunset at a time. Thirty years later, their evening ritual has become a symbol of the love they share.

Releasing the Power of Positive Emotions

Positive emotions have powerful benefits for couples. They enable partners to experience a wider range of thoughts and solutions when faced with challenges. Maintaining positive emotions enables partners to be more aware and perceptive of what's happening in their relationship. A couple's experience of positive emotion brings resources to their relationship on two levels:

- **Physically:** Health and longevity are associated with enduring positive emotional experiences. Positive emotional responses correct the physiological effects of negative emotional responses, calming escalating heart rates and respiration that may have increased in the midst of a conflict or argument.

- **Psychologically:** Positive emotions are related to optimism and a hardiness in facing difficult situations. Positive emotions promote endurance in the face of negative experiences and enable better coping with adversity.

Finding strengths and focusing on positive attributes in your partner can promote positive emotional experiences in your relationship. Take a moment to look at the following list of partner qualities. Circle the three words in the list that first jump out at you when you think about your partner. Now think of situations in which you've recently seen each of these characteristics in action.

Loving	Attractive	Exciting
Nurturing	Sensitive	Interesting
Thrifty	Warm	Brave
Supportive	Intentional	Virile
Intelligent	Funny	Shy
Kind	Thoughtful	Considerate
Vulnerable	Gentle	Generous
Affectionate	Committed	Practical
Loyal	Athletic	Involved
Relaxed	Silly	Flexible
Sexy	Graceful	Calm
Rich	Sweet	Beautiful
Imaginative	Active	Powerful
Interesting	Reserved	Graceful
Strong	Adventurous	Caring
Elegant	Responsible	Energetic
Faithful	Spontaneous	Organized
Receptive	Lively	Dependable
Decisive	Tender	Expressive
Understanding	Best friend	Truthful
Fun	Assertive	Protective

After you've identified these positive attributes and experiences, take turns sharing them one at a time. Allow time for each of you to "take in" these positive experiences. Look each other in the eyes, or take hold of each other's hands as you do this exercise. Being intentional in sharing your positive emotions is an investment in the security of your relationship.

Too often, couples take for granted their positive attributes and experiences, either dismissing their partners' compliments or minimizing their importance. So, take a deep breath, create some space, and allow room in your conversations for the power of positive emotion.

Sharing positive emotions and experiences offers couples an example of what it's like to enter an emotional experience together. For example, if you see the delight in your partner's eyes as he expresses how much he appreciates your creativity, you can begin to experience that delight as well. In essence, you get his delight because it's now something you both share.

The power of emotions to transform your relationship is not a matter of having more positive than negative emotions. It's about how you work together with the emotions you have. When you're able to work together in meeting at an emotional level, there is a deeper awareness of the bond you share. This is the power of attachment. It's the emotional glue that holds couples together.

Chapter 15

Working with a Couple Therapist

In This Chapter

▶ Considering whether couple therapy is for you

▶ Understanding what happens in couple therapy

▶ Locating the right therapist for you

Many couples are looking for a "relationship booster shot," some way to energize their relationship a little. They aren't necessarily unhappy — they just want to inject some more understanding and happiness. These couples may go to weekend enrichment workshops or buy self-help relationship books like this one.

Other couples may find that they simply can't work through a book like this because they get too angry or hurt, and find it too difficult to continue. The activities in this book and others like it can be painful. If you find it increasingly difficult to do the activities in this book, or if you've completed all the activities and you still want more, you may benefit from seeing a couple therapist.

In this chapter, we explain what couple therapy usually looks like, and help you figure out if it's right for you. We also offer suggestions on finding the right therapist for you.

Identifying When You May Need Couple Therapy

Couple distress (an increasing level of emotional strain between partners) is the single most common reason for seeking couple therapy. It undermines family functioning and is strongly associated with depression, anxiety disorders, and alcoholism.

But not every couple needs couple therapy to be happy and content. Some therapy can even make couples worse! (Not every therapist is proficient in doing couple therapy.)

In this section, we walk you through common warning signs that you and your partner may be ripe for couple therapy. We also let you know the kinds of situations in which therapy may not help.

Common warning signs

Monica and Dan had been married for four years when they called to make an appointment for couple therapy. They dated for two years in college, and were married soon after graduating. They reported having argued since early in their relationship, but said that in the past two years things had gotten worse.

"Since we had our son two years ago," Monica said. "Things have been bad. That first year after the birth was terrible. I'm angry and bitter — I admit it." Turns out that Monica felt she was left alone far too often with the infant in that first year. "I was up and down all night, every night!" she said. "He wouldn't help. I work full time, too!" Monica reported a year of fear and loneliness as a first-time mom. She'd gotten to a place where she didn't think she could count on Dan when she needed him most.

In turn, Dan felt he did okay "for a guy who doesn't know anything about babies." They argued continually about how to parent. Dan felt shut out. "It's her way or no way," Dan said about Monica's parenting. Monica turned to friends to help her with the baby, which Dan resented. Before long, many of those earlier college dating arguments resumed and got more intense.

By the time they came in for therapy, Monica and Dan were both fully blaming each other for their problems, and their arguing cycle had pretty much taken over their marriage. Their negative cycle was the norm. She was sleeping on the couch, and they weren't having sex.

Following is a list of warning signs of possible danger — many of which Dan and Monica had. (Many of these warning signs are based on the work of John Gottman in his book *Why Marriages Succeed or Fail: And How You Can Make Yours Last* [Simon & Schuster].) If these elements have increased in your relationship, you may want to consider couple therapy:

- Criticism
- Attacks on the other person's character
- Blaming the other person

- ✔ Persistent anger
- ✔ Bitterness
- ✔ Resentment
- ✔ Name calling
- ✔ Insults
- ✔ Mocking
- ✔ Hostile humor
- ✔ Sarcasm
- ✔ Seeing yourself as a victim
- ✔ Ignoring what the other person says
- ✔ Giving the other person the silent treatment
- ✔ Physically removing yourself from arguments
- ✔ Withdrawing emotionally and physically

The more these elements increase, the more likely a couple is to divorce. The more of these warning signs you find in your relationship, the more evident it is that you may benefit from couple therapy.

Certain life events have a strong effect on couples and families. Here's a list of common life events that can strain any relationship:

- ✔ Getting married
- ✔ Losing a job
- ✔ The death of a family member or someone close
- ✔ A serious illness or disability
- ✔ The birth of a child
- ✔ Depression or another mental health issue
- ✔ A natural disaster
- ✔ Children leaving home
- ✔ Addiction
- ✔ A crisis with one of your children

Most couples who experience one or more of these life events will experience increased stress on their relationship. Many times, couples come to therapy while experiencing these common life events, or soon after.

Sit down with your partner and read over the list of warning signs. Talk about the example of Monica and Dan. Try not to blame each other — instead, try to be honest and open with each other. Consider the following:

- Which of the warning signs are occurring in our relationship?
- Have these warning signs increased in number and intensity?
- Have we experienced or are we experiencing one or more of the listed life events?
- Are there similarities between Monica and Dan's story and ours?

Talk about whether you think you could benefit from couple therapy. Again, try to be honest and open with each other, and put your relationship first in your consideration.

When couple therapy may not help

Sometimes couple therapy is not the first line of defense. The main situations in which starting with couple therapy doesn't make sense are addiction, violence, an ongoing affair, and mental health issues.

When one or both partners is coping with addiction

John and Marie came to couple therapy because they genuinely wanted help with their relationship. In the first session, it became apparent that John had an addiction problem that he wasn't yet ready to face. "It's a real problem," Marie reported. "He drinks too much and too often." John met the criteria for having a serious problem with alcohol. In addition, he sometimes used cocaine.

John, like many people struggling with drug use, found solace in using substances to deal with his emotions. Unfortunately, he wasn't *really* dealing with his emotions at all. Addictive behavior actually stuffs emotions so that you don't deal with them. John wasn't ready to face this. For this reason, couple therapy wasn't a viable treatment at that time. First, John needed to get help for his addictions. Couple therapy would make sense only after he got his addictions under control and was able to begin dealing with emotion in a healthy way.

Time and time again we've seen couples struggling with addiction. When the emotional intensity arises, as it does in emotionally focused therapy (EFT), most often one partner will use drugs or alcohol to self-medicate and numb the emotions. When this happens, it can be very hurtful to the other partner, who may have begun to be vulnerable in the relationship for the first time in years. The non-using partner can feel hurt and abandoned.

Primary emotions can be painful and scary, but they're there for a reason. They're there to be heeded, to be learned from, and to be acted upon. When someone is caught in addiction to the point of not being able to integrate primary emotions into awareness, and instead "medicates" with drugs or alcohol to make the emotions go away, it makes mutual vulnerability and sharing of primary emotion with each other — the staples of EFT — almost impossible.

If alcohol or drug use is a primary cause of distress in your relationship, EFT is probably not the approach to start with in couple therapy. A behavioral approach, however, may be something to consider. Behavioral therapy has been found to be effective in individual and group settings when dealing with addiction. If the individual with the addiction is willing to go to individual or group behavioral therapy, a behavioral couple therapist could be of help. The therapy would probably focus on dealing with the addiction as a couple. Later, when the addiction has been contained, and you both have more confidence in that, EFT would be appropriate.

When one partner is violent toward the other or both partners are violent with each other

Couple therapy is currently not recommended when there is violence in a relationship. In addition, EFT is not recommended when either partner fears the other, or fears for his or her own safety. The main priority in these situations is protecting the safety of the victim of domestic violence.

If you ever fear for your well-being due to your partner being violent, call the police immediately.

Community-based studies (which use communities as their research population, as opposed to couples going through the criminal justice system or battered shelters) have found that interpersonal violence occurs across gender more than previously realized. These community-based research participants reported male-perpetrated, female-perpetrated, and reciprocally perpetrated violence in couple relationships. Researchers analyzed data on 11,370 U.S. adults ages 18 to 28 from the 2001 National Longitudinal Study of Adolescent Health and found that almost 24 percent of all relationships had some violence. Interestingly, this study found that half of those relationships were reciprocally violent — that is, both partners assaulted each other. When only one partner was violent, women were the perpetrators in more than 70 percent of the cases. Although more women reported perpetrating violence than men, 62 percent of those actually injured by a partner were women.

Intimate partner violence: A definition

Couple therapy is not warranted when there are certain kinds of violence in the relationship. Michael P. Johnson, PhD, at Penn State University, separates intimate partner violence into two distinct categories: intimate terrorism and situational couple violence.

Intimate terrorism is defined by

- The attempt to dominate one's partner
- The attempt to exert general control over the relationship
- Domination manifested in the use of a wide range of power and control tactics
- Violence
- Nonviolent control tactics
- Emotional abuse
- Isolation
- Using children
- Using male privilege
- Using economic control

Situational couple violence is defined as

- Often including the reciprocal use of violence
- Not being embedded in a general pattern of controlling behaviors
- Not being rooted in a general pattern of control
- Occurring when specific conflict situations escalate to violence

When one partner is having an affair and doesn't want to end it

If you or your partner is in an ongoing affair and has no desire to end it and focus exclusively on your relationship, couple therapy is not warranted. If your partner is having an affair and isn't interested in ending the affair and focusing on your relationship, you may want to talk to a therapist on your own about what this means for you and your relationship, but couple therapy won't be any help. Trust is key to therapy, and if you can't trust your partner to end an affair, you can't trust your partner to be there for you in therapy.

This may be different in couples who have mutually agreed to a non-monogamous relationship.

When one or both partners have unresolved mental health issues

If either partner has a history that includes one of the following issues and he or she hasn't been through treatment or therapy for it, or if it still affects that person on a regular basis, individual or group therapy that specifically addresses the issue is usually warranted before beginning couple therapy.

- **Post-traumatic stress disorder (PTSD):** You don't have to be a war veteran to have PTSD. You could experience PTSD as an ongoing effect of trauma from sexual abuse, emotional abuse, or physical abuse. Treating the PTSD should be the first priority. Then, after the PTSD has been treated, you can consider couple therapy for your relationship.

✔ **Depression:** If you're clinically depressed, you need to be treated for that first. When you're in a good place in terms of your mental health, you can better cope with couple therapy.

✔ **Personality disorder:** A personality disorder needs to be treated before you can devote yourself to couple therapy.

People with these conditions can be seen in couple therapy if they're being treated separately in their own therapy and if these issues are under control. If mental health issues are overtaking your relationship, individual or group therapy is warranted before beginning couple therapy.

Knowing What to Expect in Couple Therapy

If you're thinking about seeing a couple therapist, you may have lots of questions about what you're getting yourself into. How long will it last? What does a typical session look like? In this section, we fill you in.

How long will it last?

Couples therapy is usually 50 minutes per session, and people typically go once a week. The length of therapy (the number of sessions) can vary depending on the level of distress you're in and the model of therapy a therapist employs, as well as the approach of the therapy itself (see Table 15-1). Ask any therapist you're considering seeing which models he or she uses most often, and how long he or she usually sees couples.

Table 15-1		Duration of Therapy	
Duration	*Therapeutic Approach*	*Typical Length of Treatment*	*Treatment Focus*
Very brief	Solution-focused, strategic therapy	1 to 5 sessions	Solving or relieving the surface problem
Brief	Emotionally focused therapy	8 to 20 sessions	Relationship closeness, emotions driving cycles of interaction
Long term	Psychodynamic therapy	1 or more years	Unconscious processes and individual dynamics

No pain, no gain

Couple therapy will be trying and painful at times. You can expect to feel the gamut of emotions. Often, couples experience increased distress before they begin to improve — so don't head for the hills the moment things get tough.

Many of our clients tell us that the process of opening up and getting their complaints, fears, and needs on the table and eventually heard and understood by their partners is very painful and scary. These same couples report that doing this made all the difference in their healing. As one couple recently said, "We got everything out, and we heard each other. It hurt like heck sometimes, but we were brutally honest, and it made us closer. Now we aren't afraid to talk about anything. Now we are one."

Remember: Things don't get better overnight. It took you and your partner a while to get where you are in your relationship, and it'll take a while to get back on the right track. During couple therapy, you'll sometimes leave sessions angry or hurt, and sometimes you'll wonder what you're even doing there. Other times, you'll know that you're making progress and feel much closer to each other.

If you commit to honestly doing the work, going weekly, and being patient with the process of therapy, you stand the best chance of growing into the couple you long to be.

Will the therapist see you and your partner together or individually?

Most therapists trained specifically in couple therapy will see both of you together in session. If a therapist typically separates couples and sees them individually, that can be a sign that he or she is more versed in individual therapy techniques and is focusing on treating the individual over the relationship itself.

Over the past 15 years, the emerging field of couple therapy has moved away from placing individually oriented models of therapy onto couples in favor of treating relationships themselves. Relationships involve two people intimately working out their lives together with their own arguments, patterns of interactions, and much more. We're definitely biased toward the couple relationship itself being "the client" in couple therapy, and we firmly believe that couples should be seen together in session. Individual sessions along the way are expected, but the vast majority of sessions should be focused on the relationship with both partners present.

What does an emotionally focused therapist do?

An emotionally focused therapist works similarly to what you read in this book. The difference is that a therapist helps you go deeper into your emotions than you likely can go on your own. Plus, you have a trained professional there to be with you and guide you through the process that we lay out in this book.

An emotionally focused therapist makes each of you feel comfortable and safe to open up in therapy. He or she makes sure that you know that you're understood. He or she knows the road through the EFT process, and helps you walk down it together. If you get stuck, or if there is too much for you to know how to proceed, help is there. An emotionally focused therapist doesn't assign blame to one partner — he or she puts the emphasis on how the relationship has gotten negative over time, which is something neither of you wants. Both you and your partner are responsible, and it'll take both of you working together to make things better.

Some men don't want to go to couple therapy because they're afraid that they'll be blamed. With an emotionally focused therapist, that shouldn't be the case. Sometimes, one partner may have done something that stands out as hurtful to the relationship, but most often, both partners have played roles in things going awry — whether they realize or admit that or not. In EFT, *the relationship itself is the client,* which means that the way partners interact, along with the secondary and primary emotions underlying their interactions, become pivotal. The focus is on what's keeping the partners from connecting emotionally rather than on who's most to blame.

The emotionally focused therapist slows things down, and helps each of you find the powerful emotions underneath the surface that are driving your behaviors with each other. When these deep emotions become tangible, the beliefs and thoughts wrapped up in them also become clear.

"It's really like a different world," David said during the latter stages of EFT. "I didn't know my own internal emotional world. Maybe I thought I did, but I had no clue. Now I'm in touch with it, and I can rely on it to help me tune in to my own needs and those of my wife. I never want to go back to how it was before."

Perhaps the most important aspect of an emotionally focused therapist is that he or she will work for the success, health, and positive growth of your relationship. We can't overstress the importance of this. Emotionally focused therapists see human beings as being at their healthiest when they're in close, safe, and emotionally intimate relationships with their partners and loved ones.

Focusing on the present to heal the future

Most of psychology today views people primarily in an individualistic manner. This view sees people at their best when they're standing alone, solidly on their own two feet. The emotionally focused therapist sees optimal health as occurring through close relationships. It's through emotionally close relationships (infant, baby, child, adult) that we learn who we are. This, in turn, leads to being able to be healthy individuals — not the other way around. This point of view makes for a big difference in terms of a starting point. Emotionally focused therapists believe that human beings never outgrow the core need for emotional connection with each other.

An emotionally focused therapist focuses on how you and your partner relate to each other, how you emotionally miss each other, how you push each other away, how you hurt each other and tick each other off! The emotionally focused therapist doesn't think that delving into your childhood and uncovering the unconscious is the key to helping you. He or she doesn't blame your parents for your current behavior or see you as a walking mental health diagnosis.

Yes, things from your past and your partner's past probably do make it difficult for the two of you to connect. And yes, you may have learned a way of relating from your parents that makes it difficult to do something different today. But the focus of EFT is on your present adult love relationship and what prohibits you and your partner from relating better and feeling closer today.

How do you know if the therapist is any good?

A good emotionally focused therapist is a keen observer of, and ally with, emotion. He or she understands the difference between reactive, secondary emotion and vulnerable, primary emotion. But more important, he or she works from within emotion in session. That means you *feel* it — and the therapist does, too. You know that the therapist feels it with you because you feel him or her there with you in the session.

Even in the first session of EFT, emotions usually come forth that are not normally talked about between partners at home. The way you interact with your partner around key issues of connection and disconnection are traced, along with the surface and underlying emotions, which often remain hidden. This usually allows partners to re-experience these key exchanges in part. With the help of the therapist, you can slow down and access what is actually happening emotionally for you in the session. People are often surprised to discover these emotions, and the impact it has on their partners can be an even greater surprise.

If you go three sessions and you haven't uncovered some vulnerable emotions and felt them — not just talked about them, but *felt them in-session* — it may be time to find another emotionally focused therapist.

Your best bet is a Certified EFT Therapist, although a therapist doesn't *need* to be certified in the approach to be proficient in it. The certification process does include a high level of commitment, rigor, and supervision. To find a Certified EFT Therapist, go to www.iceeft.com/index.php/find-a-therapist.

A good emotionally focused therapist helps you

✔ Uncover underlying emotion

✔ Make sense of your emotion

✔ Get the message your emotion is sending

✔ Get clarity on your relational wants and needs

✔ Act on the message of your emotion

✔ Directly share emotions and needs with your partner

✔ Hear and understand the emotions and needs of your partner

✔ Work together to defeat a negative cycle of disconnecting

✔ Work together to create a positive cycle of connecting

A good emotionally focused therapist works to help you feel

✔ Safe to discover and open up

✔ Heard

✔ Understood

✔ Pushed when needed

✔ Supported

Notice that we said you should feel "pushed when needed." The emotionally focused therapist is active — he or she isn't simply listening and supporting. When something doesn't seem to make sense, or when he or she thinks it's time for you to risk being vulnerable, the emotionally focused therapist will support and push you and your partner.

You're paying for a therapist to help heal your relationship, not just give you a warm and fuzzy hour every week. The emotionally focused therapist is busy helping you discover and share with each other. He or she will regularly have you turn and share directly with each other. That's vital to the model. EFT works inside and in between you and your partner.

A good emotionally focused therapist is extremely helpful in knowing when to have you share directly with your partner, helping you stay on track when doing so, highlighting the critical elements shared by each of you, and then helping your partner hear and respond to the sharing from the heart. The therapist helps create the safety, support, and gentle prompts to aid in this happening between you and your partner as needed. He or she then helps each of you make sense of these powerful emotions and needs in light of the past, present, and future.

How does change happen?

Change happens in EFT as you and your partner come to know the primary, vulnerable emotions that underlie and govern your relationship. As these emotions become more accessible and come into regular awareness, they give in-the-moment meaning and prompts to action.

REAL WORLD EXAMPLE

What success looks like

As Walt became aware of how deeply he felt like he was failing as a husband, he also discovered feeling deeply ashamed and sad about it. The shame and sadness had been there for quite some time, but facing those feelings is painful, so Walt had a pattern of immediately distancing from them internally. Instead of dealing with these painful emotions, Walt threw blame back onto his partner, and withdrew when they started to argue with any intensity.

"I couldn't handle the arguing after a while," Walt shared. "We'd get into it, I'd feel blamed, and I hated that feeling, so I'd quickly blame her back, or say something mean, or just get out of there. In EFT, I learned that I was running away from my deeper emotions of sadness and shame about failing to be the husband in the marriage I really wanted. All I was previously aware of was that there was a lot bubbling down there when we got into arguments, but I had no idea what my gut was trying to tell me." This is a common scenario in EFT — the process happens for both partners.

"When I heard and felt what Walt was going through," Patricia said, "everything started to change for me. I used to see him as someone who didn't listen. Someone who just blamed me, or withdrew when we needed to talk or face something. In EFT, I saw him uncover his deeper emotions of sadness and shame, a fear

of failing me as a husband. I could feel that in session. I knew it was real. It didn't change overnight, but that started real change."

When partners begin to see each other in light of their core emotions and relationship needs, it pulls them closer to each other. Emotions strongly propel us to move, to act.

"When I saw her fear that maybe I don't love her like I used to, or her deep fear that maybe she isn't the woman I want anymore, man, that lit a fire under my butt," Walt said. "I didn't know that woman still existed! I thought she was just fed up with me and everything about me."

As partners see and feel these core emotions and relationship fears and needs, they want to reassure each other. They want the relationship to be one of mutual openness and sharing. Many couples report leaving EFT much closer than they ever were.

"Of course, we were romantically close and in love early on," Patricia said. "Part of that is hormonal and wrapped in the newness of it all. But the love we have now is so much more solid, so much deeper and wiser. We still tap into those early infatuation-type feelings from time to time in a fit of passion, but our baseline connection itself is just so much more mature now."

That's a very good description of successful EFT.

The other significant part of change occurs as part of directly opening up and sharing with your partner. Sharing primary emotions has an impact on the partner sharing, as well as on the partner receiving. It's usually powerful for both. Change in EFT isn't just about emotional change inside each individual; it's always about emotional change between the two of you as well. The approach is relational in nature, rather than individual, so the sharing between partners stemming from previous inside work must happen in order to change the relationship itself.

Finding the Right Therapist

Both you and your partner need to feel comfortable with your choice of therapist. Regardless of the therapist's approach, if you don't feel comfortable, chances are, it won't work as well as it could. You're not the only one who sees this as a priority — therapists themselves prefer working with clients who are comfortable with them.

Having one session with a couple therapist isn't a commitment to continue with that therapist. Let the therapist know that you're looking for an emotionally focused therapist, and you want to have a session with a few of them to find the best fit. This approach is standard, and it just makes good sense. You don't have to decide right after the session either. Let the therapist know that you want to go home and talk about it. You can give it several days if you aren't sure. Tell the therapist that you'll call back if you want to continue therapy with him or her.

When you're looking for a couple therapist, here are our recommendations:

✔ **If you can, opt for a marriage and family therapist.** Marriage and family therapists are trained specifically for couples and families. If you don't go with a marriage and family therapist, at least find someone whose graduate training had a focus on treating couples. (You can ask about this when you call to make an appointment.)

Look for someone who has received advanced training in couple therapy beyond graduate school. You also want someone who spends at least 50 percent of the time treating couples (not individuals). This is a sign of the person's interest in treating couples.

If the therapist mainly sees individuals in therapy, keep looking.

✔ **Look for someone who sees you and your partner together, as opposed to separately.** As we mention earlier, relationships involve two people. We believe that couples should be seen together in session. You may have occasional individual sessions along the way, but the vast majority of your sessions should be focused on the relationship with both partners present.

✔ **If you're comfortable with the approach we outline in this book, specifically look for an emotionally focused therapist.**

Your best bet is a Certified EFT Therapist. To find a Certified EFT Therapist, go to www.iceeft.com/index.php/find-a-therapist.

✔ **Find someone whose rates are competitive in your area.** Various factors can affect how much a therapist charges. For example, someone with a PhD may charge more than someone with a master's degree, or someone who has certification in a particular specialty (say, a Certified EFT Therapist) may charge more than someone who doesn't. Of course, therapists decide for themselves how much they'll charge, so someone with a master's and no advanced certification may end up charging more than a PhD with lots of other initials after his or her name. Call around and see how much other therapists in your community charge, and make sure you feel comfortable with what you're paying.

Turn to Chapter 16 for ten questions you should ask a therapist before making that first appointment.

A helpful website for finding marriage-friendly therapists is the National Registry of Marriage Friendly Therapists (www.marriagefriendlytherapists.com), which is full of helpful questions and insights into how therapists think and work. The site only registers therapists who have advanced training in couple therapy. Of course, many solid couple therapists may not know about this site or may choose not to be listed there, so that alone shouldn't turn you off from a particular therapist. But the site is still a valuable resource.

Part V
The Part of Tens

The 5th Wave   By Rich Tennant

"My wife and I were drifting apart, so we decided to go back to doing what we did on our honeymoon. We called her parents and asked them for money."

In this part . . .

Here, you find quick tips and information to guide you further in exploring and investing in your relationship. We include ten questions to ask a therapist before making an appointment, ten rituals that will strengthen your commitment, ten myths about emotion and relationships, and ten myths about sex. If you're short on time but you still want something meaty, this is the part for you!

Chapter 16

Ten Questions to Ask a Therapist Before You Make an Appointment

In This Chapter

▶ Looking into couple therapy

▶ Finding a couple-friendly therapist

▶ Getting a look inside a therapist's approach

*F*inding a good couple therapist can be a difficult task. A simple search for a marriage counselor on the Internet can turn up a lengthy list of therapists, counselors, and coaches, all claiming to be willing to work on relationship issues. Important differences exist, though, and you want to pay attention to these differences, especially if you're looking for a competent emotionally focused therapist.

In this chapter, we offer important questions that will help you spot a therapist who has real relationship expertise and a passionate commitment to working with couples.

What Is Your State License and Professional Affiliation?

Various mental health professionals — from psychologists to counselors to social workers to marriage and family therapists — offer therapy services to couples, and their qualifications can vary greatly. One way to sift through the numerous names you're likely to find is to ask the professional about his or her state license and professional affiliation.

You should not work with a therapist unless he or she is licensed by your state. That's the most basic qualification you should look for.

Finding a qualified professional also includes identifying whether the professional is a member of a leading professional organization. Membership in a professional organization indicates that the therapist is more aware of recent developments in his or her field of study. Common professional affiliations in the United States include the following:

- ✔ American Association for Marriage and Family Therapy (www.aamft.org)
- ✔ American Association of Pastoral Counselors (www.aapc.org)
- ✔ American Counseling Association (www.counseling.org)
- ✔ American Psychiatric Association (www.psychiatry.org)
- ✔ American Psychological Association (www.apa.org)
- ✔ National Association of Social Workers (www.socialworkers.org)

Other organizations certify and promote couple therapists who meet specific standards and qualifications. These include the following:

- ✔ Association for Behavioral and Cognitive Therapies (www.abct.org)
- ✔ International Centre for Excellence in Emotionally Focused Therapy (www.iceeft.com)
- ✔ National Registry of Marriage Friendly Therapists (www.marriage-friendlytherapists.com)

What Approach Do You Use in Couple Therapy?

Numerous approaches to couple therapy exist. Some therapists use a specific approach like emotionally focused therapy (EFT) or cognitive behavioral therapy. Others describe their approach as "eclectic," which can mean integrating more than one approach or using techniques from a variety of approaches.

We believe that if you're going to put your relationship and your money in the hands of a professional, you should know that the therapist is working from a clinical approach that has been research tested and demonstrated positive results. Three couple therapy approaches have achieved strong research support:

- ✔ Emotionally focused couple therapy
- ✔ Behavioral marital therapy
- ✔ Integrated behavioral couple therapy

What Kind of Training Have You Had in Couple Therapy?

Make no mistake about it: Working with couples in therapy is much different from working with individuals. The training a therapist has completed in couple therapy gives you a better understanding of the level of investment he or she has made in developing expertise in working with couples. Some therapists may mention specific conferences or workshops they've attended. Others may point to certification programs they've completed.

A therapist's response will tell you whether her work with couples is something she has invested time and energy in developing or simply something she offers as a general part of her practice.

Professional knowledge changes over time. Be wary of therapists who are still practicing what they learned in graduate school ten years ago. When you ask a therapist about her training, she may mention where she went to grad school, but she should also talk about other training she has received in the years since.

What Percentage of Your Practice Is Working with Couples?

The answer to this question will tell you whether a therapist specializes in treating couples or does it as a part of his or her overall practice. It also gives you a clear way of gauging the amount of current experience the therapist has with couple therapy.

Look for a therapist whose weekly caseload is at least 50 percent couple therapy. That way, you know that, day in and day out, the therapist is working with couples. Experience is important, particularly in EFT, where therapists actively learn from the couples they serve.

Do You Mainly Meet with Partners as a Couple or as Individuals?

When we teach therapists couple therapy, we often say, "The relationship is your client." That may be obvious to you — after all, we're talking about couple therapy — but many therapists have been trained to work with individuals rather than with couples. They're used to having a relationship with one person in the room and seeing problems as located in or with an individual — not two people.

The dynamics of couple therapy are different and can be quite demanding. As a result, some therapists start by seeing a couple together and then move to a series of sessions with each individual. This approach may help the therapist focus on each partner one at a time, but it inhibits the therapist's work on the relationship. In individual therapy, the couple's relationship is missing from the room.

Contemporary couple therapy professionals don't recommend treating couples by working with individuals in isolation. Without the relationship in the room, it's more difficult for partners to know or experience what's changing at a personal level or in their relationship. EFT is an interactive approach where couples often share their experiences with each other and take risks to talk together in new ways. The power of change is in the present moment, and this is greatly reduced when one partner is missing.

Your therapist may use individual sessions in couple therapy to address specific issues. For example, we may use an individual session to check out concerns about a partner's safety or gain a better understanding of a past traumatic experience not involving the other partner. Many emotionally focused therapists use an individual session at the beginning of therapy as a part of their routine assessment. Other times they may use an individual session to focus more on a specific individual concern. We make it clear to both people why we're meeting separately and address how we'll honor what's shared in an individual session and tie that back into the couple therapy.

Do You Focus More on Strengthening the Couple or on Each Partner Individually?

The answer to this question tells you something about how the therapist sees change happening in therapy. Does change happen through helping individuals to grow and become more psychologically healthy? Or does the therapist use sessions to focus on the couple's relationship as the basis of change? An emotionally focused therapist focuses both on couple and individual experience, but the primary basis for change is the couple's relationship.

A stronger relationship brings resilience to both partners individually and to the couple. As a couple's relationship changes and more emotional security and positive emotion are felt, couples are less reactive when dealing with difficult situations. They're better problem solvers in part because they can use their emotional experiences more effectively in addressing the typical issues that couples confront. Relationships are a resource for resilience and change. Emotionally focused therapists make working with the relationship a central focus of their work.

What Do You Focus on Most When Working with Couples?

Some therapists may be surprised by this question, but that's okay — you should know what to expect from your therapist, and this question helps get you there.

Some approaches focus on communication skills and behavior change. These therapies often teach couples new ways of communicating using practice exercises and homework to help them incorporate these new behaviors into their everyday lives. Other approaches emphasize new understanding and insights. Partners increase their understanding and awareness of specific dynamics influencing their relationship; these insights are the focus of sessions and a primary basis for change.

An emotionally focused therapist focuses on emotional experience. There is a "here and now" focus to this model where primary attention is given to what's happening in the therapy room. EFT is focused on working with emotion, helping couples make explicit that which is often not spoken, and using therapy as an opportunity to work with these experiences in new ways.

What Do You Do If a Couple Isn't Sure They Should Stay Together?

Some therapists are more "marriage friendly." Other therapists are more "divorce friendly." William Doherty, a professor and marriage and family therapist, warns couples that couple therapy can be hazardous to your marriage if your therapist doesn't view marriage in the same way that you do. He encourages couples to pay attention to the values a therapist has about couple therapy before beginning therapy.

Knowing whether your therapist will be totally neutral on whether your relationship makes or breaks can be vital. Many therapists take a neutral response to this question. Ask yourself, "Do I want a therapist who will help us fight for this relationship?" If so, listen carefully to the therapist's response to this question. The decision about your relationship is your own, but so is the decision to choose a therapist who will give you what you need.

We don't believe that a therapist should make this decision for you, but we do propose that the therapist not be neutral when you're sure you want your relationship to work out.

When Should Couples Stay Together or Break Up?

Typically, a therapist will say, "It depends on the couple." This isn't a bad response, because, ethically, therapists don't make decisions for their couples. But see if you can push the therapist to talk a bit about when a couple should break up.

For example, if a relationship involves domestic violence, which is harmful to victims and children who are exposed to violence, divorce may be the best option. If a partner refuses to address destructive patterns of addiction or engages in repeated affairs that destroy trust, divorce may be best.

Beware of therapists who see divorce as a solution unto itself. More often the issues behind a breakup are more important than the decision to stay or go.

What Percentage of the Couples You've Seen Would Say You Helped Them Improve Their Relationship?

This may seem like an obvious question, but few clients actually ask therapists about their success rates. Granted, judging success in therapy is often difficult, and many factors can influence treatment outcomes. However, two-thirds of people show improvement in psychotherapy, so you should be looking for a percentage at least this high.

In studies of emotionally focused couple therapy, rates of improvement are as high as 90 percent. These rates are based on clinical research studies conducted with selected couples and highly supervised therapists, but you should expect a good couple therapist to say that at least 75 percent of his or her clients would say they've been helped.

Chapter 17

Ten Rituals to Bring You Closer

Couples often do things together that give them a feeling of togetherness. Whether it's a regular date night or a weekly tennis match, these events when repeated over time can provide a deeper sense of unity. They also mark what's unique about you as a couple. Simply put, they give meaning to your relationship.

Shared activities create memories, stories, and experiences, especially when they're done intentionally. In this chapter, we offer ten ways you and your partner can be more intentional in expressing attachment in your relationship. Each ritual we talk about provides opportunities for expressing love, care, and value. The key is finding a ritual that works for both you and your partner, as well as one that you can commit to.

It's better to postpone or reschedule than it is to skip your ritual altogether. Be careful to both agree on resetting the ritual. Inconsistency breaks the power of a ritual, but flexibility is necessary to make consistency a reality.

Hello and Goodbye

Greeting rituals can be an important and brief way of communicating love and dedication to your partner. These repeated gestures of importance can be as simple as a hug, kiss, or special word or phrase used when saying hello or goodbye. Some couples develop more elaborate or distinctive ways that signal to one another that they're special. The key is that the gestures are consistent — they become part of a couple's own language of love.

Ritual versus routine: It's all about intention

The difference between ritual and routine is the meaning you give to the activities.

William J. Doherty, author of *Take Back Your Marriage: Sticking Together in a World That Pulls Us Apart* (Guilford Press), and a leading expert on improving marriage, encourages couples to be intentional in expressing their commitment to each other and to take steps to make their rituals more effective. The more formal and involved a ritual activity, the more important it is for you to be intentional about expressing your commitment to each other — otherwise, it could just end up feeling like routine.

Here are some keys to creating effective rituals:

✔ **Include a clear signal to mark the ritual.** Communicate to one another that this activity is intentional, not just a random act. Include a clear starting point for the beginning of this activity.

✔ **Practice consistency and predictability in your rituals.** In order for something to become a ritual, you need to do it regularly. If you let it slide because you get busy, that's a sign that the activity — and, therefore, your relationship — isn't important enough. Consistency is key.

✔ **Be clear on responsibilities for the ritual.** Both of you need to be actively involved in making the ritual happen. It can't fall entirely on one person's shoulders. Make sure you both know your parts.

✔ **Conclude the ritual with affirmation.** Tell each other what you appreciate about the ritual and each other.

Rituals require more than spending time together — they involve specific action. Some rituals require planning, while others are more spontaneous. When rituals are repeated, they become part of a relationship and are noticed when they're missed. Rituals help you practice expressing love and sharing value in your relationship. Taking time to experience and reflect on your rituals makes them more meaningful.

Think about how you can almost relive a vacation by looking at pictures and talking together about the experience you shared. The effects of a vacation can have a life of their own, and this comes from making meaning from your shared experience.

Carolyn and Nathan have a "secret handshake." It involves a number of movements in sequence and ends with three squeezes. These squeezes signal the words "I love you." They do the handshake at the airport when departing or in front of their kids when they feel like it. It's a sign of affection, and it's unique. Sometimes they abbreviate it with three squeezes. It's their shorthand for reminding each other that they're special to one other.

Scheduling Regular Date Nights

When was the last time you had a great date with your partner? If you're busy or you've fallen into a routine that's all about work and family, taking time to schedule a regular night out — for just the two of you — can be a proactive step in easing the demands of a time-starved relationship.

The ritual of a date night doesn't have to be elaborate — it just has to be consistent and intentional. Setting aside time for each other is key. Making an appointment for your relationship means you're giving it priority. Keeping your date means *keeping* your relationship a priority.

After you've made time for your date night, make sure you also take time to talk about what would make the time special. Think about your most memorable dates, if you need direction. Finding examples from the past may give you new ideas for future dates. Being intentional about sharing expectations keeps you tuned into the needs and desires of your partner.

Sending Notes and Cards

Writing a note or sending a card tells your partner that he or she is important to you. Taking time to write a note shows that your partner is on your mind. Thinking about your partner when you're away is a common sign of a strong attachment bond. Taking the extra step of communicating your thoughts by sending a text message, e-mail, or handwritten note makes obvious to your partner what you're feeling. Written expressions of affection have the power of showing your partner that he or she counts.

These notes often mean more when you're separated by time or distance. When you tuck a note into your partner's suitcase before he or she heads out on a business trip, it can be a welcome surprise for your partner. It shows that you're intentional and that you're thinking about him or her. This simple action can trigger feelings of love and affection, even though you aren't in the same room (much less the same time zone).

These notes don't have to be long — they just have to be personal. Let your partner know something you appreciate about him or her. Or mention something you're thankful for. Notes of gratitude and appreciation help you express what can so easily be taken for granted in a relationship.

Setting Aside Time to Talk

Couples with small children or limited resources often find it difficult to get away for a date night. In these cases, setting aside 15 minutes to talk on a regular basis is more realistic. If this is a better option for you, find a consistent time that both of you can count on. Set boundaries — for example:

✓ No interruptions.

✓ No electronic devices.

✓ No discussions of work or children.

Your goal is to keep the time focused on each other. Keep the time manageable but also meaningful.

Start with quantity, and trust that the quality will show up. For some couples, just ten minutes in the same space without stress and demands reminds them of what's good in life.

When you feel pressured and the ritual feels forced, trust the process. Setting aside a period of time without demands and with your partner can give you a breather — even if it isn't the most romantic 15 minutes of your day.

Tim and Jack set aside 15 to 20 minutes after they put the kids to bed. They light a candle in the front room and bring a cup of tea or a glass of wine. This is their way of signaling the start of their time together. They keep the focus of their conversation on their day and how they're feeling. They try to focus on something in their day that was positive and something that was disappointing. Sometimes they have a lot to talk about, and other times they allow moments of silence, just having some quiet time together. Neither of them has energy to plan an outing or a date, but they do have 15 minutes to find each other in the midst of a busy schedule, demanding jobs, and raising children.

Learning Something New Together

Rosa and Fred found that they had more free time after their youngest child graduated from high school. Fred played golf on occasion and admitted he wasn't good at it, even though he enjoyed hanging out with his buddies. Rosa also enjoyed the sport but she'd had little time to develop her game, what with running between work and their son's school activities. The couple decided to take a series of golf lessons. They were at different skill levels, but they scheduled their lessons at the same time and made a ritual out of their weekly golf lessons. This included driving together to the club, taking their lessons, and then having a drink together to talk about what they learned.

For couples like Fred and Rosa, learning a new activity or skill gave them something to focus on together. The challenge of furthering their skills demanded more out of each of them, and they found ways to share their triumphs and defeats. They also found the process of learning together rewarding. As they improved their handicaps, they rewarded each other.

Keeping a focus on learning and growing as a couple helps partners bring new energy and ideas to their relationship. Learning together can deepen a couple's shared sense of accomplishment and the pride that goes along with it. Learning also involves taking risks — couples who are able to take risks together find ways to bring this risk taking into their relationship. Taking chances, failing, and succeeding brings couples together as they practice ways to support and celebrate their personal challenges and shared successes.

Investing in Activities to Strengthen Your Relationship

Dedication is an important aspect of commitment in a thriving relationship. Couples who have strong levels of dedication are more likely to be happier, to be more open, and to have less conflict in their relationships. They're more likely to take steps to improve and sacrifice for their relationship. One way to increase your commitment is to take active steps to invest in your relationship.

Reading a book on relationships can spark new ideas for growth and improvement. Sharing these ideas and participating in exercises can help you take steps of deeper commitment.

Hold Me Tight: Seven Conversations for a Lifetime of Love, by Dr. Sue Johnson (Little, Brown), includes a series of structured exercises that lead couples through intentional conversations to strengthen their attachment bond. These exercises provide practical resources for improving your relationship and growing a stronger bond.

Couples who make a routine of improving their relationships may also attend workshops and retreats for couples. These retreats give couples time away to focus on each other and strengthen their commitment. These intentional steps provide opportunities for couples to recommit to the purpose of their relationship.

Other couples find less formal opportunities to focus on their relationship. David and Joy have a commitment to spend one weekend a year discussing their relationship. They call it their "summit," and they use the time to discuss the year ahead and important decisions they need to make as a couple. On one of the nights, they give themselves a relationship "checkup." Each person has time to talk about his or her joys, concerns, and needs.

Couples' needs change over time. Taking the time to intentionally address your relationship makes space to invest in the commitment you share.

Celebrating Important Events

Rituals can be a powerful way of spanning time. Planning and remembering special days have a way of marking the importance of people and relationships over time.

Heather and Corbin take time on their wedding anniversary to look at pictures from the past. They use this ritual as a way of remembering all they've shared and the memories that shape their relationship.

Anniversaries can be a source of celebration and a marker of the importance of your relationship in your lives. Birthdays can also be special opportunities to communicate value. Making a special effort to express appreciation for your partner communicates how important he or she is in your life. This strengthens your attachment bond.

Be careful to discuss expectations surrounding these rituals. Partners bring different family experiences to their relationships, and with these experiences come different expectations. A missed birthday or anniversary can be seen as a lack of care or concern. It may also just be a difference in how rituals were practiced in one partner's family versus the other. Taking time to discuss your different experiences and to share expectations can help you avoid hurt feelings and misunderstandings in the future.

Finding an Interest You Can Share

Familiarity and boredom are intimacy killers. Securely attached couples find time to play together. Attachment rituals should be life giving to both of you. If not, it's time to find a new ritual.

Vital couples find fun activities to share. Having fun together is a source of renewal and refreshment for them. For example, physical activity can be energizing and provide you an opportunity to stay fit and healthy. Hiking, dancing, or sharing a sport offers you a chance to organize around activities that combine leisure time and companionship.

Other activities may involve artistic expression and creative expression. Dean and Jeanette pride themselves on their elaborate English garden. This involves a series of rituals that include planning and planting the garden, as well as an annual dinner party to show off their shared creation. They take pride in what they've done and in having others enjoy their creative effort.

Other couples organize around common artistic interests such as ballet, culinary arts, or literature. Others involve being fans of a sports team. Couples who are able to find a shared interest that they can invest in find new ways of investing in the bonds they share.

Brock and Jada love movies. On their monthly date night, they take turns choosing the movie they'll see. Whether it's an action/adventure film or a romantic comedy, each partner's choice stands — no complaints. Sometimes they have time for dinner beforehand, but they always end the evening with dessert or a drink to talk about the movie. During these times, they laugh, complain, critique, and appreciate the film — but most important, they show their love of movies and each other.

Serving Others

Taking time to help others or give to those in need offers couples a unique opportunity to invest in their relationship for the sake of others. Serving a common goal helps a couple find a deeper sense of unity by transcending their personal interests.

Carl and Shari take time each month to serve at a local soup kitchen. "I like this about us," said Shari. "It's our way of giving back and it's something we do together."

Serving others helps you see beyond your own needs and, as a result, can provide a deeper meaning for your relationship. When you make a shared decision to dedicate your time or resources to others, you make a joint expression of your values.

Several times a year, Paul and Linda give a weekend to an organization that builds homes for the underprivileged. "We talked for some time about making a difference in our community," Paul confessed. "Then Linda suggested we give it a try. We're better for it because it gives us each a way of giving back, and we do it together. I like that we feel better about ourselves when we give to others."

Couples find many ways to serve. Some couples focus on caring for the environment, while others get involved in efforts to conserve and improve their communities. Volunteering as a couple expresses a common purpose that others see and affirm. Many couples find value in more sacred pursuits, sharing in religious and spiritual activities that include serving others. These activities may also benefit a couple by being faithful to deeply held values.

Being Affectionate

Making love is an important ritual of connection. Sexual contact in a relationship of care, trust, and vulnerability communicates a deep level of intimacy. Couples who keep a focus on each other and expressions of sexual affection find greater meaning in these rituals than those who focus mostly on their sexual needs. Keeping romance in sex often requires couples to find ways of being intentional about expressing both their physical and emotional desires.

Taking time to share loving words or special actions that show intention and affection can set the stage for romance. Focusing on the relationship and how important your partner is to you helps create a sense of safety and security. Sex becomes more free and playful when partners feel safe with one another.

Keeping fun and play in your relationship helps make sex a vital part of your relationship and an important way of communicating love.

Everyday moments of sharing physical affection also create rituals of attachment. Hugging, kissing, and holding hands show partners that they're important and special. Deliberate acts of affection are subtle and effective reminders of care and kindness, and a demonstration that you hold a special place in each other's life.

Chapter 18

Ten Myths about Emotion and Relationships

In This Chapter

▶ Identifying the common myths you may have bought into

▶ Focusing on reality instead of on myths

Myths about emotion and relationships can stand in the way of using your own emotion for a more clearly informed and healthy life. You have emotions to instantly reveal what you need in a situation. You can learn to better integrate the "instant messaging" of your primary emotions into your life, instead of trying to control or change your emotion, which is an outdated understanding of how healthy and helpful emotions are to you.

Learning to heed the meaning of your underlying emotions will help you be a better partner, parent, friend, and employee. Your primary emotions are already working to help guide you. The degree to which you're aware of them and listen to them depends on you.

In this chapter, we put an end to some of the glaring, outdated misperceptions about emotions. Recent findings in affective neuroscience and a greater understanding of the healthy centrality of emotion in the fields of marriage and family therapy and psychology now have lots to say in erasing old misunderstandings. Sometimes misbeliefs can hamper progress in many areas of your life. As you move toward a fuller life emotionally, these errors no longer need to impair your progress.

Myth #1: Men Don't Do Emotions

This sentiment is taught to many boys very early in life. Statements such as, "Boys don't cry," "Dry it up!", and "Don't be a sissy!" can begin a trajectory of dissociating from emotion for males, making it difficult for them to intimately relate to their partners as adults.

We've seen many men in therapy learn the truth about how important emotion is, and as they begin to tap into their own emotions, they're stunned to learn that an entire world exists that was previously outside their awareness. "I can't believe how powerful this is," Stan said of his own growth in listening to his bodily felt emotions. "All these years, I pushed my emotions away, stuffed them down. Now as I allow myself to feel, listen, and accept my emotions, I'm finding a whole new world of wisdom that I never dreamed was there. And it's been there all along!"

Women sometimes don't understand the lengths that some men go to in order to avoid emotion. The socialization of girls and boys can be strikingly different. Listening to and trusting primary emotion really can be an entirely new language for men. Ali was shocked at how little Geoff knew about emotion. "When things got sad or vulnerable," she said, "it was like he suddenly didn't even speak English. It's like the way I talked with my girlfriends at age 7 was beyond any level of emotional conversation he had experienced. He was so shut off from my — and his own — emotional worlds. It was killing us."

The fact is, men can become aware of their emotions and integrate them into their daily lives. But men must learn to *integrate* their emotions, rather than trying to *change* them, which is the message of emotional intelligence proponents. What we're saying is different — it's more holistic. You can learn the difference between secondary, reactive emotion and primary, adaptive emotion. You can be a wiser man because of this. Men who incorporate this approach into their lives become better partners, better dads, and better employees. In short, they become better people.

"My life has more color now," Don said. "I'll never be a poet. I realize that. But life is richer and clearer now that I listen to and let my emotion say its piece."

Myth #2: Women Are More Sensitive than Men

Women are often socialized to be more emotionally aware and demonstratively sensitive than men. Researchers have consistently found that even young girls are much more concerned with how others feel, whereas boys are more concerned with competing.

But too often, society accepts this as an inborn genetic reality. Being born female doesn't automatically make you emotionally aware. We've worked with plenty of women who struggle with effectively integrating their emotions. The good news is that everyone can learn to better integrate emotions into everyday awareness.

What's commonly thought of as women being "more sensitive" than men is more a case of women being more in tune with their emotions. That's healthy.

Myth #3: Emotions Are Irrational

Many people have the misguided belief that emotions are irrational. Usually what is referred to as "irrational" is someone who's had a secondary emotional meltdown. For example, John finds his partner in bed with someone else, for example, and John goes berserk, loses his temper, and does something stupid. That's "irrational."

When emotions are referred to as irrational, it's usually about someone doing something stupid while awash in a pool of reactive secondary emotion. If you're reacting to something deeper — some kind of emotional pain, for example — but you aren't aware of what that deeper emotion is, then you are, in effect, responding from your secondary emotion. Such responses do, in fact, often seem irrational. But don't blame that irrationality on emotion.

The point is, you can trust your primary emotions. When you ignore them and, instead, react out of your secondary emotions, you may get yourself into trouble. This is what the vast majority of people are talking about when they say emotion is irrational. If John had the personal maturity, for example, to listen to his primary emotion when he saw his partner in bed with another man, he would've slowed down and felt that he was, in fact, angry — and for good reason! But he would've also realized that he was in a world of hurt, too. And by slowing down and listening to his primary emotion, John would've allowed his thinking to catch up to his primary emotions, and he would've stopped himself from charging in and playing the fool.

[handwritten margin notes: "Can trust Primary, Can't trust secondary emotion"]

Myth #4: Emotions Get in the Way of Making Good Decisions

Statements such as "Don't be emotional when making decisions" and "Take the emotion out of it" are common. This kind of thinking stems from not understanding the different layers of emotional processing. When people talk like this, they're almost always referring to secondary emotional reactions, like anger and frustration.

But heeding primary emotion has the opposite effect. When primary emotion is brought into awareness, you get clear on your needs and wants. And you get clear on when you feel you're being taken advantage of or when a business decision just isn't good. These gut-felt responses or intuitions can be streamlined into immediate awareness and used to help guide you.

You don't need to "control" your primary emotions. Just the opposite: You need to learn to let them guide you more. That's why primary emotions are there — and why they've remained there across time. Ignore them at your own peril!

Myth #5: Your Thoughts Are in Charge of Your Emotions

In this day and age, if someone says that you can control your emotions with your thoughts, he's simply unaware of mounds of neurological research — or maybe he has too much invested in the myth to let it go.

Today we know that emotions *set up* our thinking. They arrive in lightning-fast fashion and set the stage for the later-occurring thoughts. When we're in danger, for example, we simply don't have time to think it out. Your emotional system reads the situation and sends you signals of fight or flight before you can consciously think and reflect on the situation.

We need both emotion and cognition to function at our best. Trying to love and make decisions without both can be dangerous. But cognition has been so overemphasized in comparison to emotion that it's the emotional part of the equation that many people simply don't yet understand and use. We could give example after example of clients who "know" how they should be thinking and behaving differently, for example. But so many of them report, "I know what I should do in my mind — I know it — but when I get afraid or worried, I just can't do it. My emotion is too strong. It stops me."

Emotions are powerful. When you ignore them by pushing them away, they can leave you paralyzed to behave in ways that you know you should. Often, that's because you aren't clearly experiencing what your deep, primary emotions are trying to tell you. You aren't receiving the clear meaning from your emotions. When you do, you get clearer in your head, too — and your primary emotion moves you to act, instead of being stuck in fear or worry.

Myth #6: Painful Feelings Are Always Bad

Tom recently went to a funeral. Tom hates funerals. That's pretty normal, actually — ask 20 people, and you won't find one who *likes* funerals. Funerals are sad, depressing, painful, and sometimes cruel. They run the gamut of painful emotions. But painful feelings aren't all bad. "When my dad died," Tom said, "it reminded me of what my life is really about. The pain of losing him got me back on track with what matters to me." Tom shared with us how, as he sat in his sadness at his dad's funeral, he gained more clarity into his life and how he wants his future to look.

Painful emotions can ground you. We say "can" because if you run away from them and refuse to feel them, you're refusing their message to you. If you allow yourself to feel painful emotions, they remind you what's important in your life. When you emotionally hurt, you feel firsthand what's important to you. You don't get sad and cry over something that doesn't matter.

When you say something you regret to your partner, for example, it's not long before it begins to emotionally tug at you. As you feel emotionally disconnected from your partner, your primary emotions of hurt and loneliness emphatically tell you that your current state isn't good. The pain compels you to go do something about it, to go find resolution and reconnection. And if you're able to do this, your pain is washed away by the equally powerful emotions of happiness and joy, stemming from acceptance, connection, and emotional harmony with your partner. The funny thing is, if you refuse to feel your pain deeply, you also make it impossible to feel your happiness and joy deeply. You can't have one without the other.

Myth #7: Experiencing Emotion Makes It Worse

Some people think that if they let themselves feel their painful emotions, it will make the situation worse and make their pain more painful. In more extreme cases, these people may turn to alcohol and drugs to ward off their emotions.

"I keep my pain as far away from me as possible," Becky said. "If I let myself actually feel, I might die." What Becky needed most was to face her painful emotions, learn from them, and then begin living in a manner that no longer evaded them. She had lived her life numbing herself to her emotions. If she felt them coming on, she would start drinking or find some drugs to knock her out.

The opposite of this myth is true: When you face and fully feel your emotions, they get their message across to you, and they begin to dissipate. Mission accomplished. It's like putting hydrogen peroxide on a wound. When you first apply it, it hurts a lot. But as the hydrogen peroxide does its job of cleaning the wound, the stinging goes away. If you ignore your emotion, just like refusing to clean a wound, the pain only grows and returns another day, with more strength.

Emotions are there to get your attention and to let you know what's important.

Myth #8: Emotions Get in the Way of Business Decisions

When people say, "Don't take it personally — it's just business" or "You have to remove emotions when making business decisions," they're usually referring to someone's secondary emotional response of aggression or defensiveness. Sure enough, someone caught in secondary emotion can be difficult to work with. And it's not a good idea to make decisions when you're feeling the effects of secondary emotions like anger or frustration. But that isn't helpful in intimate relationships, parenting, or friendship either.

Being aware of your own and others' primary emotions is a great asset when making business decisions and in being an effective leader. Effective leaders — those who garner loyalty from others — are most often the ones who are well tuned in to their own emotional worlds and those of others. People can tell that they care because they show genuine empathy, which is only possible by demonstrating emotional sensitivity.

Myth #9: Anger Is Always Bad

Like all emotions, anger is a signal with a message. It tells you when something is wrong, and it prepares you to make it stop — to protect yourself. Anger, in the right context, is there because you need it. When you feel infringed upon, your boundaries crossed, taken advantage of, and so forth, anger immediately organizes you to protect and assert yourself to stop the intrusion. Anger, in and of itself, is helpful.

It's how you *respond* to your anger that leads to the myth that anger is always bad. If you get out of control in anger, it's never helpful. If you use your anger to assert your proper boundaries or to let others know when their behavior is harmful to you, those are proper uses of anger.

Couples can learn to recognize their anger with each other and discuss it without attacking each other's character. A goal of removing anger from a relationship is an impossible one. Often, simply naming the anger as it's happening ("I'm angry right now") can help you contain it.

Myth #10: Happy Couples Don't Argue

This myth should have been dead 20 years ago. John Gottman, a leading couple researcher, found that even his "master" couples — those who stayed happily married over many years — argued with each other. His couples who divorced argued. In fact, the only couples who *didn't* argue had grown distant, and even though they never argued, they were headed for divorce.

A pivotal difference between happy couples and divorcing couples is the *way* they argue. Happy couples argue without criticizing each other's character. These couples don't fall into the extremes of what Gottman refers to as "The Four Horsemen": criticism, contempt, defensiveness, and stonewalling. Extremes in these categories were found to reliably predict divorce. Arguing itself was not a factor in divorce. Arguing without falling into "The Four Horsemen" categories was a common trait of the "master" couples Gottman followed over two decades. In fact, he noted that some "master" couples were arguing about the same exact issues 20 years after he had initially interviewed them!

As couple therapists, we aren't especially alarmed when couples argue in our offices. In fact, it's the couples who never argue that worry us most. Too often, they no longer care enough to argue.

Chapter 19

Ten Myths about Sex

Human sexuality is so often misportrayed in movies, TV shows, magazines, and the media overall that it's no wonder so many couples are confused and misguided when it comes to understanding what makes up a realistic, healthy sex life. Generally, men are taught very little about the relational dimension of sexuality. All too often, it's driven into a man's mind early on that sex is about performance — ejaculation. And as men get older, that sometimes includes orgasm for their partners.

A problem with this is that men grow to see sex as individualistic, as in "I perform right, and she has an orgasm." Men can be very focused on their own performance and miss a crucial element of sex: It's about two. And that doesn't just mean she orgasms and you ejaculate. It means the world of sex is about the two of you. In a session, a woman said to her husband, "We have each other. Let's sexually play together. Discover together. The playground is there for us. Let's block out the world, drop our fears, and just have fun together on our own sexual journey."

Women in this culture more often view sex in terms of closeness and relationship. "Sex is the glue that holds us together," one of our clients said. "It's like we have all these tough times in our marriage, but if we're having sex somewhat regularly, we can better weather the tough times. When we aren't having sex, the tough times become much tougher."

Michael E. Metz and Barry W. McCarthy, authors of *Enduring Desire: Your Guide to Lifelong Intimacy* (Routledge), specialize in researching and writing about healthy sexuality for couples. Their model of "good-enough sex" and writings on key sexual learning for men are highly recommended. Many of their findings are in this chapter.

Myth #1: All Men Care About Is Sex

Researchers have found that men between the ages of 18 and 25 think about sex once every five minutes. Between the ages of 26 and 55, 25 percent of men couldn't go five minutes without sex popping into their minds. But even though men think about sex *often,* that doesn't mean that sex is *all* they care about.

Most men learn early on that they have to learn to take control of their sexual thoughts and urges. This is what Michael Metz refers to as regulating sexual drive and arousal. According to Metz, men must learn to

- ✔ **Acknowledge, accept, and respect their body's *biological imperative.*** In other words, men have to accept the fundamental power of sex and learn to accept the need to self-regulate.

- ✔ **Learn to manage their biologically natural tendency toward visual *sexual objectification* when faced with external sexual stimuli.** Men can move beyond this tendency with self-discipline, reminding themselves that women are not sexual "objects." A man can personalize his sexual thoughts and urges toward his partner and his sexual relationship.

- ✔ **Differentiate general emotions (such as loneliness, worry, or anxiety) from sexual feelings.** Keeping your focus on your experience and your partner will help you stay with the pleasure in the moment.

- ✔ **Place their ultimate sexual focus on *intimacy.*** Sexuality is relational.

Men who learn and incorporate these things often find themselves freed to enjoy a deeper sexuality with their partners that they never knew could exist. This is the opposite of the hokey sex seen in pornography, which is often drug fueled, intensity faked, and emotionally bankrupt, offering a destructive view of healthy sexuality for both women and men.

You can help each other counteract our culture's misunderstandings and find each other on your own sexual playground. Don't take our culture's erroneous bait — men are *not* just about sex.

Myth #2: Good Sex Always Leads to Orgasm

Good sex takes many different forms. It can be a time of

- ✔ Emotional pick-me-up
- ✔ Shared pleasure

✔ Stress relief

✔ Emotional closeness

✔ Boosting self-confidence

✔ Reinforcing the greatness of feeling wanted and desired

✔ Quick release of anxiety

✔ Humor that brings closeness and reinforces playfulness

Sex can involve all these things and more. But one thing that good sex is never limited to, cannot always involve, and doesn't have to be obsessed with on every occasion is orgasm.

In reality, both men and women can feel shackled by such a misperception. It's one thing to always have to help your partner orgasm. And it's quite another to be expected to orgasm for your partner so that your partner can feel good about himself.

Try reassuring each other that it's not important every time. And speak up when it's not going to happen, or when you simply aren't feeling it. Many partners report being fine with sex, but not with always needing to orgasm. Take away that requirement and it can free up each of you to more sex and playfulness without unrealistic expectations.

Myth #3: Most Couples Have Sex Four Times a Week

Research on sex in married couples breaks into three categories:

✔ **Marriages without sex:** In these cases, sex occurs less than ten times a year. Twenty percent of married couples fall into this category.

✔ **Low-sex marriages:** In these cases, couples are sexual less than every week — less than 25 times a year. Fifteen percent of married couples fall into this category.

✔ **"Average" marriages:** On average, married couples have sex a little more than once a week, according to the 2005 General Social Survey conducted by the National Opinion Research Center. Frequency of sex for married couples varies by age: Couples 18 to 29 report having sex 109 times a year, while couples in their 60s report 32 times yearly.

You and your partner need to agree on what's best for you, and not worry about what everybody else is doing.

Myth #4: Unmarried Couples Who Live Together Have More Sex Than Married Couples Do

This seems to be one of the biggest myths out there today. The reality is that one in three unmarried couples who have been together over two years report having a relationship without sex (defined as less than ten times a year). Recent research has found that living together means different things to men and women. Women often see moving in together as a trial period — a prelude to possible marriage. Men, on the other hand, often see moving in together as mainly a way to increase the amount of sex. Men usually don't see living together as a prelude to marriage.

Myth #5: Simultaneous Orgasms Happen All the Time

The reality is, simultaneous orgasms don't happen all the time. Most women require direct clitoral stimulation to reach orgasm. In fact, one in three women never experience orgasm during intercourse. Orgasm most often occurs with partner stimulation apart from intercourse.

Setting up simultaneous orgasms as a goal or standard means you're doomed on many levels. It hurls both partners into a performance trap.

"I wish you would understand," Sarah said to her husband, Raymond. "I love having sex with you without my having an orgasm, too. I like having orgasms, but I'm not going to have them every time we're close. And that's fine. You put so much pressure on yourself. Let's get away from that."

Raymond thought that he had to bring his wife to orgasm every time they were intimate, or else she would be disappointed. If Sarah didn't orgasm, Raymond felt he was failing as a lover. It wasn't long before this started affecting Sarah. As she became more anxious, orgasm became almost impossible. Orgasm is about letting yourself go — not tightening up. This can become a vicious cycle for couples. Together, Sarah and Raymond had to work hard to create their own "normal" for their sex life.

Myth #6: Women Are the Ones Saying, "Not Tonight, Honey"

Researchers found that when couples aren't having sex, it's most often the man who has cut it off. Women say no occasionally, of course, but when the relationship is devoid of sex, it's almost always the man who has determined this.

Myth #7: Sex Equals Intercourse

Couple sex researchers stress that couples have to learn that sex is about so much more than just intercourse. According to Barry McCarthy, healthy sexual functioning is made up of

- **Desire:** Anticipation builds desire. Sometimes, sex really does start in the kitchen in the morning. Little comments like, "You look great in that suit!" and "Have a great day today — I'll be thinking about you" can begin building desire first thing in the morning. Sending each other thoughtful text messages or e-mails during the day, picking up something small at the store that your partner will like — all these things build desire.

- **Arousal:** Being open and receptive to the touch and caress of your partner increases arousal. Make a note to go slow and enjoy each other without rushing to intercourse or orgasm. McCarthy refers to couples allowing men to "wax and wane" through erections, which allows partners to slow down. Some couples believe that when a man is erect, his arousal has peaked, but this isn't the case. Touching and caressing while allowing his erection to wax and wane can greatly build the arousal of both partners. Similarly, when a woman's vagina begins to lubricate, it doesn't mean that her arousal has peaked.

- **Orgasm:** Whether it be by partner stimulation, oral sex, or intercourse, letting yourself go emotionally and physically with your partner builds intimacy. Get lost in the experience, and try not to hold back. It's not about performance. It's about allowing yourselves to be open and receptive to each other.

- **Satisfaction:** Sex in this way leaves you feeling emotionally and physically bonded. That is the essence of healthy couple sexuality. You each risk allowing yourselves to know and be known by your partner.

Couple sexuality is most healthy when the feelings and needs of both partners are heeded and respected. The key is integrating intimacy, pleasuring, and eroticism. McCarthy uses a wonderful metaphor of a five-gear car to illustrate this:

- The first gear is affectionate touching (kissing, holding hands, hugging, and so on).

- The second gear is sensual, non-genital pleasuring (cuddling, body massage, touching as you fall asleep or upon awakening, and so on). Non-genital pleasuring can take place clothed, partially clothed, or naked.

- The third gear is playful touch with both non-genital and genital touching. This can occur anywhere (within the law that is!) or in any room of the house.

- The fourth gear includes manual, oral, or rubbing stimulation to arousal and orgasm for one or both partners.

- The fifth gear combines erotic and pleasurable touch with intercourse. Intercourse becomes a natural extension of a pleasure orientation — another touching experience.

When each partner is free to initiate each gear, the couple has a vast and flexible playground to connect and share intimacy and sexuality. Incorporating these five gears into your sexual pleasuring is a highly effective way to maintain a vital couple sexuality.

Myth #8: Men Understand Women or Women Understand Men

Well, sometimes.

Men and women are often socialized very differently. Boys are often taught to be tough, suck it up, and be competitive. Boys are rarely taught to understand or share their emotions. Girls, on the other hand, are often taught to share emotions with each other. Girls usually learn to prize feelings more than boys do. Thus, girls gain a kind of emotional intelligence, a sense of empathy for others that many boys do not.

Boys are often taught more of a "fix-it" mentality. "I was taught to dismiss my emotions because they only get in the way of fixing the problem at hand," Roger shared. "If I listened to my emotions, my friends would've moved on without me." This was very different from Erica's upbringing. "I was kind of just the opposite," Erica shared. "If someone got her feelings hurt, we all would put the game on hold to make sure she was okay. Once that was sorted out, we would continue with what we were doing."

You can see how this kind of socialization sets up women and men to collide in misunderstanding later in life. Somehow our culture separates boys and girls from playing with each other until they're older, so they miss out on learning from each other through their formative years.

At the end of the day, you just have to learn to understand your own unique partner, not all women or all men.

Myth #9: Hot Sex Based on "Romantic Love" Should Never Fade

The lure of this myth can draw partners into affairs. It feels good to be recognized as sexy and wanted again by someone new. And the unfamiliarity of sex with someone new can ignite a wild passion and a flood of feelings that you had early on with your partner.

Couple sex researcher Barry McCarthy breaks through the illusion and points couples into a more mature love and sex that leaves early romantic love where it should stay — at the beginning stage of a sexual relationship. According to McCarthy, romantic love is inherently unstable and should never be looked upon as what healthy sexuality is. Although it's powerful and natural, romantic love

- ✔ Is inherently unstable
- ✔ Usually ends before marriage
- ✔ Seldom lasts past the first year
- ✔ Is explosive, and equally short-lived

In contrast, mature sexuality that follows romantic love means

- ✔ Sexual desire is based on emotional and sexual intimacy, not on romantic love or passionate sex.
- ✔ Comfort, attraction, and trust nurture desire after that initial heat is gone.
- ✔ Sexual desire is interpersonal, not individual.
- ✔ The goal is to build an intimate, lasting team.

Desire and satisfaction are the core of sexuality. Romantic love will pass, but being romantic with each other and having erotic sex don't have to. Mutual pleasuring, role playing, having sex in different places or in different positions, with or without sexual aids — all these things help to create erotic and passionate sex that long outlives the initial romantic love stage.

Myth #10: Pornography Is Good for Your Sex Life

People can use pornography to *avoid* intimacy, which is consistent with research suggesting that compulsive porn users may fear closeness. Most porn doesn't present sex as an intimate union that builds emotional closeness. Sexuality is bigger than intercourse, however — it's really about connection. Humans search for intimacy with another — we're hard-wired for it. Even when you're afraid of intimacy, you still desire it — just in a manner that feels safer to you. So, some people turn to porn to fill the healthy need for intimacy.

Healthy sexuality involves the two of you as a team.

According to Michael Metz, the key is in realizing that sexuality is always relational, even if you're single. Sexual performance just can't be the focus of either partner. A lot of pornography accentuates performance in sex — sex acts and orgasm — and makes it the definition of great sex. This is unrealistic, fake, and dangerous to the degree that it creates pressure and anxiety in couples. These are the very elements that block relaxing and letting go, which are necessary for orgasm in the first place.

This is not the case in all forms of pornography, however. So-called "soft porn," for example, can accentuate the intimacy of relationships, which is key. As in everything involving couple sexuality, it's vital that both partners be comfortable incorporating it.

Appendix

Resources

· ·

*T*he study of emotions continues to advance today's understanding of relationships. In years past, primary or core emotions were thought to be irrational, but the opposite is the case. Primary or "gut-felt" emotion is a powerful force that can guide couples toward more intimate and closer relationships with each other. The key is learning to tap into it. This appendix points you to additional resources that you can explore to further understand the power of emotion to strengthen your most important relationship.

Websites

The following websites provide a variety of resources you can use to find a therapist, access relationship education resources, or explore recent developments in the study of emotions and couple relationships.

- ✔ **Alan Schore, PhD (**www.allanschore.com**):** Alan Schore is a leading scholar in the study of emotion and attachment. This website includes a number of his papers for scholars and the general public. Excellent summaries of his work are available in presentations on YouTube.

- ✔ **American Association of Marriage and Family Therapy (AAMFT;** www.aamft.com**):** AAMFT is a national organization supporting the practice and profession of marital and family therapy. The site includes a number of resources, including a searchable database of therapists who meet specific standards of practice and professionalism.

- ✔ **Attachment Style Questionnaire (**www.web-research-design.net/cgi-bin/crq/crq.pl**):** This site hosts a web-based measure of adult attachment style. The assessment measure provides you a quick assessment of attachment dynamics in your life and your relationship.

- ✔ **Beyond Affairs Network (**www.beyondaffairs.com**):** This site provides resources for partners working to heal from infidelity and its destructive impact on a couple's relationship.

- ✔ **The Couple Zone (**www.couplezone.org**):** The Couple Zone is Brent's group practice located in Houston, Texas. They offer couples' enrichment workshops and therapy centered on working with core emotions.

- ✔ **Gottman Institute:** (www.gottman.com): This site includes resources and information developed by one of America's leading couple researchers, John Gottman, PhD, along with clinical psychologist Julie Gottman, PhD.

- ✔ **Hold Me Tight** (www.holdmetight.net): Dr. Sue Johnson developed a workshop for couples based on her best selling book, *Hold Me Tight* (mentioned in the following section). This site features resources and schedules for workshops based on the Hold Me Tight program.

- ✔ **International Centre for Excellence in Emotionally Focused Therapy (ICEEFT;** www.iceeft.com): ICEEFT is the home of emotionally focused therapy (EFT). Here you find information on the latest developments related to this approach and a list of therapists who have been certified in the EFT model.

- ✔ **The Mindsight Institute** (www.mindsightinstitute.com): Dr. Daniel Siegel is a leading voice in the exploration of interdisciplinary approaches to understanding the mind, attachment, and emotion. This site features a number of resources exploring the frontier of these developments.

- ✔ **The National Registry of Marriage Friendly Therapists** (www.marriage friendlytherapists.com): This site hosts a list of marital and couple therapists who have been screened for their level of training and commitment to helping couples work through issues in their marriage.

Books for Couples

The following books cover a range of topics that we touch on in *Emotionally Focused Couple Therapy For Dummies*. We recommend these books as resources that will take you farther in your understanding of emotion, attachment, and love.

- ✔ *Becoming Attached: First Relationships and How They Shape Our Capacity to Love,* **by Robert Karen, PhD (Oxford University Press):** This book takes the reader on a journey of how John Bowlby's attachment theory developed and found acceptance, against seemingly insurmountable odds. It's also a very personal book that aids in understanding your own attachment/love needs.

- ✔ *The Emotional Life of Your Brain: How Its Unique Patterns Affect the Way You Think, Feel, and Live — and How You Can Change Them,* **by Richard J. Davidson, PhD, and Sharon Begley (Plume):** In this book, a leading neuroscientist helps readers identify their unique emotional fingerprint. Based on over 30 years of research, this resource helps you determine your emotional style and its implication for everyday life.

- ✔ *Enduring Desire: Your Guide to Lifelong Intimacy,* **by Michael E. Metz and Barry W. McCarthy (Routledge):** It's impossible to go wrong in the area of sex when it's a work by Barry McCarthy. His teamwork approach is simply spot on.

✔ *Focusing,* **by Eugene Gendlin (Bantam):** A step-by-step approach to giving you new insight into how to identify your bodily experience of emotion. This approach offers great insight, awareness, and self-understanding through a set of basic practices, helping you make more of your emotional experience.

✔ *Getting Past the Affair: A Program to Help You Cope, Heal, and Move On — Together or Apart,* **by Douglas K. Snyder, PhD, Donald H. Baucom, PhD, and Kristina Coop Gordon, PhD (Guilford Press):** This book offers a cognitive-behavioral approach to understanding and moving forward after an affair. It's a research-informed and practical approach to recovering from infidelity, filled with resources that will help you make sense of how to heal your relationship following an affair.

✔ *Hold Me Tight: Seven Conversations for a Lifetime of Love,* **by Dr. Sue Johnson (Little, Brown and Company):** Sue Johnson was the co-developer of emotionally focused therapy for couples (along with Les Greenberg). This book explains attachment theory and covers key sticking points that couples find themselves struggling with.

✔ *Not "Just Friends": Rebuilding Trust and Recovering Your Sanity After Infidelity,* **by Shirley P. Glass, PhD, with Jean Coppock Staeheli (Free Press):** This is the best book available on understanding the world of affairs from the foremost expert on the subject. If there's one book to get on this subject, this is it.

✔ *The Seven Principles for Making Marriage Work,* **by John M. Gottman, PhD, and Nan Silver (Three Rivers Press):** A no-nonsense behavioral approach from the leading researcher in the field of marriage and family therapy. This is John Gottman's most well-known book for couples.

✔ *Social Intelligence: The New Science of Human Relationships,* **by Daniel Goleman (Bantam):** This book is a treasure chest full of interesting facts on emotional and social intelligence. Goleman pulls together the latest research in a reader-friendly manner that does not disappoint.

✔ *Take Back Your Marriage: Sticking Together in a World That Pulls Us Apart,* **by William J. Doherty, PhD (Guilford Press):** Doherty excels in identifying practical ways couples can intentionally strengthen their relationship.

Books for Therapy Professionals

The books in this section are excellent references for therapists looking to deepen their understanding of working with emotions. Some of these resources also explore the relationship of attachment processes and emotional experience. We also include emotionally focused resources for developing greater skill in the practice of this leading therapy approach.

- *Attachment in Adulthood: Structure, Dynamics, and Change,* by Mario Mikulincer and Phillip R. Shaver (Guilford Press)
- *Becoming an Emotionally Focused Couple Therapist: The Workbook,* by Susan M. Johnson, Brent Bradley, Jim Furrow, Alison Lee, Gail Palmer, Doug Tilley, and Scott Woolley (Routledge)
- *Descartes' Error: Emotion, Reason, and the Human Brain,* by Antonio Damasio (Penguin)
- *The Developing Mind: How Relationships and the Brain Interact to Shape Who We Are,* 2nd Edition, by Daniel J. Siegel (Guilford Press)
- *The Emotionally Focused Casebook: New Directions in Treating Couples,* edited by James L. Furrow, Susan M. Johnson, and Brent A. Bradley (Routledge)
- *Emotionally Focused Couple Therapy with Trauma Survivors: Strengthening Attachment Bonds,* by Susan M. Johnson (Guilford Press)
- *Facilitating Emotional Change: The Moment-by-Moment Process,* by Leslie S. Greenberg, Laura N. Rice, and Robert Elliott (Guilford Press)
- *Focusing-Oriented Psychotherapy: A Manual of the Experiential Method,* by Eugene T. Gendlin (Guilford Press)
- *Handbook of Attachment: Theory, Research, and Clinical Applications,* 2nd Edition, edited by Jude Cassidy and Phillip R. Shaver (Guilford Press)
- *The Healing Power of Emotion: Affective Neuroscience, Development & Clinical Practice,* edited by Diana Fosha, Daniel J. Siegel, and Marion F. Solomon (W. W. Norton)
- *The Practice of Emotionally Focused Couple Therapy: Creating Connection,* 2nd Edition, by Susan M. Johnson (Routledge)
- *The Science of the Art of Psychotherapy,* by Allan N. Schore (W. W. Norton)
- *A Secure Base: Parent-Child Development and Healthy Human Development,* by John Bowlby (Basic Books)
- *The Transforming Power of Affect: A Model for Accelerated Change,* by Diana Fosha (Basic Books)

Index

Notes

About the Authors

Dr. Brent Bradley: Brent is a tenured associate professor of family therapy at the University of Houston–Clear Lake. He is founder and president of the Couple Zone, a Houston-based therapy, training, and research institute that specializes in couple therapy (www.couplezone.org).

Brent is co-editor of *The Emotionally Focused Casebook: New Directions in Couple Treatment* and contributing author to *Becoming an EFT Therapist: The Workbook*. He conducts ongoing research in the field of couple therapy and regularly publishes in professional journals and books. Brent presents his research nationally at leading professional therapy conferences and supervises and teaches the leading relationally based experiential approaches.

Brent is a certified emotionally focused couple therapist, supervisor, and trainer. He has received advanced training in emotion-focused therapy for individuals from Les Greenberg, PhD, the author of the approach. Brent has also received advanced training in Accelerated Experiential-Dynamic Psychotherapy (www.aedpinstitute.org) under Diana Fosha, the author of the approach. He is a clinical member and supervisor of the American Association of Marriage and Family Therapy (www.aamft.org).

Dr. James Furrow: Jim is the Evelyn and Frank Freed Professor of Marital and Family Therapy at the Fuller Graduate School of Psychology in Pasadena, California. He is chair of the Department of Marriage and Family and a research faculty member with the Thrive Center for Human Development (www.thethrivecenter.org).

Jim is co-editor of *The Emotionally Focused Casebook: New Directions in Couple Treatment* and contributing author to *Becoming an EFT Therapist: The Workbook*. His clinical research and practice focus on using emotionally focused therapy with couples and families. His work also includes a focus on positive youth development among at-risk youth. His research and clinical writing has been published in leading professional journals in the fields of couple/family therapy and human development.

Jim is a clinical fellow and approved supervisor of the American Association of Marriage and Family Therapy and a Certified Family Life Educator. He is a certified EFT therapist, supervisor, and trainer. He is the executive director and co-founder of the Los Angeles Center for Emotionally Focused Therapy (www.laceft.org). He regularly gives presentations on topics related to relationships, family life, and clinical training throughout the United States and internationally. You can reach him for speaking engagement via e-mail at laceft@gmail.com.

Dedication

This book is dedicated to couples who want a happier and closer relationship with each other. We're grateful that you've given our work a chance. It was a labor of love.

Authors' Acknowledgments

We'd like to thank the team at John Wiley & Sons Canada, Ltd., for this opportunity to step away from the classroom, research lab, and clinic and explore new ways to reach couples in areas of their lives together that matter the most. Special thanks to our production editor, Pam Vokey, and our acquisitions editor, Anam Ahmed. Thanks to all the marketing and publicity folks for your efforts to get this book into the hands of those who are looking for new ways to grow in their relationships.

Thank you to Dr. Susan Johnson and Dr. Leslie Greenberg for developing an approach to therapy that's rooted in the everyday lives of couples. Your insights and disciplined discoveries have opened our eyes to the resources found in engaging emotion as a powerful means for relational growth and transformation. Thanks to all our EFT colleagues and collaborators who inspire and support the development, training, and practice of this approach. It has been a gift to be a part of this EFT community. A special thanks to Dr. Annmarie Early for serving as our technical editor; your deft insights and clinical wisdom are a gift to us and our readers.

From Brent: A special thank you to Cindi and Sophia. Thanks to my dad and brother for help in supporting my education. No time to explain but thanks to: Dean Smith, Jerry Davis, Jim Hurley, LM, Cameron Lee, Norris Frederick, Daniel Shealy, Freddie Mercury, Brian May, Wayne Blanton, Chris Washburn, Nick Lee, Jeff Hickey, Sarah McConnell, Maegan Carnew-Megginson, melmaw and granddaddy, and of course, Elvis Presley.

Thanks so much, Jim for tackling this with me.

From Jim: Words are not enough to express my appreciation and love to Louise, Colin, Alex, and Libby for being there and sharing in this adventure. Thanks for bringing joy to life. Thanks to my Fuller family and EFT colleagues who continue to inspire and inform many of the key ideas in this book. A special thanks to the couples who have shared their lives with me. Through your determination and courage, you've shown me again and again the power of emotions to build lasting connections and the importance of thriving relationships to a well-lived life.

Finally, thanks, Brent, for making this happen and inviting me to join you. Love the teamwork.

Publisher's Acknowledgments

Acquisitions Editor: Anam Ahmed

Project Editor: Elizabeth Kuball

Copy Editor: Elizabeth Kuball

Technical Editor: Annmarie Early, PhD

Senior Project Coordinator: Kristie Rees

Production Editor: Pam Vokey

Cover Image: © iStockphoto.com/iLexx

EDUCATION, HISTORY & REFERENCE

978-0-7645-2498-1

978-0-470-46244-7

Also available:

- Algebra For Dummies 978-0-7645-5325-7
- Art History For Dummies 978-0-470-09910-0
- Chemistry For Dummies 978-0-7645-5430-8
- English Grammar For Dummies 978-0-470-54664-2
- French All-in-One For Dummies 978-1-118-22815-9
- Statistics For Dummies 978-0-7645-5423-0
- World History For Dummies 978-0-470-44654-6

FOOD, HOME, & MUSIC

978-1-118-11554-1

978-1-118-28872-6

Also available:

- 30-Minute Meals For Dummies 978-0-7645-2589-6
- Bartending For Dummies 978-0-470-63312-0
- Brain Games For Dummies 978-0-470-37378-1
- Cheese For Dummies 978-1-118-09939-1
- Cooking Basics For Dummies 978-0-470-91388-8
- Gluten-Free Cooking For Dummies 978-1-118-39644-5
- Home Improvement All-in-One Desk Reference For Dummies 978-0-7645-5680-7
- Home Winemaking For Dummies 978-0-470-67895-4
- Ukulele For Dummies 978-0-470-97799-6

GARDENING

978-0-470-58161-2

978-0-470-57705-9

Also available:

- Gardening Basics For Dummies 978-0-470-03749-2
- Organic Gardening For Dummies 978-0-470-43067-5
- Sustainable Landscaping For Dummies 978-0-470-41149-0
- Vegetable Gardening For Dummies 978-0-470-49870-5

WILEY

GREEN/SUSTAINABLE

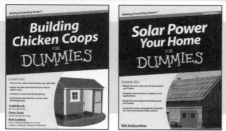

978-0-470-59896-2   978-0-470-59678-4

Also available:
- Alternative Energy For Dummies 978-0-470-43062-0
- Energy Efficient Homes For Dummies 978-0-470-37602-7
- Global Warming For Dummies 978-0-470-84098-6
- Green Building & Remodeling For Dummies 978-0-470-17559-0
- Green Cleaning For Dummies 978-0-470-39106-8
- Green Your Home All-in-One For Dummies 978-0-470-59678-4
- Wind Power Your Home For Dummies 978-0-470-49637-4

HEALTH & SELF-HELP

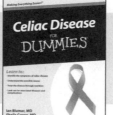

978-0-471-77383-2   978-0-470-16036-7

Also available:
- Body Language For Dummies 978-0-470-51291-3
- Borderline Personality Disorder For Dummies 978-0-470-46653-7
- Breast Cancer For Dummies 978-0-7645-2482-0
- Cognitive Behavioural Therapy For Dummies 978-0-470-66541-1
- Emotional Intelligence For Dummies 978-0-470-15732-9
- Healthy Aging For Dummies 978-0-470-14975-1
- Neuro-linguistic Programming For Dummies 978-0-470-66543-5
- Understanding Autism For Dummies 978-0-7645-2547-6

HOBBIES & CRAFTS

978-0-470-28747-7   978-1-118-01695-4

Also available:
- Bridge For Dummies 978-1-118-20574-7
- Crochet Patterns For Dummies 97-0-470-04555-8
- Digital Photography For Dummies 978-1-118-09203-3
- Jewelry Making & Beading Designs For Dummies 978-0-470-29112-2
- Knitting Patterns For Dummies 978-0-470-04556-5
- Oil Painting For Dummies 978-0-470-18230-7
- Quilting For Dummies 978-0-7645-9799-2
- Sewing For Dummies 978-0-7645-6847-3
- Word Searches For Dummies 978-0-470-45366-7

HOME & BUSINESS COMPUTER BASICS

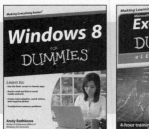

978-1-118-13461-0

978-1-118-11079-9

Also available:

- Office 2010 All-in-One Desk Reference For Dummies 978-0-470-49748-7
- Pay Per Click Search Engine Marketing For Dummies 978-0-471-75494-7
- Search Engine Marketing For Dummies 978-0-471-97998-2
- Web Analytics For Dummies 978-0-470-09824-0
- Word 2010 For Dummies 978-0-470-48772-3

INTERNET & DIGITAL MEDIA

978-1-118-32800-2

978-1-118-38318-6

Also available:

- Blogging For Dummies 978-1-118-15194-5
- Digital Photography For Seniors For Dummies 978-0-470-44417-7
- Facebook For Dummies 978-1-118-09562-1
- LinkedIn For Dummies 978-0-470-94854-5
- Mom Blogging For Dummies 978-1-118-03843-7
- The Internet For Dummies 978-0-470-12174-0
- Twitter For Dummies 978-0-470-76879-2
- YouTube For Dummies 978-0-470-14925-6

MACINTOSH

978-0-470-87868-2

978-1118-49823-1

Also available:

- iMac For Dummies 978-0-470-20271-5
- iPod Touch For Dummies 978-1-118-12960-9
- iPod & iTunes For Dummies 978-1-118-50864-0
- MacBook For Dummies 978-1-11820920-2
- Macs For Seniors For Dummies 978-1-11819684-7
- Mac OS X Lion All-in-One For Dummies 978-1-118-02206-1

PETS

978-0-470-60029-0

978-0-7645-5267-0

Also available:
- Cats For Dummies 978-0-7645-5275-5
- Ferrets For Dummies 978-0-470-13943-1
- Horses For Dummies 978-0-7645-9797-8
- Kittens For Dummies 978-0-7645-4150-6
- Puppies For Dummies 978-1-118-11755-2

SPORTS & FITNESS

978-0-470-88279-5

978-1-118-01261-1

Also available:
- Exercise Balls For Dummies 978-0-7645-5623-4
- Coaching Volleyball For Dummies 978-0-470-46469-4
- Curling For Dummies 978-0-470-83828-0
- Fitness For Dummies 978-0-7645-7851-9
- Lacrosse For Dummies 978-0-470-73855-9
- Mixed Martial Arts For Dummies 978-0-470-39071-9
- Sports Psychology For Dummies 978-0-470-67659-2
- Ten Minute Tone-Ups For Dummies 978-0-7645-7207-4
- Wilderness Survival For Dummies 978-0-470-45306-3
- Wrestling For Dummies 978-1-118-11797-2
- Yoga with Weights For Dummies 978-0-471-74937-0